This book is a must-read for anyone who cares about the state of the world we are bequeathing to our children and grandchildren, and the role that education can play in rewilding hearts and minds, and in foregrounding young people's voices, especially girls.

– **Sandi Toksvig**, *Danish-British writer, comedian, broadcaster and TV and radio presenter*

The education system in this country and beyond needs all the help (all the wild) it can get right now.

– **Robert Macfarlane**, *University of Cambridge, UK*

For schools that are serious about sustainability and nature-based learning, this book is essential reading. Whatever role you have in a school, Professor Cremin's work gives you the capacity to think and act differently. Scholarly, passionate, and provocative, *Rewilding Education* presents a deeply compelling case for reimagining a child's learning journey.

– **Philip Keech**, *International School of Luxembourg*

Children need you to read this book! Hilary's incisive diagnosis of the challenge children face makes me angry; for too many children the experience of education is a catalyst for fragmentation and exclusion. Her bold vision for what education can be gives me courage; it can become a catalyst for wholeness and peace. Leaders who read this book with an open heart and a readiness to change will find practical guidance to think and act differently. As a result, they will transform the lives of children and the future of communities in which they live.

– **Tom Shaw**, *Carr Manor Community School, UK*

Rewilding Education: Rethinking the Place of Schools is a timely and radical challenge to educators to rethink our educational systems through the concept of "rewilding education." Cremin's work highlights the potentially damaging effects of modern schooling systems and societal structures, and calls for a more holistic, sustainable approach to education. Rewilding education emphasises the importance of peace education and the need to place relationships at the heart of our educational systems creating environments that support both academic progress and emotional and social development, preparing students for the complexities of the modern world.

– **Lee Farmer**, *Holte School, UK*

Rewilding Education is needed to address uncertain futures related to an escalated climate crisis and our lackluster, detrimental, and turtle-slow human responses. The book inspires, through arts-based and creative approaches, systems-wide interventions rooted in holism and wisdom traditions. Nature is our best teacher if we slow down, connect, observe, listen. *Rewilding Education* surely will be on my bookshelves at the office and at the cabin-- for guests, students, and for me to absorb theory and practical ideas therein.

– **Edward J. Brantmeier,** *James Madison University, USA*

Those concerned with rethinking education's role in tackling the climate crisis and building positive peace in schools and communities today will find this book compelling. The book outlines some fundamental flaws of modernity (and modernist thinking) and in turn offers several alternatives gesturing toward rewilded futures. Written in accessible language, this book is equally valuable for policymakers, teachers, students, and parents. A thought-provoking read!

– **Kevin Kester,** *Seoul National University, South Korea*

Rewilding Education

Rewilding Education calls for a radical, system-wide reinvention of education as an adaptable ecosystem; less predictable and measurable, but far more suitable for shaping the adults of tomorrow.

By encouraging us to transform how we think about education in what is left of the twenty-first century, Hilary Cremin connects directly with educators, parents, young people and policymakers to share a vision for healthy education settings and societies that nurture both human flourishing and sustainable ecosystems. Full of ideas about what rewilding might look like when applied to education, Hilary Cremin evidences how education has been, and can be, successfully rewilded in schools and classrooms, including case studies from unexpected places like Kerala in India, where literacy rates exceed those in the United States.

By combining academic research, poetry and examples from around the world, the book will inspire the next generation of educators, decision-makers and families to take practical steps towards the education our children need and deserve.

Hilary Cremin is a Professor in Education Peace and Conflict and Head of the Faculty of Education at the University of Cambridge, UK. Hilary has also published *Positive Peace in Schools: Tackling Conflict and Creating a Culture of Peace in the Classroom* (2017, Routledge) and *Debates in Citizenship Education* (2012, Routledge) amongst others. Hilary has worked in the public, private and voluntary sector as a schoolteacher, educational consultant, project coordinator and academic.

Rewilding Education

Rethinking the Place of Schools Now and in the Future

Hilary Cremin

LONDON AND NEW YORK

Designed cover image: © Getty Images

First published 2026
by Routledge
4 Park Square, Milton Park, Abingdon, Oxon OX14 4RN

and by Routledge
605 Third Avenue, New York, NY 10158

Routledge is an imprint of the Taylor & Francis Group, an informa business

© 2026 Hilary Cremin

The right of Hilary Cremin to be identified as author of this work has been asserted in accordance with sections 77 and 78 of the Copyright, Designs and Patents Act 1988.

All rights reserved. No part of this book may be reprinted or reproduced or utilised in any form or by any electronic, mechanical, or other means, now known or hereafter invented, including photocopying and recording, or in any information storage or retrieval system, without permission in writing from the publishers.

Trademark notice: Product or corporate names may be trademarks or registered trademarks, and are used only for identification and explanation without intent to infringe.

British Library Cataloguing-in-Publication Data
A catalogue record for this book is available from the British Library

ISBN: 978-1-041-04318-8 (hbk)
ISBN: 978-1-041-04315-7 (pbk)
ISBN: 978-1-003-62780-7 (ebk)

DOI: 10.4324/9781003627807

Typeset in Times New Roman
by SPi Technologies India Pvt Ltd (Straive)

For Rowan and Jude – may yours be a rewilded future

Contents

Acknowledgements	*x*
List of poems	*xi*
Introduction	1

PART I
What's wrong with schools?   9

1 In the death throes of modernity?	11
2 Tunnel vision and neglect of the climate emergency	29
3 Making us ill	39
4 Reproducing inequality	55

PART II
Rewilding education   69

5 Why rewilding?	71
6 Valuing wisdom	80
7 Nature as teacher	107
8 Health, engagement, practical wisdom and an arts-based mindset	122
9 Education for peace, justice and inclusion	148
Conclusion	165
Rewilding education: Letters to my readers	167
Index	*177*

Acknowledgements

I would like to thank all of the people who contributed to this book in large ways and small. There are those like Janice Tai Yeung Ning who sorted the practicalities so that I could sometimes take time to write, and there are those who wrote poems and case studies that are included in this book. Thanks so much to Jwalin Patel, Carlotta Ehrenzeller, Nomisha Kurian, Will McInerney, Jenny Davis, Tom Shaw and Portia Ungley. Thanks to my readers and reviewers who have been so supportive and given excellent advice. Thanks to teachers, researchers, members of the Cambridge Peace Education Research Group, members of the Positive Peace team in Kazakhstan and young people everywhere who have taught me so much.

To GD: THANK YOU

Poems

Bloodless angel	23
Mexico City	31
Second-best tears	48
COVID-inequality	49
My child	59
Awakening	76
Postscript	85
Forever changed	109
Into the forest school	115
Tree	135
Beach	136
Portia Ungley: Twice 4 a.m.	137
Will McInerney: A poem in 6 parts	141

Introduction

This book lays out what an education system might look like when it engages with fresh ideas about what it is to educate. In the book, rewilding serves as both an extended metaphor and as an opportunity for reconnection with wild spaces and nature through education. In the same way that some farmers are turning away from massification, monocultures and an over-reliance on human intervention and chemicals, education needs to turn away from standardisation and an over-reliance on modernist and enlightenment ways of being and knowing. Education, and the social sciences more generally, has tended to situate itself within an agrico-botanical way of thinking, with massification, monocultures and experimental research methods aping the methods of the laboratory with disastrous effects. Change is needed in both modern farming and in education.

Landscapes are increasingly benefitting from processes of rewilding. Education too can benefit from reclaiming teaching and learning as natural, dynamic and creative processes that are deeply embedded within complex ecosystems. This book contains poems, stories, case studies from schools and early career scholars, and collaborative writing. These are the lifeblood of the book and reinforce its emphasis on the arts, creativity and embodied and affective ways of communicating complex ideas and bringing about change. The book has two parts as well as letters to its readers at the end. The first part of the book focusses mainly on challenges, and the second part speaks about what can be done to address them.

You may be wondering where I get my ideas from and why I have chosen to speak out now against modern systems of schooling. On the face of it, I am deeply embedded within standard education policy and practice in the UK and internationally. As Head of the Faculty of Education at the University of Cambridge I could hardly be more mainstream! On the other hand I am deeply ambivalent about the ways in which schooling is organised throughout the world. It can't be denied that I currently have a platform to begin a global conversation about the aims and purposes of education, and I don't want to waste it. I am aware that, despite decades of work with tens of thousands of schools, teachers, children, students, education researchers, policymakers, education leaders and workers of various kinds in the UK and elsewhere, I will be dismissed and ridiculed by many. My position in Cambridge (and the fact that I am a woman) may draw down a particular kind of vilification.

Nevertheless, continuing to act as if schools were benign facilitators of social mobility and meritocracy no longer feels tenable. It is time to demonstrate that modern systems of schooling make people ill, reproduce and exacerbate inequality, cut young people off from nature and lead to disembodied, de-contextualised and impoverished ways of thinking and acting. It is time to share my experience of how education can be different. The case studies that I and my colleagues and students have gathered show how it is possible to dare to dream differently about education.

I call on my readers to join me in a conversation about what is wrong with schools and how they might be rewilded. Whether you are a teacher in an alternative education setting (or wanting to experiment with alternative methodologies), a home educator, a youth worker, a parent, a public or charitable sector project-worker, or someone who went to school, I hope that you will enjoy being engaged in far-reaching debate about the aims, purposes, potential and failures of education globally. Although I write as a professor of education, with many years of research and practice behind me, I hope that the debate that follows is readable by anyone with a genuine interest. I look forward to accompanying you.

Outline of the book

This first part of the book asks: what is wrong with schools? It lays out the need for rewilding education. It outlines some of the fundamental flaws of modern systems of schooling, and modernity more generally. It also spells out in some detail how education contributes to ill health, the climate emergency and inequality.

Chapter One reviews threats emanating from the worst excesses of modernity and enlightenment thinking and the ways in which education is complicit in their reproduction. Education could play a vital role in rebooting the way that we think about the world and our place in it, but so far it has succumbed to neoliberal ideology and is part of the problem rather than part of the solution. It needs to rid itself of the modernist infatuation with permanent growth, with the exclusionary practices of a professional elite, and with financial markets. It also needs to take account of AI and new post-human realities, the need to maintain healthy populations, and the globalisation and diversification of human identities and aspirations.

The first chapter explores the 'fractious twins' of modernity and postmodernity, and how they relate to education, through the related twins of capitalism / post-capitalism, humanism / posthumanism, and empirical truth / post-truth. These allegorical twins are fractious because there are tensions between them that can't be resolved. They are also deeply connected, however, and one could not exist without the other. They all impact powerfully on our understanding of what it is to be educated. The chapter discusses the modernist / postmodernist conundrum of structure and agency, and the extent to which teachers, parents, students, researchers, activists, project workers and others can take action towards desired futures without being held back by the systems that constrain them.

Chapter Two builds on the previous chapter by considering how education has impacted on ways of thinking about the natural environment. In particular, it discusses how education and the industrial/post-industrial way of life favoured across most of the planet are based on what Schumacher[1] has referred to as the false assumption that irreplaceable natural capital can be treated as income. It reveals the folly inherent in obsession with GDP and expectations of continuous economic growth. It also discusses how societies throughout the world have become indifferent to the toxic legacies of planetary degradation and consumerism that they are bequeathing to the young.

The second chapter suggests that education has played no small part in promulgating the idea that the climate emergency is subject to technical solutions and that environmental concerns must not be allowed to interfere with business as usual in the economic and educational sphere. A central obstacle to achieving sustainability is the way that education has normalised notions of an underlying 'metaphysics of mastery' over nature. This Enlightenment myth, which was taken (rather ironically) from religion, has since been twisted to suit those who have the most to gain from the idea that rationality, human will and science can impose anthropocentrism on the entire planet without consequence. Chapter Two ends by picking up the central theme of this book – that rewilding is a useful metaphor for supporting education to emerge from the stultifying linearities and binaries that normalise the destruction of the planet.

Chapter Three takes a long hard look at the poor physical and mental health that permeates education systems throughout the world. From the point of view of physical health: there is a lack of regard for bodily needs and a lack of time and space for movement and play. From the point of view of mental health: there is teacher stress and problems retaining teachers on the one hand and a lack of student well-being, anxiety, bullying, school refusal and exclusion on the other. Poor mental health applies to both winners and losers in the education system: losers through the impact of underachievement, lack of opportunity and poverty and winners through the effects of stress, pressure and diminished creativity and personal autonomy.

The third chapter goes on to discuss the ways in which the field of education has historically been dominated by the discipline of psychology. This means that change is seen as needing to come from individuals being better adapted to the system rather than the other way around. Although psychology as a discipline continues to evolve and diversify, with important developments such as social psychology and positive psychology, these have largely been ignored by education in favour of notions of deficit and the medicalisation of need and care. There is a clear problem when medication is used as a way of enabling healthy young people to interact with an ailing system. Part of the solution comes from avoiding students getting caught in an endless loop of performing vulnerability in ways that reinforce an unhealthy sense of victimhood, as well as from promoting healthy vulnerability that involves genuine encounter, healing and change.

Chapter Four discusses the ways that education reproduces inequality. It contains a poem outlining the depth of educational inequality in the UK and elsewhere. Despite the myth of social mobility, education is deeply complicit in ensuring that the Earth's resources are mainly enjoyed by global elites. Political leaders and their allies throughout the world spend an inordinate amount of time convincing parents and business leaders that the next iteration of their education system will finally deliver equality and inclusion – but the truth is that much of this activity serves to obscure rather than ameliorate the issues at hand. In many cases, schemes that seduce with promises to reduce social and educational exclusion end up delivering the opposite: with zero tolerance behaviour policies leading to increased permanent exclusions; returns to traditional academic curricula leading to disaffection and achievement gaps; and widening access to higher education leading to graduate unemployment and crippling lifelong debt amongst the poor.

Educational inequality seems stubbornly resistant to change, with marginalised groups throughout the world making painfully slow gains (or else going backwards) in comparison with those with access to wealth and power. Whether young people are marginalised due to the impact of direct or indirect racism, sexism, colonialism, homophobia, social class or simply by virtue of being young, they often find themselves falling behind due to misrecognition of non-dominant narratives and identities. When this is added to the effects of poverty and trauma (which are greatest amongst the poor and marginalised) a need for change is clear.

The second part of the book responds to these crises and suggests ways forward. It explores in more detail how a significant cultural shift towards rewilding in education might happen. It responds to fundamental flaws in modern systems of schooling by outlining ways of knowing, being and learning that might be necessary for a significant cultural shift towards rewilding in education. This part of the book goes beyond the current anthropocentric focus in education to suggest how we might embrace nature-based learning, and how we might encourage an arts-based mindset. It shows how we might tackle global inequality through education taking its place in the world as a force for sustainability, equity and human (and non-human) thriving. The second part of the book talks about the need for new social imaginaries of what the Good Life looks like, and how we might arrive there.

Chapter Five gets to the heart of the book by discussing what is meant by 'rewilding' in its original and literal sense. It discusses both the scientific rationale for rewilding, and also its historical, cultural and aesthetic factors. It draws for this on a range of writers, scientists and activists. The chapter gives reasons why rewilding is an important impetus and metaphor for education. These include that rewilding sees nature as teacher; values holism and wisdom traditions; enables humans to thrive beyond the anthropocene; and creates low impact, productive, regenerative, inclusive and efficient ways of living.

Chapter Six, co-authored with Jwalin Patel who researches holistic education schools in India, builds on the idea that wisdom involves inner work as well as an integration of affect and cognition. It discusses how it is more important for young people to be knowledgeable and wise than to be academically successful in a narrow sense. This chapter proposes that, whilst the intellect is important, so are ways of knowing that integrate sensing and feeling from the body with the processes of the mind. It offers hope in response to Chapter One, which outlined the failures of modern systems of schooling and ways of thinking. This chapter discusses how the dominance of academic knowledge and abstraction in Eurocentric scientific thought has meant that embodied, common sense, holistic and contextualised ways of knowing are seen as less valid than de-contextualised, abstract, scalable, atomised ways.

Drawing on many wisdom traditions, Chapter Six takes body, heart, mind and soul in turn and applies them to rewilded education. It suggests that the body needs to be seen as deeply connected with processes of cognition and human flourishing. Education for the heart needs to support young people to develop good relationships, empathy, compassion, self-governance and self-regulation. Education for the mind needs to go beyond the mere transfer of information to include mindfulness, critical thinking, and awareness of how the brain works. Education for the soul needs to be based on self-transformation, equanimity, inner peace and harmony, universal oneness and unconditional love. The last part of the chapter draws together body, mind, heart and soul to suggest that holistic education integrates all of them in an education fit for purpose for the 21st century. This chapter discusses pedagogical and classroom-based implications of rewilding and includes case studies from schools in both the UK and India that have rewilded their approaches to education, emphasising education for togetherness and harmony.

Chapter Seven speaks back to Chapter Two. It discusses how the need to honour nature's integrity demands a different way of thinking about education. We need to move beyond merely human considerations and place nature at the heart of processes of teaching and learning. This is not to abandon the humanities – but rather to include non-anthropocentric perspectives and study of the more-than-human in the curriculum. This demands taking the cycles and rhythms of nature as starting points for teaching and learning. Although not necessary for rewilding education, this will often involve learning out of doors and having direct experience of nature. Wild spaces can provide opportunities for young people to transition into adulthood with greater maturity and self-awareness. Many possibilities open up when we consider nature as teacher. Chapter Seven presents a case study in the form of a poetic narrative from a forest school in Germany.

Chapter Eight responds to Chapter Three. New kinds of relationships for teaching and learning are required if we are to reverse the global mental health crisis. This chapter identifies three areas of focus for achieving this: promoting self-efficacy and feelings of empowerment; practical wisdom, appropriate technology and situated learning; and imagination, narrative and an arts-based mindset. The three are linked and together they can take us from paralysis and despair to hope, creativity and change. It is essential for good mental health for people to feel in control of their lives. When they feel that their choices are limited and that they are subject to external forces, they do not thrive. The climate emergency has taken away many people's sense of agency and this has led to a kind of collective trauma that induces eco-anxiety and solastalgia (nostalgia for things that have been lost because of climate change). Young people's mental health can be restored if we can help them to move beyond depression and paralysis towards feelings of hope, engagement and biophilia (an affinity with life and living systems that can improve human health and well-being). This chapter explores how this can happen through educational approaches that foreground agency, practical wisdom, creativity and collective action.

This chapter discusses how rewilded education can support educators to develop feelings of agency and empowerment through circle pedagogy, and an arts-based mindset. Educators can work with circles and the arts to empower young people to find their voice and work towards the change they wish to see for themselves and for others. This is not a narrow view of the arts, nor is it a view that values high art over craft and local forms of community engagement. It is a view that seeks to develop an artistic mindset that allows particular ways of feeling and seeing to find creative expression. I share some of my nature-based poems in this chapter as part of this. The artistic mindset works in tandem with a scientific mindset that foregrounds practical wisdom (phronesis), innovation, imagination and hunches alongside technical skills (techne). It leads to feelings of empowerment, affirmation and achievement. This chapter shares case studies of how schools and projects in the UK, USA and India have been able to foreground agency and an arts-based mindset.

Chapter Nine, co-authored with Nomisha Kurian, who researches the ethics of care and children's safety and well-being, builds on ideas from permaculture about balance and flow and applies them to education. In counterbalance to Chapter Four, it suggests that education can be rewilded by improving the flow and distribution of social, cultural and educational resources amongst populations of the world. For this it will need to prevent resources from being sequestered by global elites. Inclusion in this chapter is envisaged as involving all young people globally in an education that is fit for purpose, rather than providing credentials for a minority who go on to exclude and accumulate.

The chapter begins by looking at education programmes that might offer promise for more balanced and inclusive education systems, building on my own peace-building work in schools. It then turns to more radical, critical and anarchic ways of educating before finally exploring a real-life example of rewilding. Our case study of sustainable development is Kerala, a small coastal state in India. What miracles and challenges emerge when a place commits to alternative ways of living and being for over a hundred years? We reflect on the autoethnographic impressions of Nomisha and then link Kerala's experience of sustainable development to the broader themes of rewilding discussed throughout this book.

Chapter Nine discusses the idea of the degrowth economy[2] and the doughnut economy,[3] linking them with Kerala, which has been acclaimed as a model of development by economists and scholars around the world. The chapter examines how and why Kerala has set out to prioritise human welfare in order to ask broader questions about sustainable development globally. How, for example, has Kerala achieved universal literacy, exceptionally low infant mortality rates and longer life expectancy despite being an extremely poor state? What lessons might the Kerala model present for global efforts to reconsider purely corporatised, profit-driven and technocratic economies? The chapter analyses Kerala as a living example of putting principles of degrowth and rewilding into practice. It is also realistic about the challenges and pitfalls of pursuing a degrowth economy. These include Kerala's low industrial development, and brain drain. Nevertheless, it concludes by emphasising the value of putting human well-being at the centre of the economy, and the fresh opportunities this presents for rewilded living and learning.

The conclusion to the book summarises the basic content of the chapters and paves the way for the final section, which is letters to the book's readers. The letters speak directly to them, engaging them in reflection on their own educational experiences and on possibilities for the education of young people in the future. Whether the reader is a teacher, policymaker, NGO worker, parent or young person, they will be invited to reflect on the implications of the book for themselves. These letters suggest how teachers can reclaim their personal and professional integrity and become 'wild' in the sense that they are freed from the modernist structures that regulate and constrain their practice. The letters draw on the ideas in this book to reclaim the heart and soul of what it means to teach and learn. Without romanticising teachers, or the teaching profession, they go beyond technicist and performative considerations to talk about ideas for change – asking the kinds of questions that might begin the rewilding journey and bring about an education worthy of its name. The final two letters – to a parent and a young person – ground and complete the book with the people who really matter.

Conclusion

As shown throughout this book, teaching in modern times has become an almost impossible task. Teachers have been subject to a constant imperative to improve themselves, their institutions and the attainment and well-being of the young people they serve. There is no arrival point, no end to the deafening clamour of multiple voices, and no rest. There is not even any agreement about the purpose of the journey or where it is heading, with actors from the Right and the Left seeking to influence social and political futures through controlling teachers. Someone somewhere is always looking to gain social and political capital from 'taking on' teachers and schools. How then to create spaces for education to find another way? How to be a change-maker who is an ally rather than an adversary? How can all stakeholders stand in solidarity with teachers to ensure that young people and parents get what they need from education in current times? Hopefully this book will begin to suggest some answers.

Notes

1 Schumacher, E. F. (2011). *Small is beautiful: a study of economics as if people mattered*. Vintage.
2 Nixon, R. (2011). *Slow Violence and the Environmentalism of the Poor*. Harvard University Press.
3 Raworth, K. (2017). *Doughnut Economics: Seven ways to think like a 21st century economist*. Random House.

Part I

What's wrong with schools?

Chapter 1
In the death throes of modernity?

Introduction

In this chapter I outline some of the fundamental flaws of modern systems of schooling and modernity more generally. I suggest that, whilst modernity has brought about certain benefits, such as improved life spans, and the Long Peace over past decades[1], it has also been catastrophic for many people globally. More specifically, I show that the grand narratives and effects of capitalism, patriarchy and colonialism have wreaked havoc amongst the least advantaged of the world and that the planet and its ecosystems are heating up due to humanity imposing its will over nature through industrialisation and agribusiness. New ways of thinking and acting are needed if we are to rise to the challenge of reversing some of the excesses of modernist thinking. Education could be a key player in this. Unfortunately, however, not only are schools globally not up to the task, but they currently serve to perpetuate these excesses and to exacerbate the toxic effects of modernity. The modern school is an 'intolerable' institution[2] that is beyond redemption in the usual sense of school improvement and education research. In making this claim, I am not of course arguing against education – only against what we have allowed our modern schools to become.

Whilst it is up for debate whether we are in the death throes of modernity, or whether its institutions continue to thrive, it is nevertheless the case that the values and assumptions of modern systems of education are beginning to break down. In this chapter I will define modernity generally and how it applies to education. I will then review some of the problems associated with modernity and modern systems of education before taking a postmodern turn in order to reflect on what might be 'post' (or after) modernity and the challenges of bringing about change.

Defining modernity

But first I must define modernity. What is it that we are in the death throes of? We often use the word modern to talk about things that are up-to-date and contemporary, but in fact, modernity goes back as far as 18th-century European

Enlightenment. The Enlightenment was about replacing religion and superstition with science, rationality and reason. For centuries the Church and State had worked together to benefit from ensuring that people saw Heaven and an afterlife as compensation for their struggles and hardships on Earth. Now, a growing urban population was encouraged to think about redemption in terms of modern science, the industrial revolution and the achievements of 'man' (and it was mainly rich white men whose achievements were recognised).

The 18th and 19th centuries saw increasing valorisation of the humanities and growth in global exploration, anthropology and colonisation. The 'modern' view was that civilisation could be brought to 'lower classes' and indigenous populations of the world through science, industry and reason. Thomas Arnold's Rugby School in the UK was the model for how a school might prepare the sons of elites for the task of bringing Enlightenment and rationality to the world. It is this model of schooling that dominates to this day and that remains so toxic.

The origins of modernity, then, involved global reach, mass production, industrialisation and the logic of the machine. This was taken further in the 20th century, with scientific, social and technological revolutions, which are associated with the modernist movement in art and architecture and massive expansion of markets following the Second World War. Events such as the moon landings, the contraceptive pill and the advent of the internet really did make people think that humanity had transcended its messy organic limitations. I was a child when the first person set foot on the moon, and I remember thinking that it was only a matter of time before we could take a pill instead of eating a meal and have robots doing all our chores! I can't remember why I thought that this would be desirable.

Modernity then, implies straight lines, simple binaries, and the methods of the laboratory, workshop and high-rise building sites – none of which are particularly favoured by natural ecosystems. The laboratory is designed to keep complexity out, the workshop is for machines, and concrete is used to keep nature at bay. It is for these reasons that I am arguing here that we are in the death throes of modernity. It is not that laboratories and workshops and high-rise buildings are no longer significant – it is more that these spaces are seen as less and less useful and desirable. The laboratory's scientific results often fail to translate into real life, workshops have been replaced by IT suites and many high-rise apartment blocks are soulless and neglected. It's interesting to reflect that workshops nowadays tend to refer to people engaging in personal or professional development activities in seminar or training rooms. The word is not used so much to refer to an actual repair shop. This is rather unfortunate if you have tried to engage a plumber or engineer recently!

Self-evidently, nature is refusing to be kept at bay, with the climate emergency serving as a reminder that there are consequences from anything in nature getting out of balance, including levels of carbon and population growth. We are also, perhaps, facing the humbling reality that we cannot impose our will on nature without unintended consequences for ourselves and other species. Perhaps we are not so godlike after all. One of my favourite quotes is from Mary Midgeley, who says in *Myth and Meaning*[3] that, 'modern people might actually in some monstrous sense win their bizarre war, ... they might 'defeat nature', thus cutting off the branch that they have been sitting on.'

Problems with modernity

Modernity has had its detractors since its inception. Indeed, I suggested in 2018[4] that modernity and postmodernity have always existed in creative and dynamic balance with each other, and that, like 'fractious twins,' they were born at the same time. In the 19th century, the Romantics – poets, philosophers, artists, musicians and novelists – moved beyond an obsession with the rational mind to reclaim the heart, body and soul. In the 20th and 21st centuries, postmodernist philosophers have argued that modernity is flawed and incapable of taking account of the complexity and diversity of human existence (hence the post-).

One of the big ideas behind the philosophy of postmodernity comes from Lyotard, who argued in 1979[5] that the 'grand narratives,' or 'métarécits,' of modernity no longer hold sway. This was partly a result of new discoveries in science and partly a result of changing ideas about time, space, and language. These grand narratives include, for example, international development, Marxism and democracy. Grand narratives are not as galvanising as they were. This is because they often imply a universal way of looking at the world that is based on a particular perspective. Rationality and scientific thinking are not able to produce a narrative that can encompass everyone. So, for example: what a 'developed' nation might look like is not agreed upon by everyone[6]; it is more difficult to ascertain who are the oppressors and who the oppressed than historical Marxism implies; and democracy might not be as emancipatory and just as many had hoped.[7] One of the biggest 'grand narratives' of them all is education.

The grand narrative of education

Education is at the heart of the modernist project. It really got going in the West after the Second World War through universal secondary-level provision. This was a time when there was a lot of faith in modern industrial methods, new social contracts and modern welfare states. Education, so the grand narrative goes, builds human capital through providing the citizens and workers of the future with the knowledge, values and skills that they need to be useful to society and live a fulfilled life (and not put unnecessary strain on the taxpayer). Education can (so the narrative continues) pick out the brightest and the best – rich or poor – to be future leaders, whilst equipping the less academic to nevertheless be of service. Any correlation between wealth and academic achievement is (of course!) purely coincidental.

It is difficult to imagine modernity without education. This book is about whether we can imagine things the other way round – education without modernity. Can we let go of the grand narratives that surround education, and its associated accoutrements, including traditional ways of schooling? One of the most downloaded *Ted Talks* of all time is by Sir Ken Robinson[8] and concerns this very issue. In it he argues that education policymakers are trying to solve the problems of the future by using the methods of the past and that large numbers of young people are alienated as a result. He points out that schools are organised around the principles of the factory – with children divided into batches according to age-group and moved around the building (which is organised as cells) throughout the day by a series of bells. This production-line mentality leads to standardisation and conformity (or rebellion / exclusion / medication) and disincentivises the very diverse thinking that is vital if populations are to survive into the next century. It is necessary, according to the logic of the factory, for young people to tolerate boring and repetitive tasks, to always be punctual, not to question their line managers, to be neat and contained in their personal habits, and to learn to conform to rules and regulations that are imposed on them. The problem is that the factory is a modernist institution that is, for the most part, on the decline. Why are we continuing to educate young people as if they were factory workers?

I argue that, in addition to the factory, the modern school is organised around the principles of the military. The wearing of a school uniform is an example, as well as lining up, being punished for expressing individuality, and obeying people in authority without question. Despite the fact that even the military is trying to distance itself from these old-fashioned methods, many policymakers, voters and parents continue to believe that education-as-bootcamp is a good thing, especially for disadvantaged youth who find it harder to conform than their parents and grandparents might have done. I wonder why? As Ken Robinson points out, schools are not this way because teachers want it – they are as they are because it 'just happens that way.' These methods, he suggests, are in the gene pool of education. I would counter that they are not in the gene pool of education per se – they are rather in the gene pool of modern systems of schooling.

Both modernity and postmodernity

In order to understand why schools 'just happen that way' it is necessary to focus on modernity's fractious twin – postmodernity. A slightly more theoretical postmodern way of talking about this concerns the role of discourse in questions of truth, power and knowledge. As I suggested in 2017,[9] the French philosopher Foucault is particularly helpful here with his analysis of the techniques (technologies) that decide what counts as truth and knowledge. His concepts of regimes of truth (e.g. school improvement discourse), and the 'de-centring of the subject,' suggest that power comes from knowledge and discourse, and that people (for example, students and teachers) are situated within these discourses of power, rather than possessing power.

So, what does this mean in layperson's terms? Perhaps an example. Put simply, teachers who find themselves directly opposed to what they are being asked to do in the name of school improvement (feeling, for example, that each new initiative is more about being seen to do things than about addressing the needs of students) often feel powerless to do what they know is best for their students on a Tuesday afternoon. They find words coming out of their mouths that they don't believe and that students don't believe either. It is almost as if teachers (and students) are 'being spoken' rather than speaking. They don't seem to matter as thinking, feeling, living human beings. The system of schooling has already decided what needs to be spoken on a Tuesday by whoever occupies the node at their particular intersection. Teachers' own words don't count, even though they know the students better than anyone. This is what Foucault meant by the 'de-centring of the subject.' The subject / agent / person finds that they are not at the centre of their professional life. This implies a reduced sense of agency and explains why teachers and students often feel powerless to change 'how things are' in the gene pool of schooling. This, by the way, is the big difference between a modern view (teachers take action based on rational choices) and a postmodernist view (teachers' actions are formed by structures of schooling).

So if teachers are not at the centre of systems of schooling, what is? Foucault would say that certain powerful discourses about education are, and that these discourses shape the actions of everyone affected by them – whether they stand to gain from the discourses or not. Discourses are not dissimilar from grand narratives. The difference is a question of agency. Whilst grand narratives suggest that power operates in deliberate, coordinated and structured ways, discourses are more fluid. They just are (although power plays a big part in shaping them). They are maintained by all of us. What then might be examples of Foucauldian discourse in education? There are many, and they will be immediately recognisable: a good education enables social mobility; schools must constantly improve; a back-to-basics curriculum is needed to address new-fangled ideas about education; competition between schools drives up standards; all young people must leave school with a high level of attainment; (quickly followed by ...) grade inflation is leading to a reduction in standards.

None of these discourses stand up to scrutiny, and yet this hardly seems to matter. I can easily show this. For example, education does not in and of itself provide social mobility (more about this in Chapter Four) and competition between schools often comes with perverse incentives. In the UK, this includes expensive-to-educate students with special educational needs and disabilities (SEND) being tossed between schools like hot potatoes before they eventually land in second-rate Local Authority provision[10] – if they land anywhere at all. What started as a discourse of 'parents can choose a school for their child,' has become 'schools can choose the students that make their school look good' (again, more on this in Chapter Four). In the USA, school districts engage in 'creaming' students.[11] This entails schools selectively admitting high-performing students to enhance their overall test scores and reputation. In the process, students with lower scores, often from disadvantaged socio-economic backgrounds, are left behind. This cycle of inequality limits opportunities for social mobility and results in students with disabilities or behavioural challenges finding it hard to get a place in a good school.

A discourse that is particularly perplexing is the one that states that all young people must leave school with a high level of attainment. If that were the case, could the level logically be described as high? Modernist thinking in education leads people to think that exams and grades are somehow a priori entities that are capable of discerning intelligence. They forget that the level is set by people who make assumptions about what level society wants. Levels can go up and down (and do) to include more or fewer young people. International comparators (such as PISA[12]) do little to mitigate this.

Returning to the question of whether or not teachers have agency within systems of education, it can perhaps be said that, as with most things, the truth is somewhere in the middle. Teachers are not completely powerless, but neither are they in control of what happens in education. Teachers' modern certainties have given way to postmodern complexity and the constant need to perform according to the logic of discourses that are not of their making. This makes the job very stressful. It is of course both important for teachers to feel that they can do what they know is best for their students (based on their training, experience, and knowledge of students and what works, etc.), and for stakeholders in education (students, parents, researchers, policy makers, elected representatives) to have their say. If we let go of the certainties, binaries and linear thinking of the past, then a new complex reality starts to emerge. If we can celebrate the creativity and messiness of human experience and put science, knowledge and learning relationships at the heart of education, inspiring teachers can lead by example and young people can thrive.

So how can this be achieved?

Education in modern and postmodern times

Education has a vital role to play in rebooting the way that we think about the world and our place in it, but so far it has been used to shore up, rather than challenge, the failed modernist project.[13] It has succumbed to neoliberal ideology (by which I mean marketisation, privatisation and competition) and is part of the problem rather than part of the solution. Given the hegemony of high stakes testing and accountability regimes to serve modernist education systems throughout the world, it is hard to imagine how schools might reclaim education as a 'beautiful risk.'[14]

Education will need to address not only the universalising monoculture of its national systems, but also the new realities of young people for whom the art of surfing has taken over from the art of fathoming; downward mobility has replaced the myth of social mobility; choice is reduced to various consumer options;[15] the climate emergency has replaced notions of continuous economic growth; and viable identities for large sections of the population are reduced to criminality and / or underemployment.[16] Now is the time to update processes of learning and teaching to take account of the realities of young people's lives.

More fractious twins

Unfortunately, we are educating for jobs and lifestyles that will soon cease to exist, whilst failing to educate for the jobs and lifestyles that don't yet exist. Our infatuation with modernity, the growth of markets, professional careers and urban Western liberalism has blinkered us to the likely futures that our children and grandchildren will face. Removing the blinkers will take courage.

There are no easy answers, but it might help if I introduce some more fractious twins to explore these issues. Fractious twins (like modernity and postmodernity, it will be remembered) exist at the same time and are in a complex relationship, rather than coming one after the other. This means that the first set of fractious twins considered below – capitalism and post-capitalism – are both here in the present and will continue to exist together for some time to come. Although I would not wish to come out as anti-capitalist (and for the record, this is not an accurate description of my position) I believe that it is important to debate capitalism in a book like this about education. I will claim each twin as both my friend and my enemy.

Capitalism and post-capitalism

Capitalism basically implies free trade and the accumulation and reinvestment of resources. Under the conditions of capitalism, it is expected (and even promoted) that those who become wealthy retain the rewards of their investment and enterprise. Once they spend this money, resources continue to circulate through various markets, and the process continues. Often, borrowing is needed to enable the expansion of capital and market opportunities so that continuous growth is necessary for everyone, including investors, to make a profit on activities. There are four fundamental problems with modern capitalism: firstly, that capitalism, like an ouroboros (a snake eating its own tail) is continuously depleting the resources that are necessary for its own survival[17] (more on this later with relation to externalities and sustainability); secondly, that growth is unpredictable, and can quickly shift to decline; thirdly, that capitalism needs a constant supply of capital and relatively low-paid workers to provide profits for others; and fourthly, that capitalism fuels inequality. All of these will be reviewed later in this book, but for now the emphasis is on the fractious twins of capitalism / post-capitalism.

The modernist logic of the market under conditions of capitalism states that those who experience exploitation can jump ship, or else set up in competition, and that those who disagree with the methods or products of a particular business can simply choose to go elsewhere. A post-capitalist logic suggests that neither option is viable for many people. To give an example from the UK: according to Amy Borrett, writing in *The New Statesman* in 2021,[18] the average house price was 65 times higher than in 1970, but average wages were only 36 times higher. This means that many people who would have purchased their own home in the past are currently renting because their salary is not enough for a bank to consider a mortgage. The rental sector in the UK has expanded dramatically at the same time. This is largely fuelled by banks giving mortgages on a buy-to-let basis to those who already own capital and resources. The result of this is that investors (many of them using the money to provide a retirement income) are inflating house prices so that fewer young people are able to buy.

This means that many older landlords, who may have benefitted from lower house prices in the past, now own at least two properties whilst many young people don't own one. What is more, young people are paying more than they would have done if they had a mortgage, but the money they pay each month for housing is funding someone else's capital accumulation rather than building up their own capital. It is hard to imagine how the logic of the market will prevail without seriously negative consequences for some.

The situation is still worse for countries who have faced the negative effects of both capitalism and colonialism. For example, according to the World Inequality Report, in 2022 the richest 1% of the population in India owned over 40% of the country's total wealth.[19] Owning property has been a right historically enjoyed by only a few wealthy families, with land inherited through the generations. As a result, only a small percentage of the population own the vast majority of India's land, while many precarious workers struggle to find affordable housing. Women remain especially unlikely to enjoy the right to inherit due to traditional practices of passing property down to the eldest son. Complex intersectional inequalities mean that, despite state-led land reform and housing schemes for low-income families, marginalised communities still struggle to own property and build wealth.

The issue here is that despite the myth of meritocracy and stories of rags to riches, capital breeds capital. The vast majority of people who are born poor will die poor and the same with those born wealthy. The ways in which this happens are many and complex, but, as I argued in 2016,[20] education plays a major part in maintaining and obscuring the social conditions of capitalism. The discourse linking social mobility with education, for example, serves as a fig leaf for inequality. If it can be argued that academic achievement leads to the accumulation of capital, 'people who fail to climb the social ladder have only themselves to blame.'[21] Michael Apple[22] argues in a similar way that the political Right in the USA has benefitted from the social mobility myth. He cites one of its major 'achievements' as having shifted the blame for unemployment and economic stagnation 'from the economic, cultural and social policies and effects of the dominant group to the school and other public agencies.' Similarly, in England, Richard Pring[23] points out that ministers and policymakers hold schools and colleges responsible for the effects of wider social problems because it deflects blame away from themselves, and because it perpetuates the modernist myth that education reform will lead to continuous growth in achievement and in the economy. The combination of capitalism and education, then, exacerbates the toxic effects of modernity for many of the poorest of the world. Not only do they have limited access to resources, but they also come to believe that this is the 'natural' result of them not being clever enough, or that their schools and teachers are not doing as they should.[24]

So, what of the other fractious twin – post-capitalism? Living a post-capitalist lifestyle can take many forms, from intentional communities and communes, to individual choices to reject consumerism and live more simply. For example, communities such as Findhorn in Scotland and Auroville in India organise themselves to live sustainably, share resources and make decisions without hierarchies. Such communities prioritise cooperating over accumulating wealth and possessions. Some have been around for decades, such as the Federation of Egalitarian Communities in the United States, while others are newer and more experimental. Another example is the degrowth movement, which advocates for decreasing production and consumption in favour of ecological sustainability and social justice. This movement emphasises community building, sharing and prioritising quality of life over economic growth. More on this later.

To return to the topic of housing and welfare, a post-capitalist view would start from the position that everyone should have a home and sufficient resources to live a modest and healthy life (without necessarily accumulating capital). The Tiny Houses movement is a good example of this.[25] Whether as a solution for homelessness, or as an opportunity to downsize and focus on the environment, people in different parts of the world are choosing to learn how to build their own small and simple home and to live in community with others. Whilst not a panacea, it is certainly attractive for some to simply sidestep economic pressures and re-focus on what they value most.

If capitalism leads to hard and unfulfilling lives for those whose families have not been able to accumulate significant levels of capital, it is easy to see how post-capitalist futures might involve more and more people dropping out or simply refusing to play the game. It is not as if they were ever going to win anyway! Perhaps, as Zygmunt Bauman[26] points out, people are sick of being 'prodded, forced or cajoled to buy and to spend – to spend what we have and to spend what we don't have but hope to earn in the future.' If this is the case, it is imperative that we begin to educate for alternative futures to the ones that dominate our modernist, capitalist, neoliberal education systems. This is not to say that everyone wants to live in a post-capitalist world – but some do. Many will end up on the wrong side of capitalism in any case, with diminished quality of life, and it is surely better to support people to make conscious choices about their priorities and well-being than to leave them to suffer as losers in the system. As has been shown here, modern systems of education have not yet started to consider what this might look like, and often contribute to the problem in the first place.

Humanism and posthumanism

Two more fractious twins that will be considered here before the chapter concludes are humanism / posthumanism, and truth / post truth. Humanism is defined here in its Enlightenment sense of valorising the achievements of 'man' (democracy, justice, reason). Posthumanism, on the other hand, does not place these achievements centre stage. On a postmodern, posthumanist stage, humanism is criticised for perpetuating a monolithic idea of what it means to be human. Predictably this human is white, male, European and heterosexual. Qualities that this human might possess have been universalised across the whole of humanity with negative consequences for many women, people of colour, people living in low- and middle-income countries (LMICs)[27], and people in LGBTQ+ communities.

Several non-Western theorists have critiqued this careless universalism. They argue that traditional humanism has excluded and silenced the voices and experiences of non-white, non-male, and non-European peoples and cultures, perpetuating a monolithic idea of what it means to be human. Cameroonian philosopher Achille Mbembe,[28] for example, argues that Western humanism has been used to justify colonialism, slavery and other forms of oppression and that a posthumanist perspective is needed to challenge this socio-political domination and to promote more inclusive and egalitarian societies. Similarly, Indian postcolonial scholar Gayatri Chakravorty Spivak[29] has critiqued humanism for being complicit in colonialism and failing to address the specific experiences and struggles of women, people of colour and other marginalised groups.

Posthumanism, then, critiques this essentialist idea of what it means to be human. It also troubles the notion of the biological human as the pinnacle of the evolutionary process. The next chapter will look at the need to move beyond anthropocentric ways of seeing the world, but here I briefly consider a central concept of posthumanism – what it might mean to transcend the limitations of the human through AI.

Yuval Noah Harari[30] in his book *Homo Deus* shares some ideas about what could happen in the future as the interface between the biological human and technology gets blurred. In many ways, the future is already with us as diverse examples show. Implants generate data about levels of insulin and the regularity of heart beats and act before the 'patient' has become aware that there is a problem, for example. Facebook and Google know more about our likes and political preferences than we do, and driverless taxis could soon be on the roads. Biotechnology is a significant growth area, allowing scientists to manipulate living organisms at the molecular level, and augmented reality technology, which overlays digital information onto the real world, is changing the way we experience our embodied realities.

Life expectancy has been subject to rapid growth, and this will continue with some wealthy humans eventually able to live almost indefinitely. Today more people die from obesity than from starvation, more die from old age than from infectious diseases, and more commit suicide than are killed in war. Tomorrow, if the ageing process continues to be countered through technological interventions, the main cause of death for the relatively wealthy technologically assisted human will be a catastrophic accident. Harari suggests that after four billion years of organic life, the era of inorganic life is now beginning, and that the main products of the 21st-century economy will not be textiles, vehicles or weapons, but bodies, brains and minds.

There is an increasing need to address human worklessness, as networked algorithms and machines replace human labour – intellectual as well as physical. Richard and Daniel Susskind[31] predict the decline of today's professions, including doctors, teachers, accountants, architects, the clergy, consultants, lawyers and many others. They suggest that increasingly capable technologies – from telepresence to artificial intelligence – will enable everyone to have the expertise of specialists at their fingertips, and that this will often be without cost or face-to-face interaction. This challenges what they call the 'grand bargain' that has enabled the monopoly of professionals and their ability to operate under conditions that are antiquated, rent-seeking, opaque, unaffordable and only available to a wealthy minority.

The beginning of the decline of traditional professions has led to collective and cooperative attempts to address worklessness. For example, platform cooperativism seeks to create democratic, worker-owned alternatives to the kind of platform economy that companies like Uber and Airbnb tend to use. Platform cooperatives are owned and operated by the people who use them, rather than by outside investors. They thus aim to provide fairer pay and working conditions. Another example is open-source software. Such software challenges the traditional model of corporate-owned proprietary software and aims to democratise access to technology. Similarly, community-owned energy projects, such as solar or wind farms, aim to offer lower prices than those charged by large energy companies. Since it is local communities who own and operate them, they aspire to promote energy independence and create jobs in the community. The common thread across these examples is the desire to take ownership of technology, creating equitable and community-led systems of production and distribution. By challenging the monopoly of traditional professions and business interests, these approaches suggest new opportunities for collective ownership and decision-making in the rapidly altering landscape of work and technology.

The implications of all of this for education are clear. Firstly, as previously stated, we are educating for jobs that will soon cease to exist. Secondly, it seems important to consider basic existential questions, such as the value of a permanently extended life. Without the humanist ideas of justice, liberty, equality and freedom, what will give meaning and purpose in the posthumanist world? Thirdly, as Harari points out, humans will need to navigate their changing relationships with machines and algorithms, probably without understanding what is at stake or how they work. Our current inequalities will be nothing compared with the gap between those who are able to take advantage of these new possibilities and those who are left behind. As some humans seek immortality, happiness and powers of creation, what will become of the majority who will ultimately be rendered superfluous (whilst continuing to negatively impact on the planet)?

It is concerning to consider these questions whilst taking account of the ways in which the basic rights of poor and marginalised people are being ignored, even now. There is already a global reluctance to protect people who have little use value. For example, a global estimate suggests that there were 27.6 million people in forced labour in 2022, of which 12% were children.[32] These children often find themselves cut off from basic human rights. Barely accessing education and healthcare, they are seen as disposable labour, rather than as children who deserve protection and care.

Another example is the plight of refugees and displaced persons. Forced to flee their homes due to conflict, persecution, or environmental disasters, many refugees live in overcrowded and unsanitary camps or informal settlements. Hostility from local inhabitants is often more prevalent than basic services such as healthcare, education and legal protection. Vilified as unwanted outsiders, the basic humanity of refugees is often ignored.

Yet another example of dehumanisation emerges in the global supply chain. Many multinational companies rely on low-wage labour in LMICs. However, the very labour that fortifies these companies can be built on unsustainably long hours, low pay and dangerous environments. Factories may lack basic safety standards and expose workers to toxic chemicals. Treated as replaceable cogs in the machine of economic growth, these workers often go unrecognised as individuals with dignity and rights. This is the dark side of posthumanism.

Truth and post-truth

Finally, I will consider the fractious twins of empirical truth and post-truth. Modernity was built on the foundations of empirical truth, which postulates that the reality that is revealed through our observations and experiments is the same as the reality that exists outside of human exploration (or very close to it). Empirical truth then, is based on a certain view of objective reality. In recent times, the dominance of this 'epistemology' (or way of knowing the world) has been challenged. Not only is it seen as favouring a view of reality that is grounded in disembodied thought and intellect, it is also seen as favouring a modern, urban, liberal, Western view of the world. Some refer to this as the epistemology of the North, meaning the societies that own most of the Earth's resources. Boaventura de Sousa Santos[33] suggests that 'cognitive justice' can be achieved through foregrounding the 'epistemologies of the South,' which challenge the dominance of the Eurocentric thought of the global North. I will explore this in more depth later, but in the meantime, the following poem expresses these complex philosophical ideas in a non-traditional way that speaks to the heart as much as to the mind. I wrote it for a conference on the topic of representation in education research at the Faculty of Education in Cambridge in 2018, and I'm including it here because it hopefully demonstrates the power of poetry, and because it resonates with the methods of the global South, where poetry is often linked with activism for social justice.

Bloodless Angel

I am a bloodless angel. I float in airy efficacy
I exist outside of history, outside of time.
I have no place,
I speak from nowhere in particular.
I speak from everywhere.

I have no thoughts
I convey what is thought
I have no feet,
so I leave no footprint.
I have no hands,
so I do not act.
I have no body
Prick me, and I will not bleed.

They say that god is dead
That his palace in heaven is vacant.
That wind blows through empty rooms
And mice chew on velvet curtains.

I say that god's palace is occupied.
Its rooms are full, its curtains intact
It is occupied by reason, science,
rationality, Enlightenment.
It is occupied by me.

I rest on my canon.
My validity, my reliability, my rationale.

I consort with kings,
With prime ministers, presidents
Philanthropists.
They lend me their ears
They ask me what is true
What is valuable
And what is right.
They are eager to know.

The subjects of my research are not kings,
Or presidents, or angels.
The subjects of my research
Are gendered, ethnic, gay, disabled, poor.
They have bodies.
Entangled in the messiness of time and space,
Grounded in clay.
Prick them, and they bleed.

These bodies are fascinating to me
I wish to know every intimacy.
What does someone with your gender think?
What choices would someone in your ethnic group make?
How is your life impacted by poverty?
My view from nowhere
Pierces their somewhere.

I bestow voice upon them
I give them the gift of the word.
I represent them.
I work for social justice, peace and sustainability.
I turn their utterances into gold.

I have heard that there is another
Coming through
She unsettles me
She (oh the arrogance)
Speaks only for herself.
She stands in the mud
And the clay
Of her positionality,
Bizarrely proud

> Of her bricolage.
> Her participatory methodology.
> Her new story
> Her research journey.
>
> She speaks of postcoloniality
> Patriarchy,
> Elitism.
> She renders me an actor
> In this world,
> Gendered, embodied, classed.
> She dares to colour me white.
>
> I am starting to feel unsettled.
> And yet,
> What is there to fear?
> What harm, what truth
> Could possibly be held
> Within the arms
> Of one
> Simple
> Poem.

This poem expresses so much of what I want to say about what is wrong with the dominance of modern, urban, liberal, Eurocentric ways of knowing. The fractious twin of truth, however, – post truth – is far more dangerous. At least, notions of empirical truth are grounded in attempts at grasping something universal (however flawed). Post-truth is not so well intentioned. Whilst we engage in poetry and dialogue about how to access truth, the post-truth twin is hatching an evil plot. Lee McIntyre[34] has defined post-truth as 'an assertion of ideological supremacy by which its practitioners try to compel someone to believe something regardless of the evidence.' As I argued in 2022,[35] the decline of traditional media, the rise of social media, and the use of fake news for political ends have created the ideal conditions for widespread denial of facts surrounding all kinds of things, including smoking, vaccines, evolution and election results. Cognitive biases that are hardwired in humans can easily be exploited by those who have much to gain politically and economically from this new form of propaganda. Particularly concerning is the use of these methods to scapegoat minoritized groups and refugees for political ends. The issue for education is that we can no longer rely on dialogue to further the aims of peaceful coexistence. If behaviour can be influenced by the clever techniques of marketeers, behavioural psychologists and spin doctors, then education will struggle to compete. As a rule, people will act in predictable ways if they are incentivised or frightened, regardless of what they have been taught in school. How then do we break through to address the need to understand how to weigh up the relative validity of various truth claims?

Conclusion

This chapter, then, has explored the 'fractious twins' of modernity and postmodernity, and how they relate to education, through introducing the related twins of capitalism / postcapitalism, humanism / posthumanism and truth / post-truth. The chapter has made it clear that these twins exist at the same time, with neither of the twins coming before nor after the other. They are fractious because there are many tensions between them that cannot be resolved, but they are also deeply connected, and one could not exist without the other. They all impact powerfully on our understanding of what it is to be educated.

These fractious twins have new relationships with space and time. They are ubiquitous, with no part of the world unaffected by them. They also stretch out time – reaching back into the Enlightenment past as well as forward into the unknown future. The present is therefore more dynamic and unstable than ever. From beliefs about the rational power of humans – and their ability to know and educate from the universal values of democracy, progress and freedom – to new realities concerning cyborgs, permanently deferred mortality and workless populations, education, and even time itself, has taken on new meaning. The twins find themselves overstretched and lacking definition, but they can't step out of the game. Not only do they stand in relation with each other but also with the other twins. Marketing consumer products (capitalism) morphs into the manipulation of behavioural psychology (post-truth), for example, and post-capitalism and posthumanism have much to learn from each other. All of the twins need to inform the ways we think about what it is to educate – and what we are educating for.

This chapter has discussed the modernist / postmodernist conundrum of structure and agency, and the extent to which teachers, parents, students, researchers, activists, project workers and others can take action towards desired futures without being held back by the structures that constrain them. There are no easy answers to these questions, but it seems imperative to take action anyway, trusting that, to the best of our knowledge and ability, our actions have integrity and purpose. Learning how to trust ourselves to make these decisions is the very stuff of education. We can't allow our postmodern angst to paralyse us into inaction – but neither can we afford to direct our efforts purely towards the modernist goal of emancipation, with the 'other' viewed as an object to be acted upon. Education policy needs to stop asking what the poor can do and how they can learn to be more 'developed.' It needs to consider instead what 'we' can do in order to begin to dismantle modern education systems that sustain global inequality. Drawing on concepts of rewilding, then, I am arguing here that the dominance of monocultures of modernity, capitalism, humanism and empirical truth needs to be tempered. Their related posts- are not proffered here as the solution. They are offered as a means of beginning to understand the ecosystem of our new global realities.

Notes

1 Pinker, S. (2011). *The better angels of our nature: why violence has declined*. Viking Books.
2 Ball, S., & Collet-Sabé, J. (2022). Against school: an epistemological critique. *Discourse: Studies in the Cultural Politics of Education*, 43, 6, 985–999.
3 Midgley, M. (2007). *The myths we live by*. Routledge. p.171.
4 Cremin, H. (2018). What comes after post/modern peace education? *Educational Philosophy and Theory*, 50(14), 1564–1565.
5 Lyotard, J.-F. (1979). *La condition postmoderne: Rapport sûr le savoir*. Les Editions de Minuit.
6 Illich, I. (1980, December 1). *The De-Linking of Peace and Development* [Opening Address]. First Meeting of the Asian Peace Research Association, Yokohama.
7 Arendt, H. (2006). *Between past and future* (Fourth). Penguin.
8 Ken Robinson (2015, June). Do schools kill creativity? [Video]. TED Conferences, accessed January 2025 https://www.ted.com/talks/sir_ken_robinson_do_schools_kill_creativity.
9 Cremin, H., & Bevington, T. (2017). *Positive peace in schools: tackling conflict and creating a culture of peace in the classroom*. Routledge.
10 This is not to imply that local authority schools are second-rate – quite the opposite. Local authorities are often left to provide individual learning plans for out-of-school young people with inadequate resources.
11 Perrucci, R., & Wysong, E. (2008). *New class society: goodbye American dream?* Rowman & Littlefield.
12 PISA stands for 'Programme for International Student Assessment.' It is a study conducted every three years by the Organization for Economic Cooperation and Development (OECD). PISA assesses how 15-year-old students around the world perform in reading, mathematics, and science literacy. The results are often highly publicised, with PISA measures used by governments, educators and researchers to evaluate how different education systems compare to one another and the strengths and weaknesses of each country's system.
13 Smith, D. G. (2020). *Confluences: intercultural journaling in research and teaching. From hermeneutics to a changing world order*. Information Age Publishing.
14 Biesta, G. (2016). *The Beautiful Risk of Education*. Routledge.
15 Bauman, Z. (2012). *On education: Conversations with Riccardo Mazzeo*. Policy Press.
16 Giroux, H. (2009). *Youth in a suspect society: Democracy or Disposability?* Palgrave Macmillan.
17 Bauman, Z. (2012). *On education: Conversations with Riccardo Mazzeo*. Policy Press.
18 Borrett, A. (2021). How UK house prices have soared ahead of average wages, *The New Statesman*. Accessed Jan 2025. https://www.newstatesman.com/politics/2021/05/how-uk-house-prices-have-soared-ahead-average-wages.

19 Chancel, L., Piketty, T., Saez, E., Zucman, G. et al. World Inequality Report 2022, World Inequality Lab.
20 Cremin, H. (2016). Peace education research in the twenty-first century: three concepts facing crisis or opportunity? *Journal of Peace Education, 13*(1), 1–17.
21 Bauman, Z. (2012). *On education: conversations with Riccardo Mazzeo*. Policy Press. p.72.
22 Apple, M. (2013). *Can education change society?* Routledge. p.ix.
23 Pring, R. (2013). *The life and death of secondary education for all*. Routledge.
24 Allen, A. (2014). *Education in and beyond the Age of Reason*. Palgrave Macmillan.
25 Wikipedia, accessed January 2025. https://en.wikipedia.org/wiki/Tiny-house_movement.
26 Bauman, Z. (2012). *On education: conversations with Riccardo Mazzeo*. Policy Press. p.29.
27 This book uses the term 'lower- and middle-income countries' throughout to refer to less structurally and materially advantaged parts of the world, choosing not to employ terms such as 'developing' or 'developed' nations.
28 Mbembe, A. (2019). *Achille Mbembe*. Duke University Press.
29 Sharpe, J., & Spivak, G. C. (2003). A conversation with Gayatri Chakravorty Spivak: Politics and the imagination. *Signs: journal of women in culture and society, 28*(2), 609–624.
30 Harari, Y. N. (2017). *Homo Deus: a brief history of tomorrow*. HarperCollins.
31 Susskind, R., & Susskind, D. (2017). *The future of the professions: how technology will transform the work of human experts*.
32 International Labour Organisation, accessed January 2025. https://www.ilo.org/topics/forced-labour-modern-slavery-and-trafficking-persons/data-and-research-forced-labour.
33 de Sousa Santos, B. (2018). *The end of the cognitive empire: the coming of age of epistemologies of the south*. Duke University Press.
34 McIntyre, L. (2018). *Post-Truth*. The MIT Press. NP.
35 Cremin, H. (2022). The next 40 years of peace education. *Rauhankasvatus Instituutti*. Accessed January 2025. https://rauhankasvatus.fi/professor-hilary-cremin-the-next-40-years-of-peace-Education/.

Chapter 2

Tunnel vision and neglect of the climate emergency

Introduction

This chapter builds on the previous chapter by considering how education (within the failed modernist project) has impacted on ways of thinking about the natural environment. In particular, I discuss here how the industrial way of life favoured across most of the planet is based on what Schumacher[1] has referred to as the false assumption that irreplaceable natural capital can be treated as income. I reveal the follies inherent in obsession with GNP, economic growth and consumerism, and in inadequate responses to exponential population growth. I discuss the role that education has played in all of this, both through its neglect of the climate emergency and through perpetuating false ideas about a human 'mastery' over nature. The chapter considers alternative ways of thinking about truth, reality, and the good life beyond the tunnel vision of modernity and consumerism. It asks whether the toxic legacies that we are bequeathing on the young are inevitable, or whether we can find ways of educating as if young people mattered.

Personal reflections and nature-based stories

But first, why am I writing this book about rewilding? It is grounded very much in my love of nature, and natural processes of learning and teaching. My love of nature started young. My earliest years, up to the age of 7, were spent in a new town on the edge of the countryside. My sister and I joke that we were feral – our parents let us play out as much as we liked and required only that we came in for mealtimes. There were meadows nearby, and a stream, and I remember the delight that I felt in buttercups and dandelion clocks and cow parsley. Sometimes today when I meditate, I try to get back the feeling of wonder and timelessness that I felt then (it is hard). There were no adults supervising us, and we did get into scrapes, but I think my resilience comes from this time. I remember one such scrape involved making a 'train' by tying several bikes and trikes together with skipping rope and launching down a hill. This particular scrape was resolved with a liberal use of plasters, tissues and antiseptic cream (snook out of the house because we 'big ones' were supposed to be looking after the 'little ones'), but more widely we learned to solve problems and make sense of the world away from the adult gaze and largely in nature.

From there we moved to an urban space where there was a lot of poverty. I remember my astonishment when I left my bike outside to go inside for dinner only to find it gone when I came back out again. I remember the parks and green spaces that we found to play in. After that we moved to a small town on the edge of the Birmingham conurbation on the one side, and the Severn Valley and its woods, hills and rivers on the other. The woods near our house were our playground. We ate blackberries and sweet chestnuts, climbed trees, and created extended fantasies about who lived in the witches' wood and beneath the lightning tree. My parents were mature students throughout much of this time, and so there was very little money, but we spent a lot of time together walking and camping. I remember that my dad would sometimes point to the fields around us and say, 'just look at that green!' And we did.

I went back to the woods where I used to play recently and discovered the same people there enjoying the green space. The key difference, however, is that these people are now, like me – in their 60s. They had dogs on long leads and assiduously picked up their poo. There were no children. The woods felt silent and barren without the sounds of children echoing around the trees. Why have we decided that these beautiful green spaces are safe for people in their 60s, but not for children?

In 2018, Robert Macfarlane and Jackie Morris[2] produced a book called *The Lost Words Spells*. They wrote the book because so many words about things in nature have disappeared from young people's everyday language. Since 2007, for example, the editors of the Oxford Junior Dictionary have been removing words from the dictionary that no longer seem relevant to the modern child. These words include acorn, bluebell, ivy, fern, moss, blackberry, dandelion, lark, raven, heron, starling, hazel, heather, goldfinch, grey seal, otter and kingfisher. These words were removed to make way for other words like attachment, blog, broadband, chat room, database, committee, and voice-mail. My heart breaks when I read things like this.

In recent years I have been travelling a lot for work, including to Colombia, Brazil and Mexico. The irony of how my carbon footprint would have contributed to global warming does not escape me, but I remember feeling heavy and depressed when I was confronted with environmental degradation in that part of the world. In particular, I remember the sugar cane plantations near Sao Paulo in Brazil. The blow to my heart came twice. First, because I realised how extensive the slave trade was, and how many lives would have been blighted and lost on those vast expanses. Second, because of the eery bleakness of such a massive monoculture. Anything that was not sugar cane was not tolerated for mile after mile after mile. This would have been an area where, for centuries, indigenous people would have taken care to protect the delicate ecosystems that sustained their way of life. Pacifist as I am, I feel like shooting the colonialist who, in the nearby city which is named after the joining of two rivers where the fishes used to play, decided to divert the rivers through a concrete channel. The waters now flow along straight lines, and are black and poisonous and dead. This for me is the perfect image of the cold dead heart of modernity. The original genocide of the indigenous people, the brutality of slavery and the destruction of natural ecosystems combined on that visit to make me feel overwhelmed with sadness and a sense of hopelessness. This feeling comes to me sometimes and feels a bit like homesickness. It has been called 'solastalgia' by Glen Albrecht[3] who used the word to denote homesickness, whilst still at home, because of losses due to climate change. I wonder how much longer we can continue to impose our will over nature, depleting so much of our biosystem and damaging the planet itself. This poem that I wrote in Mexico City about Quetzalcoatl, the Aztec snake god, expresses some of this:

Mexico City

Beneath the concrete
The land lies sleeping
Holding close
Cherished bones.

Above the concrete
Cars and people swarm.
Eating plastic food
Shedding plastic skin.

Incessantly sweeping
tending, repairing,
They feel their victory
uncertain.

For the land lies waiting.
Ancestors
And sun gods
Lie waiting.

For the time
When no one will sweep,
Or tend or repair.
Or subdue.

> For the time
> When the snake
> will break
> through concrete.
>
> And the rivers will flow,
> And their banks will breathe.
> And the land will rise
> And the jungle will fill with birds.
>
> And the humans
> Will fall back
> And take their place
> once more.
>
> Amongst the ones
> Who slither, and creep
> And leap and fly
> On brightly coloured wings.

In summary then, these issues are deeply personal. This book is my attempt to grapple with them to try to make things better for myself and for at least some people for some of the time, especially children and young people who have inherited such a toxic legacy. I could have started this chapter with a series of shocking statistics about the imminent danger that we face due to the climate emergency, but I trust that my readers are already versed in such statistics. Sometimes, personal stories and poetry are more powerful because they bring these issues into the everyday. We all have stories like this. Perhaps most disturbing are those that concern humanity's unwillingness to reverse the trends that will ultimately make the planet uninhabitable for us and many other species. Readers will no doubt remember Donald Trump's mocking words about Greta Thunberg in Switzerland in 2020 at the United Nations Climate Action Summit. Trump said that she appeared to be, 'a very happy young girl looking forward to a bright and wonderful future,' after she had just delivered an impassioned speech about world leaders having stolen her dreams and childhood by pretending that mass extinction due to climate change can be solved with technical solutions and business as usual.[4] Her powerlessness in the face of his dismissiveness is heartbreaking.

It feels as if we have forgotten that our most important task is to leave the planet in a good state for our children. My exasperation at our inertia is perhaps best summed up in the Netflix film *Don't Look up*, by Adam McKay in which an astronomy student and her academic supervisor (Leonardo

DiCaprio) discover a comet that's on a direct collision course with Earth.[5] Just as with the climate emergency, the problem is that no one seems to care enough to act, with senior politicians and the media only interested in exploiting the situation to promote their interests and to protect their usual ways of doing things. The idiocy and self-destructiveness of humanity are laid bare in this movie, and it serves as a useful focus for discussion about the situation in which we find ourselves.

The roots of the climate emergency

I will now turn to three important thinkers who discuss some of the roots of the climate emergency and the ways that these have been naturalised and made invisible – Satish Kumar,[6] Rob Nixon[7] and E.F. Schumacher.[8] The roots of the climate emergency will be shared here as a series of broken relationships: with economics, with nature, and with time. The final section will consider how education has contributed to this state of affairs.

The economy

Many successful industrialists and businesspeople have become rich on the basis of natural resources that they have claimed and depleted. Whether this is oil, or water, or land, or forests, or fish, the logic of the market mandates that they are free to keep the profits that they accumulate, whilst others meet the costs. Costs include both the wider infrastructure that is necessary for their trade (roads, water systems, electricity, a literate workforce), and the costs of cleaning up or caring for the sick and displaced. Whilst many benefit, others also pay the costs in terms of diminished quality of life. Some of these have not yet been born. And what goes unnoticed is the cost paid by the environment.

Schumacher points out the folly of a globalised economy that is built on the idea that irreplaceable natural capital can be treated as income. Supporters of the modern industrial system ignore the fact that production consumes the very basis on which it has been erected (back to Bauman's ouroboros from Chapter One). Production also requires permanent growth and globalisation. This has become so much part of our modern way of living that we see it as natural and inevitable, despite the catastrophic consequences for the environment and the quality of people's lives. The Ganges river in India, for example – a well-worn site of pilgrimage for Hindus – has become the world's fifth most polluted river, with its water not even safe for bathing. This sacred river has made many people wealthy through the transportation infrastructure that was needed for India's global trade and regional industrialisation, but the associated pollution has impoverished the lives of many more people, including the poor.

Global trade also threatens the planet due to war and nuclear threat. It depends on competition, protectionism, militarisation and the accumulation of weapons, including nuclear bombs. This is because our need to trade across the world makes us vulnerable – both in terms of our dependence on fossil fuels for imports and exports, and in terms of the products themselves. The Syrian conflict, for example, resulted in pipelines that transport oil and gas from the Middle East to Europe being targeted by militant groups, disrupting global supplies and damaging local ecosystems. As Kumar points out, if we remain dependent on oil from the Middle East, gas from Russia, and tea, gadgets, cooking oil, out-of-season fruit and vegetables, coffee and clothing from everywhere in the world, it is easy to see how we can be implicated in cataclysmic global events, such as the war in Ukraine or conflict in the Middle East. Whether this results in nuclear war, or 'merely' the forms of warfare that destroy cities and habitats, the environment is always a forgotten victim.

Schumacher is particularly concerned with threats to the planet due to the ways in which an industrial mindset has been applied to the economy of agriculture. Not only does this deny people the opportunity of working with soil and farming naturally and seasonally, it also leads to the mismanagement of land, animals, food storage and food processing. As agribusiness confines animals to cruel and unnatural pens and cages and maintains monocultures with pesticides and artificial fertiliser, the rights of animals, humans and the entire ecosystem are subjugated in favour of profit. Schumacher points out that this is not due to lack of resources or to ignorance of how to do things better. Feeding the global population is entirely possible. It is due to the fact that 'as a society, we have no firm basis of belief in any meta economic values, and when there is no such belief the economic calculus takes over.'[9]

The need for new ways of thinking about the economy of agriculture is vital if we are to take the climate emergency seriously and move forward with compassion for animals, humans and the natural environment. We must learn from initiatives such as permaculture and agroforestry. This must start with education. If we fail to educate young people to work with their hands and produce more goods locally for local consumption, we will continue to be dependent on imports and exports, and to perpetuate the abuses and risks listed earlier.

Distance from nature

Humans have forgotten how to be humble and proportionate, and how to maintain reciprocal, respectful and reverential relationships with the rest of nature. Kumar uses the word 'speciesism' to refer to a worldview that sees humans as superior to all other species. In this worldview, animals, forests, rivers and oceans exist only to fulfil the needs, greed and desires of human beings. This is a 'shallow ecology', whereas a deep ecology might 'recognise the intrinsic value of all life, small or large.' Thus, 'a blade of grass, an earthworm, an insect, even a mosquito has the right to life; so have trees, rivers, birds and fish, irrespective of their usefulness to humans.'[10]

Kumar suggests that our indifference to nature is partly due to disconnection. The modern way of life is designed precisely to keep us away from nature – with homes and offices artificially lit, heated and cooled. Any ills that we face from our sedentary lifestyles, such as poor diet or lack of time spent in nature, are dealt with through the use of pharmaceuticals that prolong our lives, despite multiple comorbidities. This disconnection leads to a lack of ethical and moral responsibility towards nature. It is hard to protect something that we do not know and love.

Kumar speaks of a moral imperative to protect the soil and the oceans, pointing out that no ethical standards would permit us to fill the oceans with plastics or the biosphere with carbon dioxide. It is the moral responsibility of every generation to leave the land as we found it, but it is also the moral responsibility of every generation to honour the rights of other species, who are also members of Earth's community.

Time

Our changing relationship with time is another way in which the root causes of climate change are naturalised and made invisible. Nixon talks about environmental degradation as slow violence. Whereas we tend to think of violence in terms of quick, dramatic, one-off episodes, climate change involves 'long dyings.'[11] Whilst shallow graves, burning towers, terrorist bombs, avalanches, volcanoes and tsunamis have visceral, eye-catching qualities, slow violence, unfolding over years, decades, even centuries, struggles to gain the attention of the media. Stories of toxic build-up, greenhouse gases and accelerated species loss due to ravaged habitats are just as cataclysmic, but the casualties are postponed, often for generations. For example, in the Himalayan mountains, climate change is causing glaciers to melt, which in turn puts populations at higher risk of flash floods and landslides, but this is not being addressed by policymakers or the media because glacial melt is so slow and gradual that no one is ever fully held to account. Casualties from slow violence are often out of sync with electoral cycles. Even if politicians do engage with environmental issues, they tend to put off any action until they themselves will have to face the immediate consequences of restraint, repair or long-term investment.

This lack of care about the ways in which slow violence is meted out on future generations (and on the poor, even now) has its counterpart in the lack of care about the speed of turbo-charged capitalism. As Nixon[12] says, 'the present feels more abbreviated than it used to – at least for the world's privileged classes who live surrounded by technological timesavers that often compound the sensation of not having enough time.' Kumar makes a similar point, asking where all the time has gone. Centuries ago, when people were less well-off materially and economically, they were able to build magnificent cathedrals, mosques and temples. Now we prefer prefabricated buildings and feel that we have no time, despite labour-saving devices in our homes and workspaces. Somehow the impression is being created that there is never enough time and that tackling climate change will have to wait.

Education

Many questions arise from all of this for education. If education aims to prepare young people to be economic citizens, why is such an unsustainable view of the economy at the heart of schooling? If education aims to produce young people who are aware of their moral and ethical responsibilities, why does it ignore the moral imperative of protecting the planet? If education aims to eradicate sexism and racism, why does speciesism go unchallenged? If education aims for global peace, why are the ways of war promoted in classrooms? If education aims to enable problem-solving and innovation, why are the problems of the medium- and long-term future systematically ignored? Why do so many young people think that the climate emergency will not happen in their lifetime?

Many will say that some of these things are covered at least some of the time in schools. It is my contention, however, that this is done superficially, that it amounts to tinkering around the edges, and that there is something fundamentally wrong with a system of education that continues business as usual in the face of so much destruction. This serves to naturalise the causes of climate change and render them invisible. Education is one of the major contributors to the unsustainable mindsets that threaten not only our own continued existence, but also that of other species. I will end this chapter by suggesting three ways in which education is complicit in this.

Firstly, education deals in abstractions. Abstraction can be seen in the ways that living systems are taught in schools in subjects like biology, but it can also be seen in the epistemologies (ways of knowing) of the various academic disciplines. Children and young people are taught to associate abstraction with intelligence and academic success. Contextualised learning is often associated with failure and less-able learners, despite the obvious benefits of apprenticeships and practical on-the-job training.

This overvaluing of abstraction means that many young people are denied opportunities to connect with nature in their locality and to explore the specifics of place. They develop the language and concepts of universalism, rather than the language of connection, appreciation and love. They become less likely to express the depth and richness of experiences in nature and more likely to objectify and violate it. The links between abstraction and extraction cannot be ignored. If the natural world is set up as a universal resource separate from direct human experience, it can be objectified and made available for human exploitation. Education is an important means by which this idea is normalised.

Secondly, education supports a metaphysics of mastery. It does this throughout the curriculum,[13] but when this is applied to nature, it implies that global warming can be dealt with by human ingenuity and technology. An impression is created that there is no need to learn from nature, or to inhibit our industrialised way of life, because one day a clever person will emerge from school and show us how to sort all this out. This kind of thinking has been called 'technological utopianism' or 'techno-optimism.'[14] It can lead to arrogance and poor decision-making. Hornborg gives the Bank of America's 55-story skyscraper in Manhattan, New York, as one such example. Billed as one of the world's 'most environmentally responsible high-rise office buildings' and 'the most sustainable in the country' in 2010, it was assessed as producing more greenhouse gases than any similarly sized office building in Manhattan a mere two years later, and as using more than twice as much energy as the 80-year-old Empire State Building. If education perpetuates shallow perceptions of technology as a quick fix, then this can reinforce the trend of businesses only talking about sustainability for the purposes of greenwashing rather than for anything more fundamental. Education must not be allowed to fetishise technological advances for their own sake.

Thirdly, education serves to normalise violent, exploitative and unsustainable relations. Science education in the UK, for example, often builds narratives of voyages of discovery and exploration whilst remaining silent about exploitation of native people and natural resources.[15] Education fundamentally refuses to question the paradoxes, omissions and falsehoods that maintain the status quo. It serves instead to teach the young to be proficient at sleepwalking like the rest of us. Bonnett[16] calls this 'normalising catastrophe.'

Conclusion

This chapter, then, has outlined some personal and theoretical roots of what I feel is the urgent need for rewilding. It is not possible to take action, or to educate differently, if we are not aware of the ways in which climate change is normalised and rendered invisible. The first step is to see things as they are. Many people in the global North are reluctant to do this because modern civilization has set their identities as mere shoppers and consumers, and they have a high standard of living that they don't want to have to give up. Kumar points out, however, that the economic advantages that capitalists and former colonisers continue to enjoy may well be short lived. Stable societies with happy and prosperous people require more than the kinds of knowledge and skills that are the stuff of modern systems of education. They require knowledge and skills that enable sustainable and equitable lifestyles and a mentality that gives dignity to makers, growers, creators, builders and workers.

Notes

1 Schumacher, E. F. (2011). *Small is beautiful: a study of economics as if people mattered*. Vintage.
2 MacFarlane, R., & Morris, J. (2018). *The lost words: a spell book*. House of Anansi Press Ltd.
3 Albrecht, G. (2019). *Earth emotions: new words for a new world*. Cornell University Press.

4 Mark Landler and Somini Sengupta. (2020). *New York Times*. Accessed January 2025. https://www.nytimes.com/2020/01/21/climate/greta-thunberg-trump-davos.html.
5 McKay, A. (2021). *Don't look up*. Netflix.
6 Kumar, S. (2017). *Soil soul society: A new trinity for our time* (3rd ed.). Leaping Hare Press.
7 Nixon, R. (2011). *Slow violence and the environmentalism of the poor*. Harvard University Press.
8 Schumacher, E. F. (2011). *Small is beautiful: a study of economics as if people mattered*. Vintage.
9 Schumacher, E. F. (2011). *Small is beautiful: a study of economics as if people mattered*. Vintage. p.93.
10 Kumar, S. (2017). *Soil soul society: a new trinity for our time* (3rd ed.). Leaping Hare Press. p.19.
11 Nixon, R. (2011). *Slow violence and the environmentalism of the poor*. Harvard University Press. p.2.
12 Nixon, R. (2011). *Slow violence and the environmentalism of the poor*. Harvard University Press. p.8.
13 Bonnett, M. (2013). Normalizing catastrophe: sustainability and scientism. *Environmental Education Research, 19* (2), 187–197.
14 Hornborg, A. & Martinez-Alier, J., (2016). Ecologically unequal exchange and ecological debt. *Journal of Political Ecology 23*(1), 328–333.
15 Gandolfi, H. E. (2021). Decolonising the science curriculum in England: bringing decolonial science and technology studies to secondary education. *The Curriculum Journal*, 32(3), 510–532.
16 Bonnett, M. (2013). Normalizing catastrophe: sustainability and scientism. *Environmental Education Research, 19* (2), 187–197. p.187.

Chapter 3

Making us ill

Introduction

In this chapter I build on the previous chapter by turning the focus from harm to the planet to harm that we are doing to ourselves. I take a long hard look at the poor physical and mental health that permeates education systems throughout the world. From the point of view of physical health, there is a lack of regard for bodily needs and a lack of time and space for movement and play. From the point of view of mental health, there is teacher stress and problems retaining teachers on the one hand; and a lack of student well-being, anxiety, bullying, school refusal and exclusion on the other. Poor mental health applies to both winners and losers in the education system: losers through the impact of underachievement, lack of opportunity and poverty; and winners through the effects of stress, pressure and diminished freedom and personal autonomy. These issues will be reviewed here, with a particular focus on the UK, as well as issues surrounding the field of psychology and its application to education.

Poor physical health in schools

Despite a focus on healthy lifestyles in school curricula throughout the world, schools are contributing to poor physical health amongst young people and teachers. They are failing to impact on the unhealthy lifestyles that result from poverty and from modern industrial ways of life. This point will be made here by focussing on just two aspects of physical health: exercise and toilets. Others that I could have chosen include a general lack of education about diet and cooking and a lack of high-quality sex and relationships education.

To start with exercise, in the UK, according to government statistics, between November 2001 and April 2010, approval was given for the sale of 246 playing fields in England. Some of this was to release capital to improve the infrastructure of school buildings, some was to provide land for housing, and some was because of closure or merger of schools. Since 2010, almost 300 school playing fields have been sold.[1] The GMB, the union for amateur and semi-professional footballers, warns that this places England's footballing future at risk, as well

DOI: 10.4324/9781003627807-5

as flying in the face of the need to tackle childhood obesity.[2] According to statistics from the British National Health Service[3], the percentage of 4–5-year-old children who are obese increased from 9.9% in 2019–20 to 14.4% in 2020–21. Amongst 10–11-year-olds, it increased from 21.0% in 2019–20 to 25.5% in 2020–21. The impact of lockdown and the closure of school buildings because of the pandemic can be seen in these statistics, but levels of obesity in primary children remained unacceptably high in 2023–24 at 22.1%. These figures point to the dangers of young people's sedentary lifestyles.

In Australia, similar threats to children's health and well-being have emerged; at just five years of age, one in five Australian children experience obesity.[4] Public health experts have flagged the role of shrinking spaces for children to play and exercise freely; over half of 300 state schools surveyed reported sacrificing playgrounds to build new classrooms. Studies of paediatric obesity in Australia have flagged that children need more playgrounds, parks, bike paths and green space, because longitudinal studies show that providing children opportunities to be mobile (e.g. walkable or bikeable paths to school) lowers body mass index and counters childhood obesity.

Another risk for childhood obesity can be found in reduced time for physical education (PE). In February 2018, the Youth Sport Trust[5] published a report on shrinking PE provision in UK schools. The report was based on results from an online survey of teachers in 487 secondary schools. The report's findings concluded that the average number of curriculum PE minutes had declined over time, with Key Stage 3 (11–14-year-olds) declining by 20% over the last five years, and Key Stage 4 (14–16 year-olds) declining by 38%. Research published in the *British Medical Journal*[6] links losses of PE lessons in schools with reductions in health-related fitness (HRF) over this same period. The losses include muscle strength, cardio-vascular fitness, ball-catching skills and jumping. They conclude:

> Adolescent HRF has declined in recent years, in parallel with PE lessons. Declines were observed across all young people and particularly those of low fitness and normal BMI. To reach the majority of young people, policy makers could increase PE in schools to increase activity and prevent worsening fitness and health in future generations.

There is not the capacity in this chapter to review every aspect of school life that contributes to ill health, but it does seem important to discuss the frequent lack of adequate toilet facilities, as this is an often-neglected area for discussion. Children's needs for safe water, sanitation and hygiene are still going unmet globally. In 2018, UNICEF[7] found that over 620 million children lacked basic sanitation services in their school. Parts of the world affected by the ravages of colonialism, chronic poverty or conflict can be particularly vulnerable: for example, 1 in 3 primary schools in Ethiopia did not have facilities to dispose of solid waste in 2017.

I am concerned about the issue of toilets in schools for four main reasons. Firstly, we require children and young people to attend school. They have no choice, and so it is incumbent on adults to meet their basic physical needs whilst in school. Secondly, I know that many young people 'hold on' at school because they find using a toilet unpleasant, unsafe and exposing. Some of these young people have related health issues. Thirdly, my own research in a secondary school[8] revealed that inadequate toilet facilities were experienced by young people as an abuse of their human rights and a sign of the low esteem in which they were held. In this research school the toilets were permanently locked, and young people had to find an adult with a key if they wished to use the toilet. This was because there had been vandalism in the past. The toilets themselves were dirty and broken, and there was a pecking order amongst peers which dictated who could occupy precious private space when it could be found and who could not. This hierarchy was maintained by bullying. It is easy to see why some young people try to wait until they get home to go to the toilet, but this is not a solution, especially for young girls who may be learning to manage their periods.

Burton[9] carried out a literature review of research investigating school toilets and their role in the health and well-being of children (with specific reference to Scotland). She assessed children's experiences and reported on five themes that were raised by them: health and well-being; safety and respect; facilities and standards; adults' and children's equality of access; and issues of power and control. The review found that restricted access and poor-quality toilets can result in inadequate hand hygiene, leading to illnesses such as gastroenteritis or unpleasant conditions such as threadworm. Irregular toilet use can contribute to bladder problems such as urinary tract infections, wetting and dysfunctional voiding and to bowel problems such as constipation, soiling and dysfunctional elimination syndrome. These may have long-term health consequences, including psychological difficulties if a child suffers day or night-time wetting.

Poor psychological health in schools

In 2020, research based on data from the Millennium Cohort Study[10] in the UK found that, by the age of 17, 10% of females and 4% of males had self-harmed with suicidal intent. These are shocking statistics. If a significant number of students under 17 are so profoundly unhappy that they wish to end their life, their schools, families and wider society have failed them. There are few educational outcomes more important than well-being and resilience, and many young people are vulnerable because they leave school without attaining them. It is my view that students' vulnerability is not being recognised in schools, despite the fact that it is spoken about a lot. Students can get caught in an endless loop of performing vulnerability in ways that reinforce an unhealthy sense of victimhood, and this can create an impression that vulnerability is everywhere. However, despite a lot of talk, labelling and professional development and training for teaching staff, problems persist and grow. We must take care to ensure that these practices do not take the place of genuine encounter, healing and change.

In 2020, I wrote a chapter with Kevin Kester[11] in a book about the pedagogy of vulnerability. In it, I shared a poem about one of my formative experiences as a teacher, and what a student called Michelle[12] taught me. She had a label of SEBD (social emotional and behavioural difficulties) and she was often angry. As I said in the chapter, I needed to be vulnerable to this child's anger in order to reach her – I couldn't meet her anger with my own, no matter how provoked I felt. Through making myself vulnerable to her I knew that she would find her own vulnerability beneath the anger, and it worked. I seem to remember that I missed my staff Christmas party one year to be with her whilst she sobered up before going home, having snuck alcohol into school. Our conversation that afternoon transformed both of us. I thought that she hated me, she had been so challenging, but her Christmas card to me expressed nothing but love. Michelle got what she needed that afternoon to turn a corner in her attitude towards school, and to be included in normal lessons. More immediately, she survived Christmas at home in difficult circumstances. These kinds of moments can, quite literally, save lives.

I often wonder how Michelle might fare today. I have noticed that many UK schools now have a good number of paraprofessionals (teaching assistants, behaviour mentors, etc.) and that young people like Michelle spend a lot of their time out of the classroom. When they are having a bad time, or are disruptive, they are taken away to an 'inclusion unit' so that teachers can get on with the job of teaching. Whilst many would argue that it is good for teachers to be able to focus on teaching and learning in their subject specialism and for young people to get out-of-class support, it is nevertheless a shame, in my view, that teachers don't get to respond to the 'feedback' of challenging behaviour from students like Michelle. Some of the most stressful times of my life have been spent in classrooms where students were disruptive. My craft as a teacher was shaped in the fire of these experiences. What was good for the more volatile students (usually less talking from the front) was also good for most of the others.

I worry that an increasingly exam-oriented, content-driven curriculum might force alienating teaching-styles that disproportionately affect students who find it hard to just sit and listen. I also worry that a significant minority of students are being kept out of the way and managed through their time in school by well-meaning, but often low-wage non-teaching staff. Despite growing recognition of a wide range of special needs in schools, including neurodiversity and mental health issues, I'm not sure that there is adequate recognition of the ways that schools themselves label and perpetuate the harms that they set out to address. I think that it's important for young people to feel safe to make themselves vulnerable to their teachers in ways that have the potential to bring about real change. For this, teachers also need to feel safe to make themselves vulnerable and to build strong learning relationships with the full diversity of the student population. This will not happen in schools that internally exclude, or keep apart, the students who bring the gift of challenge and the potential for change.

It is hard to know when statistics about poor mental health amongst young people and their teachers will reach a point where we feel that something needs to change. We don't appear to have reached that point. Earlier in this chapter, shocking statistics around self-harm and suicide in the UK were shared, but mental health problems amongst young people are a global phenomenon. The World Health Organisation estimated in 2024[13] that, globally, one in seven 10–19-year-olds experiences a mental disorder, accounting for 15% of disease in this age group. Suicide is the third leading cause of death among 15–19-year-olds worldwide, and depression, anxiety and behavioural disorders are among the leading causes of illness and disability among adolescents. According to the Center for Disease Control and Protection in the USA[14] more than 40% of high school students had experienced persistent feelings of sadness or hopelessness in 2023, and 20% of students had seriously considered attempting suicide. Unfortunately, poor mental health often persists into adulthood, impairing both physical and mental health and limiting life opportunities.

Distress amongst young people, then, appears to be unacceptably high. Whilst the causes cannot be isolated to schools, it can't be ignored that schools, at the very least, are not equipping young people to live well with the kinds of 21st-century stresses and problems that are reviewed throughout this book. A bolder view might suggest that schools are actively contributing to the problems faced by young people. This could be due to a lack of adequate funding, or to the toxic effects of cultures of schooling. Either way, young people are suffering.

Lack of teacher well-being

As hooks[15] has noted, there is a serious crisis in education if students don't want to learn, and teachers don't want to teach. In 2024, according to the NASUWT teachers' union[16] in the UK, 86% of teachers believed that the job had impacted negatively on their mental health in the previous 12 months. In a survey of nearly 12,000 teachers and school leaders, 87% of teachers said that in the previous 12 months they had lost sleep because of their job, 84% had low energy levels, 7% had increased or started to take antidepressants, and 3% said that they had self-harmed. Reasons behind increases in work-related stress include workload (54%), pupil behaviour (36%), monitoring and accountability measures (26%), pupil academic performance (19%) and financial worries (19%). Clearly, things are not as they should be.

The inadequacy of traditional education psychology

The preceding accounts make it clear that ill health inevitably results for millions of young people and teachers worldwide when the worst excesses of modernity are combined with the degradation of the planet and growing levels of inequality (see Chapter Four). It is also clear that many young people are struggling or unhappy, and that our modern education systems are doing little to prepare them for challenges to come. It seems that the medical profession is getting better at keeping bodies alive, but not at enabling them to thrive, and that schools are failing to begin the important conversation about what a healthy and fulfilled life looks like beyond failed 20th-century paradigms. Thriving should be the remit of education psychology, but I will argue here that it can fail young people in two key ways: firstly when it draws on traditional deficit models, rather than on models that are grounded in human thriving (e.g. positive psychology); and secondly when it is complicit in modes of pacification and control that are detrimental to mental health and well-being.

Deficit models in education

The field of education has historically been dominated by the discipline of psychology, and this has contributed to the idea that change needs to come from individuals being better adapted to the system rather than the other way around.[17] Although psychology more generally continues to evolve and diversify, with important developments such as social psychology and positive psychology, these have largely been ignored by traditional educational psychology in favour of notions of deficit and the medicalisation of need and care.[18] When healthy young people are subjected to psychological or pharmaceutical interventions to enable them to cope in a sick system, we know that we have a problem.[19]

Children at both ends of the putative ability spectrum suffer from the effects of comparison and high stakes testing, but students with special educational needs and disabilities – SEND – fare particularly badly. They are diagnosed, managed and kept apart – many of them destined for ongoing marginalisation on welfare or in prison. According to a paper in the journal *Health Affairs* in the USA,[20] among people in state and federal prisons in 2016, an estimated 66% reported themselves as disabled. The distribution of specific types of disability shows that bipolar, depressive and anxiety disorders were especially common, as well as attention deficit hyperactivity disorder (ADHD) and having been diagnosed with SEND at school. There is of course not a causal link between SEND and incarceration, and yet we cannot ignore the fact that disproportionately high numbers of young people with SEND are being sent to prison. Something is not working.

Young people who are perceived as more able are affected differently. For them, the need for continual student progress dominates their lives. This need is perpetuated by school administrators who themselves feel under pressure to constantly improve and raise student attainment, as measured by standardised tests and exams. This comes to replace the joy of teaching and learning and education for its own sake, and students are taught to value their education as something that provides certificates that can be cashed in for higher education or for good job opportunities. These pressures are not exclusive to Western nations.

In high-fee international schools in lower- and middle-income countries, for example, children from higher-income families are socialised into a Westernised form of education. Losing the opportunity to learn in their mother-tongue or access culturally relevant teaching, they are taught to follow Anglo-American curricula and examination boards from an early age. In turn, they are expected to excel academically while acquiring the social and cultural capital and credentials to leave their homelands and move overseas for a high-paying job.[21]

Education has become a commodity to be consumed like any other. Schools frame children early as consumers and as workers who must be productive and manage their own risks. They also prepare children to reproduce universalising Western norms and to live in a constant state of dissatisfaction with how things are. This renders them malleable as voters and global consumers. Human thriving will be a low priority for schools as long as this persists.

The failure of inclusive schooling

There were hopes at the beginning of the 21st century in many parts of the world that inclusive schooling might begin to move beyond an obsession with ability and attainment. Inclusion was seen as the remedy for both segregation (special schools for students with SEND) and integration (special programmes in mainstream schools for SEND children to attend classes where they 'could cope'). The aspiration in many parts of the world was for schools to include all children in mainstream classes by designing teaching and learning spaces that could cater for the full spectrum of learning needs.[22] There was a switch in focus from deficits within individuals to deficits within mainstream schools. Many special schools in the UK were closed with the aim of diverting resources and expertise into mainstream settings. Perhaps predictably, however, the savings made through closures were quickly lost, and SEND young people more than 20 years later once again experience segregated provision, this time within the same school building and without adequate resources. Genuine mixed ability teaching with differentiated learning is resource-intensive and not the norm.

Full inclusion is expensive and difficult, and there is not the political will to make this a reality in the UK or elsewhere. Spain, for example, emphasised inclusive education in its 1990 educational reform (the *Organic Law on the General Organisation of the Education System*).[23] Arising from decades of advocacy and progress in disability-inclusive legislation, Spain's 1990 reform allowed for a high number of youth with special educational needs to begin joining mainstream settings. Yet, such youth still experience multiple hurdles to true inclusion. Spanish educationalists report that students with disabilities are labelled negatively, given fewer resources and taught in separate groups while judged as lower-ability students.

It is worth restating here that this is a question of economics and resources – not of medical need. Conditions such as dyslexia and ADHD are only debilitating in education systems that need students to think along certain lines, or to sit still for long periods of time. The way that we organise schooling is as much to do with the need to manage large cohorts of young people as cheaply and efficiently as possible, and to prepare them for a modern, industrial way of operating in the world, as it is to do with any natural or self-evident way of organising education.

To diagnose and label those young people who struggle to fit in with systems of schooling is to do them a disservice. The gifts that they bring through diverse ways of thinking and acting are lost if they are made to emulate typical ways of thinking and being in the world. The costs to them in terms of mental health and well-being cannot be overestimated. For some, just being in spaces designed for neurotypical students is a real challenge. For example, children with autism can find the bright lights and loud noises of classrooms overwhelming. Sensory overload can make them anxious and distressed. They can also struggle with pressures to follow social cues in the fast pace of traditional classrooms. Creative and dynamic inclusive solutions have eluded most state education systems to the detriment of students like these.

Pacification and control

Turning now to the problem of traditional education psychology being complicit in pacification and control, I will consider here the role of behavioural psychology in schools and beyond. Behavioural psychology, as its name suggests, takes behaviour rather than mind as its main concern. It begins with the premise that behaviour alone can be observed, known and influenced. The workings of the mind are too obscure, irrelevant and complex. This means that if the behaviours of individuals and groups are to be influenced, behaviourist psychologists focus on enablers and inhibitors and not on people's minds. Behavioural psychology takes its impetus from experiments with animals – most notably Skinner's rats and Pavlov's dogs. If rats and dogs can change their behaviour because of rewards and punishments, perhaps the same can be achieved with humans?

With the rise of universal secondary education in the middle of the 20th century, the need to control the behaviour of large numbers of young people became the preoccupation of growing numbers of educational psychologists. Behavioural psychology was popular at the time, and its methodologies have become inscribed into modern systems of schooling.[24] Assertive discipline is an example of applied behavioural psychology that is popular in many schools in the UK and the USA.[25] Teachers are trained to use praise and rewards to incentivise certain behaviours and to use 'consequences' or sanctions to deter behaviour that is unwanted. It can appear to be effective, and many teachers and parents support the increased use of rewards that it introduces and the reduction in traditional authoritarian methods. It must be remembered, however, that these powerful psychological tools are being used to incentivise behaviour that is convenient for teachers and institutions and not necessarily in the best interests of the young people involved. It must also be borne in mind that the approval and rewards that young people get are conditional on compliance. This is not the same as the unconditional positive regard that is so powerful in humanistic psychology[26] and humanistic education.[27] Children learn that they gain approval and praise for doing what powerful others require and that they are sanctioned for acting out of any of their needs that are disruptive to institutions.[28]

To take the argument further – the mindset that is promoted by behavioural psychology in schools is also a mindset that is useful for governments. The need to control populations so that they ensure economic growth on the one hand and avoid impacting on the public purse on the other, is strongly felt across the different jurisdictions of the world. This can be seen in the growing propensity to use behavioural psychology and 'nudge theory' to influence behaviour.[29] Nudge theory enables policymakers to incentivise certain behaviours in public spaces without requiring constriction or education. Common examples can be seen in the placement of healthy food choices by supermarket checkouts, requests for charitable donations at cashpoints and in the wording of public announcements to take account of basic human psychology. In the UK, there are now behavioural psychologists and nudge theorists in every branch of government. Whilst this has hitherto been seen as mainly benign, there are concerns around behaviour being influenced at a population level by psychologists routinely working with the government. The UK Behavioural Insights Team, for example, use a variety of techniques to nudge certain behaviours. They use the acronym MINDSPACE to summarise these.[30] They suggest, for example, that we are heavily influenced by: the messenger (who conveys information to us); incentives (especially loss aversion); norms (what others do); defaults (default options); salience (incentives that are visible and new); priming (subconscious clues); affect (emotions); commitment (pre-commitment devices may increase buy-in); and ego (people like to feel good about themselves).

I find this chilling. During the COVID-19 pandemic for example, fear was deliberately evoked by the UK government in order to keep people at home and to protect an underfunded and badly managed NHS. Many people lost livelihoods whilst a few made money, but a terrified population remained largely compliant. Bearing in mind the concept of slow violence discussed in the last chapter, over time it is likely that the harm caused by the virus will be at least matched by the harm caused by lockdowns, social isolation, unavailable medical care, missed education and the trauma of births and deaths experienced without a loved one. Few people are holding governments to account for this, however (as they never do for slow violence), and there is a notable lack of meaningful dialogue about health, life and death, and the risks that we are, and are not, prepared to take as a population.

The following poem was written in the heart of the pandemic to try to capture the trauma of what was happening. It makes for sobering reading several years on, and yet those times must not be forgotten. Whether COVID-19 was caused by an error in a biological warfare lab, or by consumption of wild animals, or by a cross-species viral infection, or by something else, it is important to bear in mind that the factors behind the pandemic have not gone away. We must do all that we can to ensure debate about how and why so many people died and how we can avoid this happening again. Nudge psychology alone simply won't do.

Second-best tears

And the doctors
Hold a hand
As souls unclip
From claggy bodies.
Rising into the air
Like so many planes.

One then another
A macabre line.
Queued on the runway
Filling their slot.

And the watch
Is still ticking
And the text
Is unanswered
And the bookmark
Still marks
And the doctor weeps
Second-best tears.

And the souls
Float free
Of cooling bodies.
And the virus,
Deadly passenger,
Has already moved on.

And beyond
Eerily quiet
Streets lie dreaming
And birds
Nest undisturbed
And dogs whimper to the moon
And cats look to the skies
And run away
Skittish.

Schools, and society in general, have not begun the urgent task of debating risk and post-pandemic social contracts. This would require openness, wisdom, maturity and a deep understanding of science, statistics and probability. Without this, many people will again succumb to nudge policies and behavioural psychology where this is felt necessary to reduce the costs of public health. I wonder about the role of traditional behavioural psychology in schools (and the growing popularity of zero tolerance and rule-bound behaviour management regimes – see Chapter Four) in priming populations for compliance and control. I also wonder about the role of competition in schools in preparing workers for competitive working environments where they push themselves to extremes and seek approval and rewards to the detriment of their well-being.

Conclusion

This chapter has discussed the ways that cultures of schooling impact negatively on the physical and mental health of teachers and students in the UK and beyond. It has shared some ideas about how an overly psychologised way of looking at the world has infiltrated education and served to prepare young people as compliant citizens and workers. The final section focussed on the effects of COVID-19 and its associated lockdowns. It was argued that the techniques of behavioural psychology used by governments in the pandemic may have resulted in certain population-level benefits at the time, but that the harms caused over longer periods may not have been adequately taken into account. The issue at stake here for rewilding education is that the use of powerful psychological tools to ensure compliance in schools can easily slip into the same tools being used in wider society to meet the needs of governments and corporations for their own ends. This undermines health, well-being and autonomy, and reduces opportunities for genuine encounter, dialogue and ethical decision-making. The next chapter focusses on inequality, and so the final part of this chapter is a poem that provides a link from Chapter Three to Chapter Four through considering COVID-19 alongside the inequalities that it laid bare.

COVID-inequality

You isolate
In your garden,
Take sun
On your balcony,
And on country walks
Away from it all.

I isolate
In my tiny urban flat,

No garden,
Only glass,
And the window painted shut
Against thieves.

And in the park
Taking in sun
You disperse me,
Shame me, tut me,
Not staying home
For England.

You queue
At the supermarket,
Two meters apart
Even three.
The virtue
Of your civility
Signalled for all.
One in one out,
A friendly smile.
The shelves are full

I walk past
Supermarket security,
Face masked with suspicion.
Fear not smiles.
Shelves gap-toothed,
And anxious.

You teach your children.
Your global projects
Becoming living-room small.
So many books and ideas.
We see your family performances
On Facebook

I, fearful, choiceless,
Needed care-worker,
leave my children
To their iPads and crisps,
And idleness and video games.

We perform chaos
And getting by.
Trying to forget
That we share
Exam halls.

You go to your study,
Important work.
Your wife fills the slot
Recently vacated
By the ethnic female.
She re-embodies
Domestic woman,
Just for now.
A goddess of sorts.
Your god-status
Incontrovertible.

I am,
Have never NOT been,
Domestic woman.
Failing,
Of course.
Falling,
Always.
Cycles of food and faeces
And water and sweat
Never-ending.
These are my media.
My art goes unnoticed.

You eat into your savings,
A little.
A few cancelled projects,
You will pick up.

I eat store cupboard basics,
Instant noodles
Until they are gone.
Seeing the end of the month
Coming too fast
Like a brick wall.

You have always been
Your own project.
Organic food
And supplements
Health from the gym,
And Pilates at noon.
Needed restoration
After stressful responsibility.
You celebrate your immunity.

My project is survival.
Fighting asthma
And fumes from cars,
And bone-weariness
And the depression
That threatens to engulf.
My stressful responsibility
Not registering on your radar.
I fear for my immunity.

You say:
We are in this together,
Clapping the NHS,
Plucky Brits
Will meet again.

And I say:
We were never together.
Your hummus and holidays
Carried your vote,
Not the NHS.
Divided Brits
Shall we meet
For the first time?

If death is a leveller
Will you die with me?
Will you take this chance,
This unique precious chance
To be re-born,
Equal?

Notes

1. Department for Education. (2024). *Register of decisions of playing field land disposals*. Accessed January 2025. https://www.gov.uk/government/publications/school-land-decisions-about-disposals/decisions-on-the-disposal-of-school-land.
2. GMB Union. (2019). *More than 200 school playing fields sold off since 2010*. Accessed January 2025. https://www.gmb.org.uk/news/more-200-school-playing-fields-sold-2010.
3. NHS. (2021). *National Childcare Measurement Programme England*. Accessed January 2025. https://digital.nhs.uk/data-and-information/publications/statistical/national-child-measurement-programme/2020-21-school-year.
4. Hardy, L., Mihrshahi, S., Gale, J. et al. (2016). 30-year trends in overweight, obesity and waist-to-height ratio by socioeconomic status in Australian children, 1985 to 2015. *Int J Obes 41*, 76–82.
5. Youth Sport Trust. (2018) *PE provision in secondary schools 2018: Survey Research Report*. Accessed January 2025. https://www.sportsthinktank.com/uploads/pe-provision-in-secondary-schools-2018---survey-research-report.pdf.
6. Weedon, B.D., Liu, F., Mahmoud, W., et al. (2022) Declining fitness and physical education lessons in UK adolescents. *BMJ Open Sport & Exercise Medicine*. 2022:8 p.1.
7. UNICEF. (2018) *Drinking water, sanitation and hygiene in schools: global baseline report*. Accessed January 2025. https://data.unicef.org/resources/wash-in-schools/.
8. Cremin, H., Mason, C., & Busher, H. (2011). Problematising pupil voice using visual methods: findings from a study of engaged and disaffected pupils in an urban secondary school. *British Education Research Journal, 37*(4), 585–603.
9. Burton, S. (2013). *Toilets unblocked: a literature review of school toilets*. Scotland's Commissioner for Children and Young People. Accessed January 2025. https://www.cypcs.org.uk/resources/toilets-unblocked-a-literature-review-of-school-toilets/.
10. Patalay, P. and Fitzsimons, E. (2020). *Mental ill-health at age 17 in the UK: prevalence of and inequalities in psychological distress, self-harm and attempted suicide*. Centre for Longitudinal Studies. Accessed January 2025. https://cls.ucl.ac.uk/wp-content/uploads/2020/11/Mental-ill-health-at-age-17—CLS-briefing-paper—website.pdf.
11. Cremin, H., & Kester, K. (2020). Bare-foot hope for peace: vulnerability in peace learning. In M. McKenna & E. Brantmeier (Eds.), *The Pedagogy of Vulnerability*. Information Age Publishing.
12. Not her real name. Students' names in this book have all been anonymised.
13. World Health Organisation. (2024). *Mental health of adolescents*. Accessed January 2025. https://www.who.int/news-room/fact-sheets/detail/adolescent-mental-health.
14. Center for Disease Control and Protection. (2023). *Mental Health*. Accessed January 2025. https://www.cdc.gov/healthyyouth/mental-health/index.htm.
15. hooks, b. (1994). *Teaching to transgress: education as a practice of freedom*. Routledge.
16. NASUWT (2024). Accessed January 2025. *Teacher Wellbeing Survey*. https://www.nasuwt.org.uk/news/campaigns/teacher-wellbeing-survey.html.
17. Cremin, H., Mason, C., & Busher, H. (2011). Problematising pupil voice using visual methods: findings from a study of engaged and disaffected pupils in an urban secondary school. *British Education Research Journal, 37*(4), 585–603.
18. McLaughlin, C. (2008). Emotional well-being and its relationship to schools and classrooms: a critical reflection. *British Journal of Guidance & Counselling, 36*(4), 353–366.
19. Sellman, E., & Buttarazzi, G. (2020). Adding lemon juice to poison – raising critical questions about the oxymoronic nature of mindfulness in education and its future direction. *British Journal of Educational Studies, 68*(1), 61–78.

20 Bixby, L., Bevan, S. & Boen, C. The links between disability, incarceration, and social exclusion. *Health Affairs*, *41*(10).
21 Kenway, J., Fahey, J., et al. (2017) *Class choreographies: elite schools and globalization*. Springer.
22 Thomas, G., & Loxley, A. (2001). Deconstructing Special Education and Constructing Inclusion (Inclusive Education), OUP.
23 De Luis, E.C. (2016). Inclusive education in Spain: promoting advocacy by legislation. *SFL*, 3(2), 164–176.
24 Cremin, H., & Bevington, T. (2017). *Positive peace in schools: tackling conflict and creating a culture of peace in the classroom*. Routledge.
25 Canter, L., & Canter, M. (1976). *Assertive discipline: a take-charge approach for today's educator*. Canter and Associates.
26 Rogers, C. R. (1956). Clientcentered theory. *Journal of Counseling Psychology, 3*(2), 115–120.
27 Rogers, C.R., & Freiburg, J.H. (1994). *Freedom to Learn*. Prentice Hall.
28 Zembylas, M. (2020). Affect, biopower, and 'the fascist inside you': the (un-)making of microfascism in schools and classrooms. *Journal of Curriculum Studies*.
29 Dodsworth, L. (2021). *The state of fear: how the UK government weaponised fear during the Covid-19*. Pinter & Martin.
30 BIT (2010) MINDSPACE. Cabinet Office, Institute for Government. Accessed January 2025. https://www.bi.team/publications/mindspace/.

Chapter 4
Reproducing inequality

Introduction

The final chapter in Part One of this book concerns the ways in which schools reproduce inequality. Despite the myth of social mobility, education is deeply complicit in ensuring that the Earth's resources are mainly enjoyed by global elites. Educational inequality seems stubbornly resistant to change, with marginalised groups throughout the world making painfully slow gains (or else going backwards) in comparison with those with access to wealth and power. Whether young people are marginalised because of poverty or because of some aspect of their identity, they often find themselves falling behind due to misrecognition, trauma, or a lack of physical, social or cultural capital.

Inequalities do not of course originate in schools, and schools are not the only social institutions that reproduce inequality. They do, however, play a significant role – functioning more as sorting devices than as levelling devices[1]. Despite the fact that political leaders and their allies throughout the world spend an inordinate amount of time convincing voters, parents and business leaders that the next iteration of their education system will finally deliver equality and inclusion, the truth is that much of this activity serves to obscure rather than ameliorate the issues at hand. In many cases, schemes that seduce with promises to reduce social and educational exclusion end up delivering the opposite: with zero tolerance behaviour policies leading to increased permanent exclusions; returns to traditional academic curricula leading to disaffection and achievement gaps; and widening access to higher education often leading to graduate unemployment and crippling lifelong debt. In this chapter I will expose social mobility and meritocracy as myths before discussing the issues involved and moving on to explore the role of education discourse in perpetuating the very inequalities it sets out to address. I will focus towards the end on recent UK education policy changes as a case in point.

The myth of social mobility

After a century of universal primary education in many parts of the world, and over half a century of universal secondary education in countries like the UK, the world remains deeply unequal and divided. According to the International Monetary Fund (IMF),[2] in March 2022, the top 10% of the global population owned roughly 190 times as much as the poorest half of the global population. Income inequalities are not much better. The richest 10% earned 52% of all income in the world and accounted for 48% of carbon emissions. The poorest half earned just 8.5% of all global income. The report shows that progress in reducing gender inequality has been slow over the past 30 years, with women earning 30.6% of global income in 1990 and still only 34.4% between 2015 and 2020. In the UK, inequality and poverty are significant problems, especially for children. According to the Child Poverty Action Group,[3] there were 4.3 million children, or 30%, living in poverty in 2022–23. These figures are worse for children from Black and minority ethnic British families, with 47% in poverty (compared with 24% of children in white British families).

So, what is the role of education in improving the life chances of the poorest children? Every UK government for as long as I can remember has promised to increase social mobility by raising the educational attainment of the poorest children as part of their manifesto pledges, but this clearly has not worked. Despite other indicators such as ethnicity and gender continuing to have a small influence on educational attainment, poverty remains by far the strongest predictor of low educational outcomes. In the academic year 2023–24, the percentage of all pupils getting a strong pass grade of 5 or above in English and Maths GCSE (taken at age 16) was 45.9%. This percentage was 25.8% for children eligible for free school meals (a proxy for children living in poverty).[4] According to research carried out by the Sutton Trust,[5] the attainment gap between the richest and poorest children begins in the early years and is already evident when children begin school aged 5. It grows wider at every following stage of education: it more than doubles to 10.3 months by the end of primary school, and then almost doubles again, to 18.8 months by the end of secondary school.

So, schools are clearly failing to address this attainment gap, but are they reproducing or even exacerbating inequality and underachievement? In 2019, the Sutton Trust produced a manifesto for change to tackle what it saw as the drivers of the attainment gap caused by the British education system.[6] They identified several areas in need of change. For the youngest children, they called for the re-establishment of children's centres (neighbourhood-based service provision for young families living in areas of deprivation) which have declined by 30% since 2009, due to closures. They also called for an end to schools that are effectively segregated according to family income. Although this happens in indirect ways, their research shows that the highest performing state secondary schools took just half the number of disadvantaged pupils compared to average schools. The house prices in the catchment area of these schools were 20% higher than in the surrounding area – one reason amongst many why the poorest children were not able to access them. The authors note that although 27% of secondary-age children received private tuition, parents from higher socioeconomic backgrounds were five times more likely to provide this for their children; that 85% of teachers in the most deprived state schools thought that recruitment issues were affecting the quality of education in their school; and that, although only 7% of the UK school population were privately educated, they made up over half of people in leadership roles in the most selective and influential professions. Very little progress on any of these has been made since 2019.

Similarly, in the USA, students typically do not begin schooling on equal terms. Kindergarten assessments show how mathematics and science achievement gaps are stratified by socio-economic status and keep growing as students grow older. For example, a national sample of elementary school children showed that the mathematics score gap between low- and high-income students was nine points at the beginning of kindergarten. By the Spring of fifth grade, this gap widened to 13 points.[7] Disparities start from a young age as poorer children have less access to informal learning and high-quality preschools. US schools, too, face systemic barriers. A significant revenue gap emerges between high- and low-poverty school districts; high-poverty districts raised $2,710 less per student in 2022 than low-poverty districts, amounting to a 14.1% revenue gap.[8]

When it comes to access to university in the UK, the Sutton Trust report cited earlier revealed in 2019 that there were more than twice as many people from the most advantaged backgrounds on coveted degree-level apprenticeships as there were people from less well-off homes (28% vs.13%); that private school applicants were seven times more likely to gain a place at Oxford or Cambridge than those in non-selective state schools and over twice as likely to take a place at Russell Group universities; and that students from the lowest 40% of earners took on graduate debts of £52,000 compared with £38,400 in the top 20% of households. Finally, they note that over a quarter of graduates completed an unpaid internship, which would have been unaffordable for most young people who did not have the financial support of their family.

Similar patterns exist in LMICs. In Latin America and the Caribbean in 2013, only 25% of university students came from the poorest 50% of the population.[9] Opportunities for social mobility shrink when higher-income students dominate tertiary education. Public universities offering no-fee or low-fee education do exist. However, they are often underfunded, with fewer places than the number of students who need them. Higher education can thus cement rather than challenge entrenched patterns of inequality.

Schools as the problem – not the solution

It becomes clear then that education reproduces inequality in complex and interrelated ways, and that it does little to redress imbalances in household income and in social and cultural capital. Organisations like the Sutton Trust in the UK have an important advocacy role to play in bringing these injustices to light, but there is a need to avoid what I would call 'leg-up' politics which can benefit the few without addressing structural inequality. For example, the Sutton Trust has called for the top 100 private day schools to open their doors to a certain number of students each year whose parents can't afford to pay the fees. This has the effect of helping certain students whilst keeping exclusionary structures intact, and possibly even legitimising them. I feel that we need to do more than give some young people a leg up – the whole system needs to be rewilded. The structures that exclude and segregate need to be allowed to decompose so that fairer ways of educating and cultivating excellence can be allowed to grow.

Apart from neglecting structural inequalities, leg-up policies can have unintended consequences. In France, for example, the Ministry of Education has encouraged prestigious universities to offer tutoring programmes (entitled Cordées de la Réussite – Team for Success) to highly able students from under-resourced high schools, but one of these from the École Normale Supérieure of Paris (one of the world's most selective universities) was found by researchers to be counterproductive. Its programme was so time-consuming that some of the most disadvantaged students in France lost time for schoolwork and underperformed in their exams[10] (Ly et al., 2020). Researchers judged the programme as a 'pleasure that hurts'.

Leg-up politics build on two key concepts – social mobility and meritocracy. There are significant problems with these. The first is that they are reliant on a certain amount of downwards mobility, and the middle classes will not countenance that.[11] Wealthier parents are better placed to ensure that their own children are credentialised by the very best institutions, whether this is through tuition of various kinds or through funding travel and volunteering activities that look good on a personal statement or CV. As soon as disadvantaged students start to catch up, it always seems that another hurdle for excelling academically or gaining elite employment is introduced. There are not enough of these opportunities to go round, and when 'the market decides,' it is unsurprising that people of means are able to provide the resources needed to push their children ahead. The second problem with the concepts of social mobility and meritocracy is that they obscure injustice and social exclusion by providing a smokescreen of equal opportunities. They imply that if the poor fail to be socially mobile it is either because they are not bright enough or because they do not work hard enough. Global elites can settle into their privileges, believing that they are entitled to do so because they have been earned on a socially mobile playing field.

The following poem summarises the arguments to date in a visceral way. It points to the fact that there are no winners when people of means attempt to game the system to provide an advantage for their children.

My child

My child is a star,
An A star,
Yours is a B.
Not your fault,
Of course,
But a B
Nonetheless.

We had to move,
Got inheritance early.
Houses in this catchment
Are not cheap.
You stayed in your
Social housing.

Your Local School
Underwhelms.
Your child
Languishes
In mixed classes,
Chatting in corridors,
Learning maths
From a teacher
Of PE.

My child
Circulates
On the left,
In silence.
Tough love,
Buttoned up.
Graduate teachers
See her right.
She knows
Shakespeare
And Kings.

We work hard,
Sacrifice
To give her a future.
We have earned
Her privilege.

She knows.

Your hard work,
Bone tired after shifts,
Is hardly the same.

My child is destined for
Gap-year greatness.
Her work with

The poor
In Bangladesh
Will touch their lives
In ways that
Oxbridge admissions tutors
Can't fail to notice.

Your child knows
Poverty
From the inside.
Perhaps it is
Your fault?

Who will your child blame
When working shifts
To pay for 'uni'
Becomes their permanent?
The golden ticket
Does not come cheap.

My child has her
Ticket to her future.
What more could she want?

My child
My child
My child

> Is curled in a ball.
> They think
> They can save her.
> It turns out
> She doesn't know
> How to be.

'Unintended' consequences of education reform

The final section of this chapter will consider initiatives that have been presented as ways of closing the attainment gap in the UK, but that have ended up having the opposite effect. There are many examples, but a few will serve as illustration of how intractable the problems are, and how proposed solutions often end up being subverted to serve the ends of global elites. The first of these is personal. It concerns the popular ideological belief that teachers (and the people who train them) are to blame for the attainment gap, and that disadvantaged children would do better if their teachers expected more of them and gave them a properly rigorous academic curriculum.

I was one of one hundred education professors and lecturers, including top academics at Oxford, Cambridge, Bristol and the London University Institute of Education, who signed a letter in 2013 denouncing the plans of Michael Gove, the education secretary at the time, to close the attainment gap through a more 'rigorous' content-driven national curriculum for primary schools.[12] Under Gove, we wrote, children faced, 'endless lists of spellings, facts and rules' that, ironically, 'could severely erode educational standards.' We wanted young children to have longer to learn through play and to focus on skills for learning rather than on regurgitating 'powerful knowledge' such as British kings and queens, Shakespeare quotes and long-division rules. We questioned the assumption that this knowledge would somehow close the attainment gap, arguing that the reverse was likely to happen if teachers were forced to use cramming techniques to get children to pass content-driven tests.

Michael Gove's response was to come back at us a few days later in an article in *The Mail on Sunday* national newspaper. He called us 'enemies of promise' of a generation of children and said that we 'seem more interested in valuing Marxism, revering jargon and fighting excellence.'[13] He conflated us naming the attainment gap with us condoning or even causing it. The reforms were duly implemented amidst claims that the attainment gap would be significantly reduced. That was back in 2014. Readers might want to remember the statistics in this chapter, and in earlier chapters, in order to ascertain whether, more than 10 years later, Gove's reforms have indeed closed the gap.

When Michael Gove introduced the curriculum reforms in 2014, he also introduced reforms aimed at reducing disruptive behaviour in schools. This he said was aimed at improving the attainment of all students, especially the least advantaged. This is what he had to say about students who underachieve:

> It's those children who arrive at secondary school incapable of reading properly, who find they can't follow the curriculum, who cover up their ignorance with a mask of bravado, disrupting lessons, disobeying teachers, dropping out of school, drifting into gang culture, and in the worst cases, ending up in the justice system.[14]

He put forward a range of suggestions to tackle this underachievement, disruptive behaviour, and school-to-prison pipeline. These included criminalising parents who fail to send their children to school, assessing reading, making it easier for schools to exclude disruptive students and increasing the policing role of teachers (making it easier for them to search young people's property, for example, and abolishing 'no-touch' policies). Many schools have since changed their behaviour management policies to take what has become known as a zero-tolerance approach to indiscipline.

The zero-tolerance approach was originally developed as a means of enforcing weapon control policies in education settings in the USA but has migrated to other areas of school life and to other countries. Schools with zero-tolerance policies use them to enforce behaviours such as completing homework, moving around the school in silence, wearing school uniforms correctly and obeying teachers unquestioningly.[15] Many parents choose this education for their child because of the high attainment and discipline that it brings about for some young people, even though others do not fare so well under these conditions.

Consequences in some zero-tolerance schools include isolation. This can take place in regular classrooms, or else in isolation booths where children are made to sit facing the wall, sometimes for hours on end, with no social contact. Some young people with unmet special educational needs and disabilities are forced to spend unacceptable amounts of time in isolation booths. It is hard to see how this counts as reducing the attainment gap or even as providing education at all. It is also hard to see how zero-tolerance behaviour management strategies reduce the attainment gap overall as claimed. Advocates base their support on the idea that young people who fall behind are missing discipline and firm rules. The 'no excuses' policy is designed to provide them with the same hard boundaries as they believe are found in more privileged households.

Charter schools in the USA are notorious for harsh discipline in the name of promoting social mobility. For example, the Knowledge is Power Program (KIPP) charter school became well-known for ten-hour schooldays, repetitive drilling and chants, and a school year beginning mid-summer. Students receive mock paychecks called 'KIPP dollars' each week based on behaviour. If they finish homework, they receive a KIPP dollar. If they speak out of turn, leave a shirt untucked or chew gum, they lose one. Students who do not earn the required amount of KIPP dollars have to sit separately from their peers in class, on small and uncomfortable chairs. In addition to writing letters of apology, they have to wear yellow shirts, often smelly and unwashed. The school's founder justifies these measures in the name of instilling values of discipline and willpower that children are presumed not to receive at home. One teacher has compared the putting on of the yellow shirts to prisoners' jumpsuits.[16]

It is worth pausing for a moment to reflect on the assumptions that underlie these ideas. Whilst it may be true that many children living in poverty have chaotic lives, it is not the case that the adults responsible for them don't care or don't have high aspirations for their children.[17] Difficulties providing a uniform, homework space, childcare, internet, and even food and an adequate area for sleeping hinder their efforts. When this is added to the additional challenges that children living in areas of disadvantage face (gangs, drugs, violence, addiction issues) it is easy to see how they can be vulnerable to school exclusion under the conditions of zero-tolerance.

Readers will be aware by now that in the UK the attainment gap has not closed in the period of Michael Gove's reforms, but it is worth asking whether this crackdown on disruptive behaviour has resulted in less educational exclusion. In 2020, the RSA investigated this. They found that since 2015, there has been a 60% increase in the number of students permanently excluded from England's schools. By 2017–18, there were, on average, 42 young people expelled each school day.[18] The RSA also found that children from poorer backgrounds and certain ethnic minority groups, and those who have been in care, were disproportionately represented in exclusions statistics, as well as those with special educational needs and disabilities (SEND). For example, young people eligible for free school meals were four times more likely to be permanently excluded from school than their non-eligible peers, and young people with SEND were around six times more likely to be excluded. Based on a range of data, including interviews with key stakeholders, they concluded that the reasons for the disproportionate levels of school exclusion amongst the poor, and those with SEND, are threefold.

Firstly: these higher levels of exclusion are linked with wider societal factors beyond the education system, including for example increasing numbers of children with a social worker or with mental health difficulties. Secondly: they are linked with direct consequences of policymaking, such as curriculum reform making learning harder to access for some pupils. Thirdly: they are linked with unintended consequences of policymaking, such as perverse incentives caused by accountability regimes (high-stakes testing, school league tables, Ofsted), fragmentation of the education system and shifts in behaviour management strategies in schools.

Of particular interest here is a suggestion that schools are excluding disruptive and low-achieving students in order to improve the test and exam results that they are judged upon. For example, data that the RSA collected in 2019 through a freedom of information request shows a spike in admissions to Pupil

Referral Units (PRUs – alternative provision for excluded young people, and those at risk of exclusion) in the first term of their final year at school (Year 11).[19] This term marks the point where a young person's exam results can be counted towards the school's performance indicators. The authors note that if performance data were reweighted to make schools accountable for students' results proportional to the amount of time they spent on its roll, the scores of many schools and multi-academy trusts (MATs) would not come across so favourably.

As concerning as the UK exclusion statistics are, however, they may not point to the full extent of the problem. Unfortunately many young people just 'disappear' from the system – leaving a school never to return. These young people have not gone through an official exclusion process, and are therefore not captured in the statistics, but they have effectively been 'removed' from school. The RSA report's authors[20] note:

> It is difficult to know how many pupils are in this situation, or how many of these moves are against the best interests of the pupil and the will of the parents/carers. However, according to the Education Policy Institute's analysis of the 603,705 pupils sitting GCSEs in 2017, an estimated 24,000 had exited to an unknown location, not to return to a state-funded school, between Year 7 and Year 11.

My deep sadness here is that when I began my career as a teacher, I was part of a generation who believed that a child's educational needs, special or otherwise, were the responsibility of the school as a community. We felt that we had moved away from the idea that this responsibility lay with a child's family. It seems that we are now back where we started, with growing numbers of vulnerable young people being denied their right to education because they are expensive or difficult to educate. Predictably, parental choice has morphed into school choice – the tendency of schools to keep the students who make them look good in league tables and to officially or unofficially offload those students who don't.

Education that reproduces and magnifies violence and conflict internationally

Much of the preceding discussion has been about the UK, but at an international level, there has also been recognition for a long time that schooling has both positive and negative effects.[21] Whilst schooling is heralded by most people as a self-evident benefit, especially for the poorest of the world (for example UN Sustainable Development goal 4), research evidence suggests that what happens at a school and classroom level may be ineffective, counterproductive, or even harmful. Children in the poorest countries of the world, many of whom are impacted by armed conflict, often find themselves in schools that cannot protect their basic rights or provide for their needs. Whereas concerns over violence in schools tend to foreground bullying and aggression amongst students, this is only half of the story. Over many years of doctoral supervision and examination in the areas of conflict and violence in schools, I have come across far too many examples of violence perpetrated by adults against children, be they teachers, headteachers or adults who target children on their way to school. Direct forms of violence include corporal punishment and rape (including sex-for-grades). Indirect forms of violence include structural inequality and psychological harm based on ethnicity, gender or culture. These accounts have been hard to hear.

At the turn of the century, a UN Innocenti report suggested that education has two faces – one positive and one negative, and that even peace education can be manipulated to divide people, as well as to draw them closer together. They called for peacebuilding education to go further than the 'add good education and stir' approach.[22] I'm not sure that much progress has been made. In 2018, Clive Harber reviewed several peace education programmes in conflict-affected states in sub-Saharan Africa and found that desired impact was lacking because 'the traditional "intractable paradigm" of authoritarian, hierarchical and competitive schooling is deeply rooted in the minds and thus practices of education officials, head teachers, teachers, parents, pupils, and school communities.'[23] The peace education programmes were ineffective for a variety of reasons. These included the role of schools in perpetuating conflict and violence in the region; lack of adequate teacher education; lack of curriculum space or teaching materials; corporal punishment; a sanitised version of history; a lack of focus on systemic and school-wide change; authoritarian and teacher-centred methods; lack of student voice, participation or school councils; abusive and belittling language used by some teachers and students; differential treatment and discrimination; low motivation and morale amongst teachers; and gender inequality. Because of these factors and more, peace education in the region did little more than perpetuate the injustices and inequalities that fed into the armed conflict in the first place.

Conclusion

By now it will be clear that I am arguing here that education is deeply implicated in reproducing inequality, and that it does this whilst giving the impression of promoting social mobility and meritocracy. Governments, education leaders and consultants have much to gain from capturing the public imagination through promises of better things to come. The fact that this never materialised does not appear to matter. The global education consultancy industry is booming, but care needs to be taken to avoid embedding leg-up politics into the allocation of resources for education in settings of poverty, conflict and violence locally, nationally and internationally. People from (over)developed parts of the world need to avoid creating the impression that schools in low- and middle-income countries (LMICs) simply need to replicate systems of schooling from the global North in order to replicate their levels of economic success. A healthy dose of humility and accountability for the violence and exploitation of the colonial past of countries like the UK might be more useful as starting points for considering how education might contribute towards improved educational outcomes in LMIC settings. Closer to home, the UK needs to take a long hard look at the ways that schools reproduce inequality. We need to dare to dream differently about education.

Notes

1 Apple, M. (2013). *Can Education Change Society?* Routledge.
2 Stanley, A. (2022) *Global Inequalities*. International Monetary Fund. Accessed January 2025. https://www.imf.org/en/Publications/fandd/issues/2022/03/Global-inequalities-Stanley.
3 Child Poverty Action Group ((2025) *Poverty: facts and figures*. Accessed January 2025. https://cpag.org.uk/child-poverty/child-poverty-facts-and-figures.
4 UK Government Statistics (2024) *Key Stage Four Performance. National Characteristics Summary*. Accessed January 2025. https://explore-education-statistics.service.gov.uk/data-tables/fast-track/04a60084-9dff-4b28-9e9f-08dd0afc3a28.
5 The Sutton Trust (2024) Closing the attainment gap. Accessed January 2025. https://www.suttontrust.com/wp-content/uploads/2024/02/Closing-the-attainment-gap.pdf.
6 The Sutton Trust (2019). Mobility Manifesto. Accessed January 2025. https://www.suttontrust.com/wp-content/uploads/2019/12/Mobility-Manifesto-2019-1.pdf. https://www.suttontrust.com/wp-content/uploads/2022/06/Social-Mobility—Past-Present-and-Future-final-updated-references.pdf.
7 White, K., & Rotermund, S. (2020). Elementary and secondary mathematics and science education. Science & engineering indicators. National Scientific Board. Accessed January 2025. https://ncses.nsf.gov/pubs/nsb20196/executive-summary.
8 Allegretto, S., García, E. et al. (2022). Public education funding in the U.S. needs an overhaul. Economic Policy Institute. Accessed January 2025. https://www.epi.org/publication/public-education-funding-in-the-us-needs-an-overhaul/.
9 World Bank Group (2013) *Tertiary Education*. Accessed January 2025. https://www.worldbank.org/en/topic/tertiaryeducation.
10 Ly, S. T., Maurin, E., & Riegert, A. (2020). A pleasure that hurts: the ambiguous effects of elite tutoring on underprivileged high school students. *Journal of Labor Economics*, *38*(2), 501–533. p.29.
11 Reay, D. (2013). Social mobility, a panacea for austere times: tales of emperors, frogs, and tadpoles. *British Journal of Sociology of Education*, *34*(5–6), 660–677.
12 Education Professors (2013). Letters: Gove will bury pupils in facts and rules. *The Independent*. Accessed January 2025.https://www.independent.co.uk/voices/letters/letters-gove-will-bury-pupils-in-facts-and-rules-8540741.html.
13 Gove, M. (2013) I refuse to surrender to the Marxist teachers hell-bent on destroying our schools: Education Secretary berates 'the new enemies of promise' for opposing his plans. *The Mail on Sunday*. Accessed January 2025. https://www.dailymail.co.uk/debate/article-2298146/I-refuse-surrender-Marxist-teachers-hell-bent-destroying-schools-Education-Secretary-berates-new-enemies-promise-opposing-plans.html.

14 Gove, M. (2014) The purpose of our school reforms. Department for Education. Accessed January 2025. https://www.gov.uk/government/speeches/the-purpose-of-our-school-reforms.
15 Adams, R. (2016) 'No excuses': inside Britain's strictest school. *The Guardian*. Accessed January 2025. https://www.theguardian.com/education/2016/dec/30/no-excuses-inside-britains-strictest-school.
16 WHYY (2019) Don't eat the marshmallow: students from a 'no excuses' charter grow up to tell the tale. *Listen Live Morning Edition*. Accessed January 2025. https://whyy.org/episodes/s-03-ep-03-dont-eat-the-marshmallow/.
17 Reay, D. (2017). *Miseducation: inequality, education and the working classes*. Policy Press.
18 Partridge, L. Strong F.L. (2020) Pinball kids: preventing school exclusions. The RSA. Accessed January 2025. https://www.thersa.org/globalassets/reports/2020/the-rsa-pinball-kids-preventing-school-exclusions.pdf.
19 Partridge, L. (2019) Is pressure to achieve exam results contributing to school exclusions? Yes, new RSA data indicates. *The RSA Blog*. Accessed January 2025. https://www.thersa.org/blog/2019/03/exclusions-exams.
20 Partridge, L. Strong F.L. (2020) Pinball kids: preventing school exclusions. *The RSA*. Accessed January 2025. p.16 https://www.thersa.org/globalassets/reports/2020/the-rsa-pinball-kids-preventing-school-exclusions.pdf.
21 Bush, K., & Saltarelli, D. (2000). *The Two faces of education in ethnic conflict: towards a peacebuilding education for children: Innocenti Insight*. UNICEF.
22 Bush, K., & Saltarelli, D. (2000). *The Two faces of education in ethnic conflict: towards a peacebuilding education for children: Innocenti Insight*. UNICEF, p.33.
23 Harber, C. (2018). Building back better? Peace education in post-conflict Africa. *Asian Journal of Peacebuilding*, 6(1), p.23.

Part II

Rewilding education

Chapter 5

Why rewilding?

> We are fallen in mostly broken pieces, I thought, but the wild can still return us to ourselves.
>
> Robert Macfarlane, 2007

Introduction

This chapter gets to the heart of the book by discussing what is meant by 'rewilding' in its original and literal sense, so that this can be applied to education. It will discuss rewilding's historical, cultural and aesthetic factors, and the scientific rationale for it. It will draw on a range of writers, scientists, poets and activists. It starts by looking at our relationship with the wild before moving into consideration of what rewilding the environment looks like. It ends with consideration of possible futures for humanity, with and without rewilding, and discusses the urgency of educating for a rewilded future.

What is rewilding?

At the heart of the rewilding concept is the root word 'wild.' Wildness comes from the same root as 'will' – in the sense of willful or self-willed. It is easy to see how modernity in general, and modern systems of schooling more specifically, might have a problem with that. If nature and people are left to self-organise at will, human needs may not be met in ways that allow for efficiency and growth. In this view, wildness is wasteful, unproductive and needs to be brought under control. There is another story about wildness, however. This is the story where wildness enables human thriving, wisdom and well-being. It returns us to ourselves. In Shakespeare's *As You Like It*, Act II, Scene I, the banished Duke, who lives in exile in the forest, articulates this other sense of the wild:

> And this our life, exempt from public haunt,
> Finds tongues in trees, books in the running brooks,
> Sermons in stones, and good in everything.
> I would not change it.

Here wild nature is seen as a teacher. In the 19th century, the romantic poets similarly extolled the virtues of the wild and its links with wisdom and human thriving. As Robert Macfarlane[1] points out, Coleridge, for one, saw it as 'an energy which blows through one's being, causing the self to shift into new patterns, opening up alternative perceptions of life.' For Coleridge, wanderings through the landscape were essential to maintain his sanity. Likewise, in India there is a tradition of Vanvas and Vanaprastha, individuals beyond a certain age who shift to living in the forest in order to gain wisdom and enlightenment.

According to the Collins dictionary, rewilding is defined as 'the practice of returning areas of land to a wild state, including the reintroduction of animal species that are no longer naturally found there.'[2] Paul Jepson and Cain Blythe[3] present rewilding as a new and progressive approach to conservation, blending radical scientific insights with practical innovations to revive ecological processes, benefiting people as well as nature. Its goal is to restore lost interactions between animals, plants and natural disturbance that are the essence of thriving ecosystems. They note that the term rewilding was first coined in the mid-1990s by conservation biologists who were influenced by wilderness and deep ecology philosophy.

There are different versions of rewilding: translocation rewilding introduces species that can restore dysfunctional ecological processes that have been lost (e.g. European bison in the Southern Carpathian mountains[4]); passive rewilding enables ecological processes to re-establish themselves by reducing human control of landscapes; practical rewilding aims to solve social and environmental problems such as rural depopulation, flooding and wildfires (e.g. scrapes and ponds in Sussex UK that store 1,023,650 litres of rainwater and create 1 ha of wetland habitat for wildlife[5]); trophic rewilding uses large predators to regulate wilderness areas (e.g. wolves in Yellowstone Park in the USA[6]), and Pleistocene rewilding restores the evolutionary and ecological potential of ecosystems that were lost through the extinction of fauna around 10 to 15,000 years ago (e.g. the Alpine marmot in the Pyrenees).

The temporal orientation of rewilding thus varies according to the kind of rewilding that is being advocated. In general, however, rewilding sets its baseline much further back than the baseline that is usually set by traditional conservationists. In this way (amongst many), rewilding sets itself apart from conservation. The baseline for conservation is the mid-19th century across large parts of the world. This is partly because it marks the point before the impact of industrialisation, and partly because it coincides with a time when European colonists and naturalists first began to describe and value the new fauna and flora that they were encountering. Paul Jepson and Cain Blythe point out that this is an arbitrary baseline, however, and that the impact of humans on the planet goes back much further than this.

There is a danger that conservation efforts could reify a particular point in recent history, leaving unaddressed the ecological impacts of Holocene extinctions due to overkill that took place as humans began to spread across the planet between 10 and 15,000 years ago. Paleoecology, for example, reveals that for millions of years megafauna (animals weighing more than 40 kg) was abundant on the land and in the sea, before largely disappearing between 10,000 and 30,000 years ago. This is what Pleistocene rewilding aims to restore through the concept of taxon substitution: the introduction of living species from different biogeographic regions of the world that could replicate the roles of extinct species and improve nutrient availability in the soil and in the sea. This kind of rewilding is not about turning back the clock, however. It takes account of the fact that there is no way back for ecosystems, and that, as ecological interactions and processes recover, ecosystems will take on new forms. These new forms may evoke the past, but they will be different.

Many rewilding projects address the impacts of agriculture from the Middle Ages onwards – impacts that have been accelerating as farming has become ever more commercial and organised. Farmers have radically altered the landscape to grow crops and protect livestock; new categories of pests and vermin have been introduced; and forests have been felled to build fences and dwellings, and to provide logs for burning. By the mid-20th century, the growing use of agricultural pesticides was having noticeable impacts on insects, fish and birds. By the 1970s, as large-scale commercial agriculture expanded globally, extensive cattle ranching accelerated deforestation including in the so-called 'lungs of the earth' – the Amazon Rainforest.

Conservation efforts have managed to halt or even reverse some of this. Rewilding aims to do more, however. It goes beyond 'holding the line,' to try to restore dynamic interactions between the biological and physical components of ecosystems and to allow nature to take its course in ways that embrace uncertainty. In this way, it draws on systems theory, which aims to understand how complex systems behave, function and interact. Systems theory sees a system as more than just the sum of its parts, adopting a holistic lens to focus on the relationships between individual components and how they function as a whole. Whilst conservation categorises, protects and manages habitats to provide the environmental conditions for a particular species or set of species, rewilding focusses on the conditions that enable a diverse set of organisms to develop in unpredictable and non-linear ways. Conservation uses linear thinking and cause-and-effect logic; rewilding is about systems thinking and discontinuous adaptation. Conservation thinks in binaries, including wild-domestic, natural-cultivated and humane-inhumane; rewilding unsettles and blurs these boundaries. Conservation is often motivated by nostalgia and a romantic view of the past; rewilding embraces risk, uncertainty and the raw and savage elements of nature as well as its beauty and balance within chaos and uncertainty.

Paul Jepson and Cain Blythe[7] summarise rewilding's emerging ecosystemic and action philosophy as follows:

> Systems thinking involves an openness to understanding the complex systems and forces that shape our world, and a willingness to pragmatically engage with these to assemble new systems. Such thinking is based on the logic of emergence - if the right system elements are in place, desirable outcomes will emerge and persist. However, the outcomes that emerge might not be quite what was planned or indeed desired: a willingness to embrace uncertainty and a degree of risk is central to systems approaches and to rewilding's emerging action philosophy.

The certainties of the past, then, are no longer viable, and probably never were. A conservative and conservation-oriented mindset will no longer do. The future holds prospects of unpredictable and discontinuous change, and we need to take account of that. We need courage to embrace risk, uncertainty and the logic of emergence, and we need to be ready to learn from mistakes. If we act now we can create and refine the conditions that allow complex systems to unfold in ways that support sustainable futures.

Hopefully it will be clear by now why the concept of rewilding is so useful for my attempts to reimagine education in ways that go beyond mere school improvement and 'modernisation'. I too do not wish to hold the line, or to turn back the clock. I aim rather to support emergent systems that can respond to the harms that have been caused by humanity's desire to educate in binaries and linearities, and its infatuation with futures that exploit and deplete our natural and social ecosystems. I am fully aware that this 'new story' will not have the coherence or clarity of the 'old story,' but I am convinced that the best way to ensure sustainability and human and non-human thriving is to allow education systems, large and small throughout the world, to adapt to the changing embodied and existential needs of young people and their parents, within their various natural and social ecosystems.

The future of rewilding

So what does the future look like with and without rewilding? Paul Jepson and Cain Blythe[8] believe that rewilding's rapid adoption into science and popular culture has occurred because it resonates with an emerging zeitgeist. This zeitgeist can be described as 'a spirit of reassessment, creativity, pragmatism, and desire for hope that is a consequence of rapid, and often worrying, scientific, technological, social, political and environmental change.' Nature-minded people are making changes to their lives and coming together to create spaces where new concepts and techniques can be tested and refined. This is made possible by innovation in engineering, technology and AI and by new political discourses that foreground nature-based solutions.

For rewilding to scale up, however, it will be necessary for citizens, politicians, policy-makers, landowners and activists to enter into dialogue and innovate at the boundaries of nature and society. The future of rewilding is tied in with the ability to navigate precisely this boundary. Rewilding will need to capture the imagination of people living in cities as well as those living in rural environments if its ecosystemic philosophy, flexibility and action-oriented approach are to take root. The 20th-century conservation movement put wildlife at the heart of popular culture with the help of national parks and wildlife documentaries – perhaps the rewilding movement can inspire the creation of rewilding parks and renewed interest in nature recovery. Perhaps also the centralised and bureaucratic models of business and innovation that emerged in the late 20th century will give way to a decentralised network of rewilding businesses and start-ups that are located at both a local and a global level, and that share informal knowledge and skills. Perhaps with time we will see major sectors integrating rewilding and ecological recovery into their mission, approach and economic rationales.

There is of course another, less optimistic, option. In this scenario human beings continue business as usual until fire, flood, famine, runaway artificial intelligence, deadly pandemics and so on stop us in our tracks. According to the World Wildlife Fund and the Boston Consulting Group,[9] in 2020 forest fires were up 13% compared with the previous year, which was already a record year for fires. Hotter and drier weather due to climate change, and human factors such as land conversion for agriculture and poor forest management are cited as the main drivers behind the increase. Humans are responsible for starting 75% of wildfires.

It is much easier in the 21st century than in previous centuries to imagine what it might look like if humans were facing extinction. Human extinction due to their own actions is more likely than a natural event such as an asteroid hitting the earth. This is because humans have been around (albeit sparsely at first) for around 200,000 years without incident, but it is unlikely that our planet will sustain human life for another 200,000 under current conditions. Henry Gee,[10] a palaeontologist and evolutionary biologist, suggests that humans may already be facing the first stages of decline. He points out that, although the population is still increasing, the rate of increase has halved since 1968, and in most countries – including poorer ones – the birth rate is now well below the death rate. He predicts that the global population will peak around the middle of the 21st century and then fall sharply. As soon as 2100, the global population size could be less than it is now.

Of course, in many ways that is good news, but it is worth considering what the causes might be and how things might therefore play out. He lists several causes of declining population size: increasing education for women and girls and better access to birth control (good); economic insecurity leading to couples waiting too long and not being able to conceive (not so good); declining quality of human sperm; and depletion of the planet's resources. He lists pollution as a possible cause of declining quality of human sperm, as well as stress due to living in close proximity with other people – which is not something that humans have evolved to cope with. His final point is persuasive but terrifying:

> The most insidious threat to humankind is something called "extinction debt." There comes a time in the progress of any species, even ones that seem to be thriving, when extinction will be inevitable, no matter what they might do to avert it. The cause of extinction is usually a delayed reaction to habitat loss. The species most at risk are those that dominate particular habitat patches at the expense of others, who tend to migrate elsewhere, and are therefore spread more thinly. Humans occupy more or less the whole planet, and with our sequestration of a large wedge of the productivity of this planet-wide habitat patch, we are dominant within it. H. sapiens might therefore already be a dead species walking.

This final point has two effects on me. I oscillate between feeling scared and feeling disengaged. Ah well, I reason, there is little I can do, and it is probably quite good that the day of reckoning will come for the polluters and not only for climate refugees. On a more positive note, however, I find myself wondering if and how humanity might escape this fate, and how we might avoid offsetting the worst effects of climate change onto the poorest and most vulnerable populations of the world who have contributed the least towards it. As the Intergovernmental Panel on Climate Change (the United Nations body for climate science) has consistently reported, we face a less and less liveable future, and we must take action now.[11]

It seems to me that between the two extremes of a rewilded and sustainable future for humanity and no future at all, there must be a middle line. Perhaps global cataclysmic events (of which COVID-19 was a taster) will force us to think beyond business as usual. It seems inescapable that the human population will decline – hopefully with as little suffering as possible for humans and other species – but this might propel a smaller population to find a new relationship with the natural and social world.

To continue with the theme of COVID-19 in Chapter 3, I remember being struck by the folly of continuing business as usual as the world emerged from lockdown. Being forced to stay at home alone for months on end affected the way that I saw the world. I know that I am not alone in this. This is what I wrote:

Awakening

The dreaming streets stir.
Streetlamps blink
And give up their light
To the day.

> The digger shudders
> And stretches its arm,
> Resuming its clawing
> As if never stopped.
>
> The builders' radio
> Pounds the silence.
> The hum of the trunk road
> Gives a clarion call.
>
> The slithering trains
> On glistening tracks
> Imbibe and disgorge
> Their occupants once more.
>
> The cars clear their throats
> And begin to trace
> The neural pathways
> Of our collective madness.
>
> The large-headed lorries,
> Backless for a while,
> Take up the yoke anew
> And shoulder their burdens.
>
> The people emerge blinking,
> Turning outwards once again.
> Will they reclaim the insanity
> That is theirs for the taking?
>
> The circling moon
> Cries to the sun,
> And the green blue planet
> Cries to the universe
> For a vaccine.

Will we continue business as usual, or will we take heed of how we need to live if the planet is to continue to sustain us? Will we be part of the future of this planet, or will it be reclaimed by non-human species after we have gone? Will the post-pandemic trends of working from home, moving out of the city and downsizing continue? If this is the effect of the first global pandemic (and there will be others), then this may be a taste of some of the choices that affluent people will make in the future. Those who can't afford it, of course, will not have these choices. Many of these will be key workers. It remains to be seen how the relationship between the relatively affluent and the key workers they rely on will evolve over time. Continuing to ignore the basic needs of key workers is a mistake on many different levels. As with the two world wars, disaster spawned innovation and an acceleration in social justice. Perhaps the consequences of humanity's destruction of ecosystems will speed up rewilding efforts in the same way.

Conclusion

Wild and beloved landscapes are core to our relationship with nature. They shape our collective imagination and spark awe, wonder and even existential questions about the meaning of life. Wildness exists in a complex relationship with humanity, and human activity has impacted on all wild spaces. It has become increasingly necessary to ask ourselves some hard questions about what we owe to the planet as a consequence of our impact on the world. Can / should we use cutting-edge science and technology to 'rewild' according to human will? To what extent can we continue to use wild spaces as a portal into other more authentic ways of being, and to what extent should we simply move away? Rewilding education may begin to provide answers to some of these questions. It develops new ways of knowing being and doing; sees nature as teacher; values wisdom traditions; and aims to create low-impact, productive, regenerative, inclusive and efficient ways of living. It therefore has a strong contribution to make towards more positive futures for humans and the species that share our planet, as well as providing a blueprint for education. The following chapters take the qualities of rewilding and apply them to education. What could we achieve if we rewild education as part of rewilding the planet?

Notes

1 Macfarlane, R. (2007). *The wild places*. Granta. p.209.
2 Collins Dictionary. Accessed January 2025. https://www.collinsdictionary.com/dictionary/english/rewilding.
3 Jepson, P., & Blythe, C. (2020). *Rewilding: the radical new science of ecological recovery*. Icon Books.
4 Rewilding Europe (2021). *Bison rewilding in the Southern Carpathians moves into next phase*. Accessed January 2025. https://rewildingeurope.com/news/bison-rewilding-in-the-southern-carpathians-moves-into-next-phase/.
5 Sussex Wildlife Trust (n.d.). *Sussex Flow Initiative*. Accessed January 2025. https://sussexwildlifetrust.org.uk/discover/around-sussex/a-living-wetland-landscape/sussex-flow-initiative-river-ouse.
6 National Geographic (n.d.) *Wolves of Yellowstone*. Accessed January 2025. https://education.nationalgeographic.org/resource/wolves-yellowstone.
7 Jepson, P., & Blythe, C. (2020). *Rewilding: The radical new science of ecological recovery*. Icon Books. p.126.

8   Jepson, P., & Blythe, C. (2020). *Rewilding: The radical new science of ecological recovery*. Icon Books, p.148.
9   World Wildlife Fund and the Boston Consulting Group. (2020). *Fires, forests and the future: a crisis raging out of control?* Accessed January 2025. https://files.worldwildlife.org/wwfcmsprod/files/Publication/file/28zpi2e4zt_wwf_fires_forests_and_the_future_report.pdf.
10 Gee, H. (2021). Humans are doomed to go extinct. *Scientific American*. Accessed January 2025. https://www.scientificamerican.com/article/humans-are-doomed-to-go-extinct/.
11 Intergovernmental Panel on Climate Change (2023). IPCC Sixth Assessment Report. Accessed January 2025. https://www.ipcc.ch/report/ar6/syr/downloads/report/IPCC_AR6_SYR_LongerReport.pdf.

Chapter 6

Valuing wisdom

Co-authored with Jwalin Patel

> If the doors of perception were cleansed everything would appear as it is, Infinite. For we have closed ourselves up, till we see all things through narrow chinks of our cavern.[1]
>
> William Blake (1790)

Introduction

Rewilding needs an integration of up-to-date science and ancient wisdom. This chapter starts with the idea that wisdom involves an integration of affect (emotion) and cognition. It is more important for young people to be knowledgeable and wise than to be academically successful in a narrow sense. Wisdom traditions can be found in the global East and South, as well as in ancient nature-oriented traditions such as Paganism in Europe. They take the form of Buddhism, Taoism, and Song Lines amongst the indigenous people of Australia, for example. They emphasise balance and harmony and see excesses that are typical in modernity as harmful to human and non-human thriving. The chapter proposes that, whilst the intellect is important, so are ways of knowing that integrate sensing and feeling from the body with the processes of the mind. The chapter offers hope in response to Chapter One, which outlined the failures of modern ways of thinking and systems of schooling.

The dominance of academic knowledge and abstraction in Eurocentric scientific thought has meant that embodied, common sense, holistic and contextualised ways of knowing are seen as less valid than de-contextualised, abstract, scalable, atomised ways.[2] The laboratory is favoured over the field, the theoretical over the applied, the surgeon over the midwife, the physicist over the engineer, and so on, with myths (and pay gaps) surrounding the so-called relative contribution or skill of each. It is of course sometimes the case that the best approach to a problem is to isolate variables, engage with abstractions, or delve deep whilst ignoring context, but these methods are used too often when a contextualised pragmatic approach would be more fruitful. Technical and practical knowledge are often seen as less valid ways of knowing and finding out, and the body has been relegated to the sidelines of academic life.

Drawing on many wisdom traditions, this chapter takes body, heart, mind and soul in turn and applies them to non-Eurocentric ways of thinking as a foundation for rewilded education. It suggests that the body needs to be recognised as deeply connected with processes of cognition and human flourishing. The heart needs to be at the centre of education for young people to develop good relationships, empathy, compassion, self-governance and self-regulation. Education for the mind needs to go beyond the mere transfer of information to include independent thinking, critical thinking and emancipation. Education for the soul needs to be based on self-transformation, equanimity, inner peace and harmony, universal oneness and unconditional love. The last part of the chapter draws together body, mind, heart and soul to suggest that holistic education integrates all of these in an education fit for purpose for the 21st century. This chapter brings together pedagogical and classroom-based implications of rewilding and includes a case study of a holistic school in India that has rewilded its approach to education, emphasising education for togetherness and harmony.[3]

The body

Rewilding places the body centre stage. Physical education, for example, should be about more than learning to play sports. Rewilded physical education includes breathing, dexterity, training the various senses and developing healthy bodies (and stronger immune systems). It links with the arts and the sciences to support young people to use the hands creatively to make things.

The relegation of the body in Western thought is a barrier to rewilded education and goes back a long time. From Judaeo-Christian beliefs about the body as a mere vessel for the soul, to the cartesian split between body and mind that Rene Descartes ushered into Western thought in 17th-century France, to the relegation of embodied ways of knowing in modern times. This is despite the fetishisation of the body in other ways. It may appear, for example, that the body, far from being relegated, is valorised in contemporary culture at the expense of the mind, heart and soul. Certainly, the commodification of the body in capitalist and patriarchal societies has created hugely profitable industries around beauty, sex, diet and exercise. This, of course, is not what is being advocated here. What is required is a healthy rebalancing. Rewilded education can go about this in at least three ways: through taking account of embodied cognition (biology and psychology); through increasing awareness of how life is experienced differently by different kinds of bodies (socio-cultural understandings); and through preparing young people for healthier lifestyles that integrate the needs of the body with the processes of the mind.

Embodied cognition is a diffuse and growing area of scientific inquiry that rejects the notion of the mind as somehow disconnected from the body.[4] It draws on the fields of psychology, neuroscience, ethology, philosophy, linguistics, robotics and artificial intelligence to challenge the idea that the brain is a sophisticated computer and that the body serves merely to input data for the brain's computational processes (whilst also providing a means of acting on the brain's conclusions). A renewed focus on the ways that the body interacts with the mind in cognitive processes allows us to consider how the world is perceived, interpreted and experienced in different bodies. Differences might be associated with the ways that brains are wired differently (taking account for example of neurodiversity and personality traits such as extroversion, neuroticism, etc.). They might also be associated with less stable factors such as levels of hormones (oestrogen, adrenaline, or testosterone), blood sugar, or need for sleep. Whatever the reason for the difference, the world is not understood in the same way by everyone, or even by the same person over time. This challenges the idea of universal ways of knowing and the disembodied brain – so favoured in modern systems of education.

It also challenges traditional understandings of the processes by which the brain receives information in order to engage in thinking and deciding. Embodied cognition suggests that it is possible to think with the hands, with the gut, or with the heart – it is not the case that the brain alone is involved in cognition. Young people can learn to listen to their body from an early age and thus begin to solve problems and make wise choices about their physical and psychological needs and those of others.

The body then needs to be rehabilitated as deeply connected with the mind. Consideration also needs to be given to how the body is connected with the environment. Where does the body begin and end? From a philosophical point of view, embodied cognition enables us to question whether technologies such as mobile phones or 'wearables' such as hearing aids are part of our thought processes. Might an Instagram-induced dopamine hit influence my cognition, for example? Is the mobile phone on which I access Instagram part of what I think of as my body? What about my glasses? My telescope or microscope? What about the landscapes that induce feelings of calm and well-being and enable me to overcome mental blocks in my decision-making? Perhaps most importantly for education, how do we work towards equity when the bodies and brains of learners are so different, and when the bodies and minds of some learners are supplemented with devices and technologies that enable them to acquire and demonstrate high-value knowledge, and the bodies and minds of others are not? Can we continue to cling to flawed understandings of 'intelligence' and meritocracy under these conditions?

These of course are philosophical questions, but the point is that rewilded education takes account of the fact that knowledge and learning are deeply contextualised, and that much of this contextualisation originates in the body, and in the ways in which it is enabled. This implies that learners need to be better supported to reflect not only on the conclusions that they might reach, but also on the embodied ways in which they reached those conclusions and the ways that they might be thinking differently from other people. This matters because, as shown in the first part of this book, young people in schools throughout the world are routinely taught to bracket what their bodies are telling them in order to focus purely on cerebral processes. They are taught that there is one correct way to think and process information (which they will be examined upon), and that some of those who think differently, or prioritise the needs of their body, have 'special educational needs' that require intervention and support for them to put on 'the right track' within normative classrooms.

Given also that the curriculum in the normative classroom is aimed at bodies that are white, European, neurotypical, heterosexual, middle class and male, some bodies are able to flourish and others not so much. This brings me to my second point about the body: rewilded education needs to draw on socio-cultural understandings of how life is experienced differently by different kinds of bodies. Bell hooks,[5] for example, writes about how her experience of being a university lecturer differs from the experience of white male colleagues. Whilst she, as a black woman, is always conscious of herself, 'as a body in a system that has not become accustomed' to her presence or physicality,[6] her white male colleagues inhabit a body that is invisible because it is seen as universal. Hooks notes that this enables them to act as if they were disembodied and in this way to deny their power and avoid uncomfortable truths. She recalls a white male professor who wore the same tweed jacket and rumpled shirt without anyone commenting on his dress, 'because to do so would be a sign of your own intellectual lack.' As hooks points out, 'the person who is most powerful has the privilege of denying their body.' Hooks was able to address this in her classrooms by talking about the centrality of the body. This, she felt, automatically challenged the way that power was orchestrated in her institutionalised spaces. She notes that 'acknowledging that we are bodies in the classroom has been important for me, especially in my efforts to disrupt the notion of professor as omnipotent, all-knowing mind.' Rewilded education, then, encourages learners to be wise and just through enabling them to think about themselves and others as embodied beings. It also enables a wider diversity of teaching and learning styles informed by the body and socio-cultural understandings.

This wider range of teaching and learning styles might also challenge body-based oppression. Hooks points out that using the Black vernacular in academic life, for example, can offer students new ways of communicating that don't maintain the relations of oppressor / oppressed. Being comfortable with heated exchanges is another way of unsettling the idea that academic excellence is maintained by deferent and quiet students who struggle to keep awake, and certainly don't stay behind after class. Reinvigorating the classroom with passion and energy might reduce the gap between the behaviours and values necessary to 'make it' in the academy, and those that students (perhaps especially disadvantaged students) share with family, friends and community. Reciprocity, engagement and laughter are deeply embodied experiences that enable all students to speak from a knowledge base. Rewilded teachers have the skills to bring this about. They also know how to deal with confessional or digressionary narratives, manage dialogue and link with academic literature and research.

The third point to do with the body is that young people need to be prepared for healthier lifestyles that integrate the needs of the body with the processes of the mind. In classrooms throughout the world, when young people experience hunger, incongruence, a full bladder or an inability to focus, their teachers expect them to rise above these physical feedback loops and to ignore the valuable information that they contain. These unnatural ways of living in a body are therefore reinforced, and by extension, ways of being in the world that ignore the needs of environmental and social ecosystems.

Rewilded education supports young people to take account of their physical needs, and also their hunches, gut feelings and intuitions. It enables them to go for long walks in order to reflect on a particular problem, set the alarm later during the teenage years when the brain needs different sleep patterns, and organise their learning in ways that suit their preferred ways of processing information. In 2014, for example, a three-year study by Wahlstrom et al.[7] involving over 9,000 adolescents found that when schools switched to later start times, young people enjoyed greater feelings of well-being and achievement and that there were improvements in attendance, standardised test scores, lateness and even substance abuse. In addition there were reductions in symptoms of depression, consumption of caffeinated drinks and the rate of traffic accidents involving teen drivers. Even a small change to take account of the embodied realities of young people can make a big difference.

In 2023, I wrote a chapter about expressive dance in a book about doing rebellious research with Simone Erignfeld, a former MPhil student at Cambridge.[8] The chapter discusses how a workshop where we danced our academic trajectories enabled a form of embodied conversation. Circling around each other, moving in and away, connecting and disconnecting, understanding and misunderstanding each other's motions, we tested the water, built confidence, gained momentum and trust, and finally expressed our hopes and fears for the future of academia. Inhabiting together a space of ambiguity and vulnerability, we explored what resistance looks like within the space of the University, and what it means to do rebellious research. We 'discussed' how our perspectives as a senior academic and graduate student differ and what our efforts for change might bring. When the music stopped Simone and I faced each other as our breathing returned to normal (not doing, but standing) and I found the words to answer the traditional academic character in my "Bloodless Angel" poem (shared in the first chapter of this book). In my dance I had been lost in another way of being in the academy (lost or found?) and I vowed to enable my rebellious vulnerability to stay with me.

> **Postscript**
>
> Know me now
> As I stand
> In the mud
> Of my place
> In this world
> As I feel
> Blood coursing
> Breath filling
> Life lifting
> All that is me.
>
> Meet my eyes
> Know my voice.
> I am
> Researcher
> Sharing songs
> Walking with
> Dancing through.
>
> We are
> Improvising
> Calling out
> Drum beating
> World making
> Time learning.
>
> Selves as resource.

Embodied ways of knowing, then, far from being limited by mere physicality, open up new possibilities for deep exploration and change.

The mind

The word 'mind' is a slippery concept, as seen in the previous section about the body. In rewilded education the mind is seen not so much as a soul floating in a body, but as a phenomenon that is produced by a deeply embodied brain. Many wisdom traditions have a lot to say about this through the concept of mindfulness. Mindfulness is one of the areas that will be explored here as important for rewilded education. Another area that will be explored is how awareness of brain functions can support wise and mature ways of engaging with the world.

David Smith[9] writes about how mindfulness practices in education might bring about appreciation of wisdom traditions and greater levels of compassion. He suggests that distraction lies at the heart of human ills and that this has been increased by marketing that uses our psychology against us to sell products that we don't always need. Both he and Eckhart Tolle[10] write about how mindfulness might help bring about 'recollection' or recovery of the self as being in deep unity with the essential nature of the world. They suggest that a new world can be created if young people are educated to let go of fear, discover inner peace and awaken to a deeper purpose. This can be achieved through learning to use the breath and to connect with the body using practices such as yoga, or sport and the arts more generally.

There is of course a danger of mindfulness being seen as a purely technical practice. Edward Sellman and Gabriella Buttarazzi[11] warn that mindfulness-based interventions in schools and other places of learning need to avoid simply adding 'lemon-juice to poison' and serving a neoliberal agenda for education. If they are used to encourage students to cope with oppressive structures, rather than to develop awareness of how to challenge and transform them, they become part of the problem rather than part of the solution. Nevertheless mindfulness is key to the kind of rewilded education that teaches 'the joy of Being, which is the only true happiness'.[12] Mindfulness implies a deep integration of body and mind – with the mind affecting the body, but also the body affecting the mind.

Rewilded education draws on both ancient wisdom traditions and contemporary science to consider how processes of the mind can be better understood and controlled by the embodied brain. Daniel Kahneman[13] points out that the brain has two distinct systems: slow thinking, which is the system normally associated with the left hemisphere of the brain and thought in the strictest sense; and fast, automatic or unconscious right-hemisphere thinking which operates continuously in the background, constantly surveying the environment. Rewilded education needs to take account of these different ways of thinking and equip young people to understand how their brain works and how they might use an awareness of neuroscience to manage impulses, solve problems holistically and function well in the world.

Iain McGilchrist[14] researches the relation between the two hemispheres of the brain, not just from the point of view of neurology, but also as a crucial factor that shapes culture. He questions the 'left-hemisphere chauvinism' that sees the left side of the brain as dominant and practical, and the right as creative and somehow less productive. He points out that the right-hand side of the brain deals holistically with the bigger picture, whilst the left-hand side focusses on the detail of particular issues. Given that it is responsible for surveying the environment and channelling incoming data, the right-hand side is more directly in touch with the world, and therefore less reliant on the 're-presentation' of information. It is also more aware of the left-hand side of the brain than the left-hand side is about it. It could be said that the left-hand side is 'autistic' and that this creates challenges for our wider cultural lives, since the left-hand side's ways of thinking are encouraged by a capitalist, patriarchal, colonising society to the detriment of the right-hand side's holistic ways. These ways of thinking undervalue and marginalise feminised ways of being in the world.

Iain McGilchrist points out that a healthy sequence between the two hemispheres would involve the right side first seeing the whole picture before handing over anything that needs investigating to the specialist left. This would be followed by the right side receiving the processed information back, integrating it with the wider picture, and finally deciding what to do next. An unhealthy sequence would involve the left side being reluctant to hand back to the right side because it is unaware of the importance of the right and is overconfident about its ability to know the world through its own data processing.

More generally, humans vastly overestimate their capacity to predict and understand random events, and they see patterns and narratives where there are none. They get stuck in the overly cognate and rational epistemologies that dominate social and political life.[15] Unhealthy sequences between the hemispheres of our brains often dominate in our culture because of an ethic from the Enlightenment onwards that values precise, categorical thinking at the expense of background vision and experience. Iain McGilchrist argues that this has now reached a point where it is seriously distorting our ways of thinking, as well as our socio-cultural spaces and even our buildings and cities. Again, rewilded spaces would become more common if young people were taught how to understand the functionings of their brain, and how to reclaim the perspectives of the right hemisphere.

Steven Peters[16] has suggested how this might be done through his Chimp Management Mind Model which uses the metaphor of the amygdala as chimpanzee to support learners to develop strategies for robustness, inner strength and resilience in the face of their powerful, unpredictable and self-interested 'inner chimp.' Understanding, calming and managing the inner chimp within all of us (instead of allowing marketing or misinformation to prod and exploit it) will be crucial if the aims of rewilding are to be attained.

Education will need to draw on thinkers such as Iain McGilchrist and Steven Peters to support young people to think more critically about how we process information and make decisions. Thinking and learning grounded in metacognition can enable young people to do this, and to engage with their environment in more diverse and fruitful ways. Embracing mindfulness is an important part of this.

The heart

Turning to the heart, Martin Buber[17] suggests that human life finds its fulfilment in relationships, which ultimately enable a connection with a soul, or an 'eternal thou.' For most of the time, we approach others as an 'I' towards an 'it', that is towards an object that is separate. To attain depth / sacredness in our relationships, however, we need to approach others as an 'I' towards a 'Thou', that is towards another who exists as a thinking feeling subject, just like us, rather than as an object to be acted upon. In education, Philip Klaus[18] speaks about this as an alternative 'aesthetic' of learning relationships which involves being on the side of the child and seeing the world through their eyes.

So what might loving, caring and safe relationships with self and others look like for rewilded teachers, and what kind of teacher education might enable this? John Miller[19] lists nine different ways that love can be manifested and argues that each of these has a place in education. These are: self-love, personal love, impartial love, compassion and loving kindness, love of learning, love of beauty, eros, and love as nonviolence. Unfortunately, however, sentimental, stereotypical and commodified expressions of love have robbed us of valuable ways of thinking about what it is to teach and to learn.

John Miller's idea of self-love particularly resonates with the concept of rewilding, not least because he argues that nature can be used as a model for self-acceptance. For teachers, self-love involves trusting our own embodied experience of the world – that is, our body, our intuitions, and our knowhow. It comes about through 'making friends with ourselves.'[20] This can be an important antidote to being told that others know best what needs to happen in our teaching spaces and being required to ignore our judgement and hard-won expertise. When teachers experience a lack of trust and a need for outside validation, it leads to feelings of alienation, and it is hard to feel self-love and to offer positive teaching spaces to young people.

Despite what popular culture and music might suggest, romantic love is not the only way of expressing love. Love can be found in friendship, and in shared enterprises, such as extended project-based learning. Miller links this with the Japanese concept of 'en,' which is a deep connection between two people that enables them to do something that would not have been possible alone. Learning relationships that are characterised by 'en' might involve teachers being fully present and available for learners over an extended period as they explore, act, change and grow. These kinds of learning relationships might feel like friendship in that they allow both teachers and students to think aloud without fear of judgement, and to feel relaxed and at home. They might engender feelings of tenderness, magnanimity and trust. As challenges are faced and milestones reached, rewilded teachers listen deeply to young people, and feel able to respond with joy, empathy, compassion, curiosity, solidarity, disappointment or pride. This is at the heart of what draws most teachers into teaching, and what keeps them there. As John Miller[21] points out, 'our happiness and the happiness of others are connected. When we are caring for others, it can engender a sense of well-being or harmony with ourselves.' It is hard to find love or caring mentioned in current policy documentation for initial teacher education. This important element of teaching is a blind spot that has been allowed to atrophy.

There are of course two questions that typically emerge when speaking about love in teacher-student relationships: what if the teacher and learner do not get on, and what if they get on too well? Restricted understandings of 'love' might be getting in the way here. Rewilded notions of love, compassion and friendship have more in common with wisdom traditions (for example Buddhism) than with modern Western ways of thinking. If human experience can be freed from the desire to suppress, manipulate or commercialise emotion, authentic ways of teaching and relating can emerge. For example, it is possible in a Buddhist tradition to feel compassion towards strangers, and even towards people that we don't like. By setting aside our own beliefs, listening properly to people and accepting them without judgement, it is possible to offer 'friendship' (as defined earlier), even if we do not agree.

Some situations make it easy to feel compassion – others less so. It is easy for a teacher to feel instinctive compassion for a learner with disabilities who works hard to overcome setbacks, for example, but perhaps harder to extend that compassion to a challenging learner who appears lazy. It is important to cultivate this ability, however. Although this is a high bar, the Dalai Lama feels natural compassion as a teacher when he remembers that all beings desire happiness and do not want to suffer. This is independent of how they may be acting at a particular moment in time. The ability to cultivate compassion is a lifelong enterprise and is fundamental to human thriving, global justice and sustainability. This renders it essential for rewilded teaching. It differs from empathy in that it is grounded in action — in alleviating suffering experienced by all human and non-human entities. Compassion will be necessary if humans are to have a viable future on this planet. The task of the compassionate teacher as both facilitator of learning and as role model could not be more important.

But what if the teacher and learner get on too well? How do we avoid romantic associations, inappropriate friendship or the sexual abuse of children? In 2020, the UK Office for National Statistics[22] reported that (according to available information) in the year ending 2019, girls were around three times as likely as boys to have experienced sexual abuse before the age of 16 (11.5% compared with 3.5%) and that women who reported being sexually abused before the age of 16 were most likely to have been abused by a family member (40% of victims). This is followed by a friend or acquaintance (37% of victims). Around one-third (30%) were sexually abused by a stranger, 11% by a partner or ex-partner, and 10% by someone else. Only 6% were abused by a person in a position of trust or authority, such as a doctor, youth worker or teacher.[23] This research in the UK into young people and sexual abuse presents a complex picture in which teachers barely feature. This does not detract from the fact that any abuse needs to be taken seriously – it is merely to note that it is important to focus on tackling abuse perpetrated by the family members and friends or acquaintances who are the main offenders.

Of far more concern to education is the general climate in schools, and in peer culture, where girls (and some boys) are subject to daily acts of sexual harassment. For example, in 2021, Ofsted, the UK education regulator,[24] published a report that showed that 64% of girls aged 13 and above have experienced unwanted touching 'sometimes' or 'a lot,' for example in school corridors. Girls are also subject to sexist name-calling (92%) and to forms of online abuse, such as being sent sexual photos or videos that they do not want to see (88%) and being put under pressure to provide sexual images of themselves (80%). If they do send such images, 73% say that they found out later that their pictures were shared more widely without their consent or knowledge. Although the figures are lower for boys, 74% suffer sexist name-calling, for example. The young people surveyed by Ofsted did not feel that their teachers were aware of the extent of the problems or knew how best to respond.

Despite the fact that the vast majority of people who abuse children are family members or friends / acquaintances, male teachers often find themselves subject to scrutiny and mistrust as potential paedophiles.[25] This can lead to caution, avoidance, vexatious complaints and missed opportunities. When this is coupled with harm that is caused by a lack of resources to tackle abuse within families, online, and in communities, and with the daily sexual harassment that takes place in schools, this over-emphasis on male teachers is clearly an issue. In a rewilded education system, the quality of relationships between teachers and learners might mean that young people would feel more able to disclose to their teacher any abuse that was happening elsewhere in their lives.

Both John Miller and bell hooks talk about the role of eros and the erotic in education. They define it very differently to how it is usually defined, however. For John Miller eros is experienced as transcendent (or divine) energy that runs through the universe and ourselves and that connects us to something that feels larger than ourselves. It can be found in 'rapturous research' and in the appreciation of beauty that can feel like homecoming. It can be experienced as a kind of falling in love with life. Likewise, bell hooks[26] notes that:

> To restore passion to the classroom or to excite it in classrooms where it has never been, professors must find the place of Eros within ourselves and together allow the mind and body to feel and know desire.

Love and passion, then, which have been systematically erased from modern experiences of education by fear, taboos and mind-body dualism, might 'invigorate discussion and excite the critical imagination.'[27] This is education at its best. It relies on teachers and learners who allow themselves to remain embodied and full of desire for understanding, growth, connection and change.

When I showed this chapter with two practising UK teachers that I know well, they both felt that there are currently many barriers to acting from the heart in teaching and that it is currently countercultural to talk about love in the context of relationships in school. One shared her frustration at having just spent many hours entering data into a computer to provide an audit of her school's safe-guarding activities, and the other worried that I might be seen as a weird hippy! The first teacher noted unhappily that it was very unlikely that anyone would ever look at the data that she had entered. The many hours spent ensuring the compliance of the school could have been spent addressing the very real needs of the children and families in her school community – needs that were not being met because of unacceptable and dangerous delays in getting social services and mental health support for vulnerable children and families. The auditing of safeguarding had become a kind of performance that had replaced accessing support.

The second teacher is no doubt correct about me being misunderstood and vilified by some. We most certainly live in a topsy-turvy world when love, care, beauty and compassion are seen as weird, and lack of well-being and disengagement from teaching and learning are seen as normal. Roger Duncan[28] also uses the word weird but turns it on its head. For him, WEIRD (Western Educated Industrial Rich and Democratic) culture is at the heart of the developed world instead of a more compassionate beating heart. This is affecting ecosystems and human health and well-being, and is most decidedly weird.

The soul

Turning finally to the soul, this chapter shows how teachings from various spiritual traditions can support young people to experience inner peace and happiness in everyday life. As Satish Kumar[29] points out, caring for the natural environment (soil) and upholding human values (society) are incomplete as moral imperatives without maintaining personal well-being (soul). Drawing on the ancient philosophies of Hindu, Buddhist and Jain traditions of India, and on Mahatma Gandhi and Rabindranath Tagore, he points to new ways of being in relationship with nature. Everyday experiences of beauty, embodiment and stillness in nature are fundamental if we are to rewild education.

The concept of soul is universal across all times and places despite variations in how it is imagined in different parts of the world. Religions have created rituals, holy images, texts and laws to try to tie it down and build identity and meaning, but the soul itself remains an elusive concept, especially in the Western world. In the wisdom traditions the soul is seen as an entity that lies outside of the everyday – something that inheres when the clutter and bumph of living falls away. It is often felt as a private sense of purpose, continuity and meaning, and its transcendent quality enables an aesthetic of expansiveness, connectedness and peace. In education, it is a missing piece in the language that we have available to talk about teaching and learning, and education systems throughout the world are the poorer for it in my view.

It is of course dangerous when the language of the soul is co-opted by religious fundamentalists who wish to imply that only their traditions are valid, or worse, that those who have different understandings are evil. Education can be co-opted into this in deeply damaging ways. In contrast, the meaning of the soul that is used here to support rewilding is grounded in the timeless aesthetics and ethics of wisdom traditions, mysticism and love. It foregrounds happiness, peace and joy.[30] This way of thinking about the soul provides a framework for young people to find their own ways of achieving these things, rather than suggesting that a particular doctrine or religious text has all the answers.

One of the ways that the soul gets lost in modern systems of schooling is through the dominance of the ego and the need to 'be someone.' Far from being seen as a problem, the ego is nurtured and fanned so that some young people come to believe that they are entitled to success and mobility and cut themselves off from nature and the world. Avraham Cohen[31] suggests that our obsession with higher grades, promotion, better jobs, more status and more financial gains is leading to 'the burial of the soul of every student and educator.' Within an individualistic culture, those who thrive come to see themselves as important and those who fall behind as less so. The support systems of an interconnected society are weakened when the egos of the strong are allowed to grow in ways that imply a lack of obligation to others and to the planet. A focus on the soul might begin to mitigate this. Ram Dass[32] suggests that the aim of education should not be about becoming somebody – it should be about becoming nobody. He argues that the prison of self-identity valorises the ego and inhibits the joy of being 'nobody,' and of being open to the universal divine at play in the world. This is not to imply an easy journey. Pema Chodron[33] uses the metaphor of swimming in a turbulent river to depict the challenges of learning to live mindfully without ego. Those who cling to the certainty of the shore – to familiar patterns and habits – may never know the infinitely more satisfying experience of being fully alive.

Another way that the soul gets lost in schools, and in wider society, is through the push for continuous growth. Dissatisfaction with how things are, and the desire for constant improvement, are promoted as necessary for success, growth and change – whether that is at the level of the individual student or at a wider level. The Buddhists refer to this as 'duhkha,' which is often translated as suffering. David Loy[34] suggests that our sense of 'never enough' (whether it's time, accolades, money, sex, security ... even war) is at the root of our individual and collective suffering. This, he feels, is the true meaning of 'bad karma.' His 'Buddhist Revolution' calls for a radical change in the ways we approach our lives, the planet and the collective delusions that pervade language, culture and even spirituality. In a similar vein, Richard Rohr[35] draws on the life and Christian teaching of St Francis to suggest that the path towards authentic spirituality involves simplifying our lives, liberating ourselves from self-limiting biases and certitudes, and balancing contemplation with being in nature and action in the world. For this, new ways of educating are needed. But what might these new ways of educating look like?

As discussed, rewilded education for the soul would involve young people searching for peace, joy and fulfilment without succumbing to ego or dissatisfaction with how things are. This would require spaces for peace, reflection and contemplation within wider educational spaces. Avraham Cohen reminds us that we are human 'beings' and not human 'doings' and that education must create spaces where introverted ways of being are valued as much as extroverted ways. Michael Bonnet[36] asks whether current systems of schooling over-emphasise a particular cosmopolitan, urban, extroverted personality type, and whether we could do more to create spaces for withdrawal and self-awareness that do not require an 'other.' He argues that it is possible to experience one's own humanity, to 'come into presence' in these spaces, and that processes of encounter and dialogue are not always necessary for learning in the ways that are often claimed. Indeed, solitude might guard against passivity and the undue influence of others.

Helen Lees[37] notes the presence of an aesthetic of 'strong silence' in A.S Neill's Summerhill School (a child-centred, alternative school in the UK) resulting from children's freedom to withdraw or go quiet. This is in contrast to 'weak silence,' in more traditional spaces where children have been silenced or forced to be quiet.[38] Strong silence has an aesthetic quality that is both beautiful in its own right and also strongly generative. The educational outcomes of students in this alternative school are known to be extraordinary, so that silence and withdrawal are not as harmful as many teachers and parents might think. Alternative education can support individualised learning through foregrounding freedom and avoiding a one-size-fits-all approach. The uncertainty of alternative education often results in transformative spaces that are embodied, disordering, unsettling and supremely creative. Young people learn to be brave and creative if they can be shown how to embrace uncertainty, randomness and chaos. Spaces of calm and reflection are essential for navigating this territory.

Teachers need personal and professional development to create these transformative spaces. How might this happen? I have been careful to avoid the words 'teacher training' in this book in favour of 'teacher education.' The more usual term 'teacher training' perhaps epitomises how state actors think about the professional development of teachers, whereas genuine teacher education needs to engage with the messiness, paradoxes and complexity of what it means to teach. One example of this is the Mindful Teaching program developed by Dennis Shirley and Elizabeth Macdonald.[39] They point out that mindful teaching can overcome alienated teaching, but it is not a program that can be purchased, a recipe that can be followed, or a silver bullet:

> Rather it is a form of teaching that is informed by contemplative practices and teacher enquiry that enable teachers to interrupt their harried lifestyles, come to themselves through participation in a collegial community of enquiry and practice, and attend to aspects of their classroom instruction and pupils learning that are easily overlooked in the press of events.[40]

The authors developed a series of Saturday seminars in which they met to discuss readings, practise formal meditation, and explore topics of relevance and concerns for teachers. The program was based on the teachings of Thich Nhat Hanh and involved openness to novelty and multiple perspectives, sensitivity to different contexts, and orientation in the present. Sessions always began with half an hour of catching up with one another over coffee and muffins before a process with 8 steps was followed:

1 Pressing concerns. Teachers were given an opportunity to share any issues that were preoccupying them at the time.
2 Opening a topic. One of the teachers presented a previously agreed topic that was common to others.
3 Scholarly research. Teachers were given access to a range of research and materials that were relevant to the topic under consideration.
4 Meditation. Teachers were guided through meditation practice in order to achieve calm, focus, equanimity and a non-judgmental frame of mind.
5 Small group work. Teachers shared what came up for them in the stillness of meditation.
6 The listening protocol. One or two teachers for whom this topic is particularly pertinent were given time to explore it in more detail with the support of the rest of the group.
7 Debriefing. Teachers talked about the process and what they were taking away from it. They also discussed what was left unresolved and what an opposing perspective might look like.
8 Mindfulness assignments. Teachers were given a range of activities that they could do in their own settings that might build on the topic under consideration and help to embed mindful awareness in their working lives.

Not only is this mindful teaching program based on theory, practice and research that emerges from teachers' own perspectives and needs, but it also takes care to avoid perpetuating the notion that there are straightforward answers to teacher's concerns, or that 'best practice' can be transferred to any setting. It does not provide simplistic 'tips for teachers' or training in this or that new curriculum or teaching method. Rather it engages with a series of tensions, provocations and paradoxes in order to stimulate reflection and debate. Teachers might settle on a provisional resting point for their practice at the end of each session, but this is not the same as once-and-for-all solutions or off-the-shelf resources.

The mindful teaching program fits with the rewilding paradigm. It is more concerned with fitness for purpose within an ever-shifting ecosystem than with training that is seen as replacing parts in a faulty machine. The authors list seven aspects of mindful teaching that are in creative tension with each other: open mindedness; love and care; stillness; professional expertise; authenticity; integration and harmony; and collective responsibility. Open-mindedness might suggest one course of action, for example, and professional expertise might suggest another (do I keep an open mind about learners wearing headphones, or do I insist that they develop focussed study skills?). The same can be said for stillness and collective responsibility (do I take some time out to reflect on what I am seeing, or join with others to meet our original objectives?), or authenticity and integration (do I act in accordance with my beliefs or compromise to ensure consistency?). In each case a teacher might oscillate, taking account of both ends of a spectrum and using practical wisdom (phronesis in Greek) to make a judgement call. The best decisions take account of complexity, and are never set in stone.

Unfortunately most teachers in modern systems of education do not have the scope or the time to engage with programs such as this, despite multiple calls for this to be the case. Jayne Osgood,[41] for example, appeals for a 'professionalism from within' to enable the cultivation of critically reflective, emotional professionals who are able to resist the ways on which they are socio-culturally constructed. As far back as 1973, Paolo Freire[42] wanted educators to be framed as coordinators rather than as teachers due to the dangers involved in traditional ways of framing the teaching profession.

These ways of supporting teachers point towards the cultivation of wisdom through an engagement with the soul. Some feel uncomfortable with the language of the soul, but it is hard to find other ways of talking about an aesthetic of beauty, calm, transcendence and meaning beyond the everyday. Rupert Sheldrake[43] attempts to address this by showing how science validates seven practices on which all religions are built, and which are part of our common human heritage: relating to plants; rituals; singing and chanting; meditation; gratitude; connecting with nature; and pilgrimage and holy places. He argues from a scientific perspective that these practices generally make people happier and healthier, and that they lead to feelings of awe and wonder in nature. It is time to embrace these practices within rewilded education.

Holism

Despite the prior separate consideration of body, mind, heart and spirit, it is clear that these are fundamentally connected. For human beings to thrive there is a need for holism. Several holistic education scholars[44] have called for the integration of body, mind, heart and soul, as well as a separate focus on each. This resonates with Eastern scholars, for example Radhakrishnan[45] suggested that 'education has to give us a second birth, to help us to realise what we have already in us ... to emancipate the individual [through] ... the education of the whole person – physical, vital, mental, intellectual, and spiritual'.

Sadly, the epistemology of fragmentation underpins modern perceptions of the world. Living and nonliving beings are seen as independent from each other, as are individuals, human societies and nations. Real-world phenomena are arbitrarily segregated into disciplines, and lives are divided between work (working to continue living) and life (living to continue working). This results in societies divided by gender, class, caste, religion and race and classrooms divided by age and subjects. In contrast, wisdom traditions hold a deep recognition of the interconnection of all things.[46] For example, a Buddhist perspective sees all beings across the universe as interconnected, bringing obligations to reduce suffering for all.[47]

Several thinkers and schools have tried to educate holistically, including Montessori schools, Reggio Emilia schools, Waldorf schools (inspired by Rudolf Steiner), Krishnamurti schools, Aurobindo schools, home schooling, unschooling, deschooling,[48] forest schools, farm schools, and barefoot university and ecoversity initiatives.[49] Holism tends to be expressed through a lack of fixed curricula and assessment patterns and through student autonomy over content, method and pace of learning. It can also be seen in collaboration over school climate and how relationships are managed, and in schemes of work that are topic-based and link together several of the traditional academic disciplines.

Mirambika Free Progress school, a holistic education school in Delhi, India, aims to bring about an integral education, that is the education of the body, mind, heart and soul. The school is based on the educational philosophy of Sri Aurobindo and The Mother (Mirra Alfassa)[50] and the students come from a mixed socio-economic background. They integrate education of the body, mind, heart and soul by integrating it into their lesson plans; for example, lessons on photosynthesis include a focus on breathing, learning to balance like a tree, creative responses to questions of sustainability and renewable energy, and community action for protecting trees, as well as the science involved. Time is set aside for reflection on participation in group work, self-regulation, degree of critical thinking, and connection with a young person's 'inner friend.' Pedagogical practices of dialogue, project-based learning, group-based learning, embodied education, and reflection are integral to their education approach.[51] Learning is seen as multisensorial, promoting engagement through sight, visualisation, touch, object manipulation, physical movement, sound, speech, taste, smell, feeling and intuition. Holism is possible in this school and elsewhere, but sadly it is often missing in modern systems of schooling. The following part of the chapter is written by Jwalin Patel and gives a flavour of what rewilded education in an alternative school in India might look and feel like. It is grounded in his field notes from his PhD as well as ongoing post-doctoral research.

A notional day at an alternative school in India
Jwalin Patel

There is a growing body of scholarship on holistic education. Hilary and I were discussing how we could best contribute to the field, and she recommended writing a narrative that draws together elements from different holistic schools into a fictional typical day. I loved the idea; it could allow readers to walk in my shoes and experience some of the things that I did. My work[52] led me to spend extended time at over 30 alternative schools in India, some of which were set up or inspired by Indian thinkers like Aurobindo, Dalai Lama, Gandhi, Krishnamurti, and Tagore. I have put together a notional day from a set of collated experiences across such schools. They range from government-funded to low- and high-fee schools; some are residential, but most are not. They can be found throughout India, and range in size from schools for 100 to 1,000 students.

Act I – sacred silence underpinning the start of the school day

It is a warm winter morning. As I walk to the school along a sunlit path I go through an urban forest, and I am immediately drawn to various flowers that line the path. I start to lose myself to the chirping sounds of birds. My attention is drawn to a small flock of peacocks that meander the path and without realising it I have left the city behind – its sounds drowned out, its remnants left behind – nature has taken over.

I have been invited to join the school 30 minutes before the start of the day. I walk into the school and observe that teachers have gathered on the ground floor, sitting around a circular mat. I observe some of the teachers are sitting with their eyes closed in quiet meditation while others are adding flowers to bowls of water; creating mandalas. A large bowl of water with flowers has been set in the centre of the room. Everyone settles down in the circle, a few prayer handouts are distributed and everyone starts to chant prayers. I have lost track of time but as I open my eyes, I see a few children have trickled in and are nestled in the circle, around teachers, at times on teachers' laps. The chanting goes on as more students and parents join in. The prayers are followed by a short passage reading from 'The Mother's'[53] book and silent meditation / reflection time. At this point there are over 40 people in the room (including preschool students) but there is a peculiar sense of sacred silence.

I close my eyes, I am transported to another school. This is a much larger school with hundreds of students, situated in a forest. As students and parents come into the school students drop off their bags and gather in the main ground, running around playing games while parents catch up with each other. There is a single bell and everyone falls silent and gathers together, with no instructions from teachers and/or adults. As the prayers begin everyone joins in and between two prayers there is pin-drop silence. After the prayers, the air carries a similar sense of sacred silence. I can feel shivers go down my spine as it feels that this silence isn't just a silence of sounds but rather a silence of the minds – leading to a kind of sacredness. It feels as if the silence has descended from the skies, into my (our) mind, into the heart, into my (our) whole body. It feels eery that with no imposition or enforcement, silence is a natural part of the assembly. And as the prayers end, students get back to dashing around – continuing their games while making their way to the classes while the parents head back home.

Act II – a transdisciplinary 2 hour short session

After the teachers' preparation, the day begins with a sports period. After this everyone heads back into their classrooms. Once the students settle down, they observe a short spell of silence along with music being played through the school speakers. The class begins with students sharing the art pieces that they had completed at home. One of the students hasn't completed his work and a short exchange goes on between the student and teacher.

S:	"Can I do it now?"
T:	"You want to do it right now, while the rest of us work on something else?"
S:	"Yes"
T:	"But then you will miss out on what the rest of us do, can you take it home?"
S:	"No, I don't want to take it home."
T:	"See there is no school tomorrow can you do it then?"
S:	"No *bhaiya*, I don't want to take it home."
Student 2:	"He can do it in the break."
Student 3:	"But he wants to play football then."
T:	"Don't play one day."
S:	"No *bhaiya*."
T:	"See I would like you to join us in the next activity but you need to find a time to work on the drawing as well. Can you remove one of the 11 points that you have written?

I am intrigued by what these points are about. Each student has a reflection book in which they note goals that they have set for themselves for the year. These appear to be divided into academic learning goals, physical development goals, emotional goals, and cognitive goals. A child explains that each student has come up with their own goals at the start of the year, and they actively try to work on their respective goals for themselves. The student exclaims "yes, I will do it at home – it will help me achieve my goal of keeping to my commitments".

The class continues with everyone discussing the upcoming Indian festival of Ram Navami. The discussion evolves to focus on *Ram Leela*, a play that they are putting together. Once some of the pressing logistics about the play are sorted out, a supporting language teacher who is in the class asks the students to come up with short Hindi poems that can later be narrated in the play. Students have put together a series of 40 poems already and they continue building on a few more. The class teacher asks students to explore if there are any mathematical patterns in the number of words and phrases that are being used. Thereafter, another supporting teacher walks in and the whole group starts talking about the props they will need for the play. They split into groups and start designing the props; I join the group working on a cow and we intricately design and decorate the whole cow's body with various Indian motifs. Thereafter, the class teacher asks a question regarding the journey Ram would have taken across India. He asks all of us to come up to the Earth model (it's 8 feet wide!) that the students have previously designed. He asks students to point out the latitude of the school and to trace the path Ram took before the states, rivers, and oceans they would have crossed while travelling to Sri Lanka. He transitions to discussing everyone's summer trips and asking about the longitudes of a couple of other countries that the students visited over the summer. The session transitions into talking about what is meant by degrees and the mathematical underpinnings.

A short bell rings through the school – it is time for a snack break. I look up and realise that it has been 2 hours since the session began! That doesn't seem like it at all; neither the children nor I are tired. Some students still continue working on their projects. The session reminds me of an administrator's comment; she said "There is no teaching here; we chase it out". The session has been extremely participative, and students have engaged in self- and peer-learning, and in discovery-based learning. The teachers were mere facilitators and leveraged diverse students' learning to guide the group.

I decide to go up to the teacher and enquire about their trans-disciplinary pedagogical approach. He shares that they have been working on this project for the last month. It started with a student asking about Ram Leela and the whole group expressing interest in putting together a play. He describes that over time they have covered various social sciences, science, language, and mathematics topics through the project. Now they are approaching the time to perform the play for the whole school. The teacher goes on to tell me about his work supporting teachers from 30 schools across India to incorporate project-based learning into their day-to-day pedagogy.[54]

Act III – a surprising sense of onus

After the session has ended, I walk with the students to another block for another session. En route, a few of them stop and stand in a circle. They are extremely focussed and discuss in soft voices. I join their circle. A student sees me and comments, "this tree has grown weaker". I enquire "how do you know?" and another child responds "intuitively". Other students and I stand around for a while; some continue observing the tree, while others stand with their eyes closed.

As we reach the other classroom and students shuffle in, I see an elderly teacher closing a couple of half-open taps at a nearby basin. I observe what she does – she comes over and starts aligning some of the students' shoes without saying a word to the students. She walks into another classroom for her session. Later on, I decide to speak with her and she explains that it is important for safety, especially if there is an evacuation and someone trips. I further check why she did it instead of asking the students or others to do so, and she goes on, "to me school is a place where a collective is being built. It's the spirit of collective effort. It's everybody's problem, you know, where everybody is concerned about it or the fact that … we all are sharing and being collectively worried about what is happening". The teachers (and students) had a strong sense of onus, Gandhian trusteeship and collective responsibility over the school. The school wasn't just a school; it was their and our school.

I decide to go visit the principal; she has asked me to drop by when I get the chance. As I enter the principal's office I find two students sitting atop her desk. As I walk in, the students with complete confidence ask, "what do you need?" Taken by surprise I blurt "I need to see the principal". They respond "she is teaching in grade 8, she took her flute with her so you will be able to hear her". They add, "is there anything that we can help you with?" I enquire if they didn't have a class and they point at the story books in their hands and mention that it is their free period. They had come to have a discussion with the principal, but when she had to leave, they decided to stay back and read. I ask if they were meant to sit there and the students were surprised, their expressions conveying 'why not?' Later in the week, I check with other teachers and they mention that it is quite common for the students to go up and sit atop the principal's table and help run the school. One of the teachers also said when she went in, the students were able to help solve the issue that she had come there with.

Act IV – breaking bread – a caring and connected community

Over lunch, I observe students filling the lunch hall and upon finding a place to sit, they wait for everyone to settle down. A bell rings and there is a minute of silence before everyone starts eating. I find myself reflecting that such simple practices of silence can be powerful and wonder why it seems so hard to integrate them into mainstream schools. Some of the non-teaching and support staff join in for meals on a separate table. Seeing me looking at the support staff sitting together a student comments "do you know, they were going to create a separate hall for support and cleaning staff's dining, but the senior students opposed the decision". Another student comments "we like that everyone is treated equally; now all of us (teachers, students, administrators, and support staff) eat the same food, together".

I am generally a slow eater and see most of the students get up and head out. There are a few straddlers who appear to be in deep conversations. A student in a soft voice announces, "all those that are done should head out" and most of the students get up promptly. I am speaking with the student beside me and she describes that at times they get lost in conversation but if they don't get up once done then kitchen staff have to wait longer for their lunch. It occurs to me that students have developed a deep sense of community responsibility, and that they didn't feel pressured to behave in one way or another just to obey rules.

There is a genuine sense of connection and community here. It reminds me of a hike that I did in another school with grade 12 students. On the hike a couple of them were playfully throwing orange peels at each other to see if they could hit the other. However, at times the peels landed on others; but to my surprise no one reacted or got annoyed. When it landed on a student beside me; he just shrugged and when I asked "are you okay?" he replied "yes, it is just a game". Through the hike I observed students sharing everything they were carrying; water bottles, jackets, and taking turns to carry bags. They extended the same to me. It felt as if all of us were a part of a single family.

Act V – a space for flourishing for all

After lunch, I walk past a pair of students that are singing a *Bengali* song and I am awe-struck. They are hopping and skipping while singing along. While I don't understand Bengali, their melodious voice, rhythm, and control over their pitch is amazing! In the hustle bustle of students walking around, relaxing, and / or getting to another class, I realise that most of the students have smiles on their faces. There is a general chatter among students and all of them are quite happy. The school ethos and environment appears to create a space where students and teachers have the freedom to (just) be (themselves). I reflect that this is 'a relaxed hustle bustle'. Students are going their own ways, driven by an intrinsic sense of joy and aren't rushed by arbitrary pressures of class start times, grades, or examinations. As I am reflecting, I stumble across a 40-foot long mural. Students of all ages are stopping by to paint certain parts of it before walking along. It also reminds me of the various arts and craft pieces I have seen through the day (including stone sculptures, wall paintings, mounted paintings, painted pots, origami, ceiling and fan hangings, dream-catchers, and flower mandalas). The school has a thriving culture of arts. I wonder if that has something to do with the relaxed culture.

After a few more classes, once the school day has ended, teachers spend time reflecting on the day – going through incidents of the day, planning for the following day, and meditating. Teachers also reflect on the holistic development of each child, noting down key incidents of mental, vital, physical, and spiritual education. They make detailed notes on each child. They discuss their plans for a reading circle for teachers the next day, and for more extended time when they will gather to discuss project updates, explore opportunities to collaborate with each other, share critical incidents with students, and offer and receive advice and support from colleagues to help overcome challenges. This reminds me of a recent state-wide policy change in Bihar that has earmarked an hour at the end of the school day for teachers to reflect on the day and plan for the next day, and for professional development. I hope that the structures, systems, and processes from these alternative schools will be able to inform how such policies play out at scale.

Across all of these engagements, meditation and reflection remain common. Teachers frequently reflect on their own ways of living and being. In a discussion with one of the teachers, she comments, "I will stop coming to the school the day I stop growing inwards". This comment moves me and I am reminded of Krishnamurti's[55] call to his teachers at various schools across India, UK (Brockwood Park) and USA (Oak Grove School) to engage in learning to live differently for themselves, and of Maya Shakti's commentary on The Learning

Community where teachers are engaged in an ongoing process of reflection, contemplation, and meditation to understand themselves.[56] This commitment to learning to live differently for oneself means that the school is a space for learning for both teachers and students – a space to learn to live differently and to 'grow inwards'.

Act VI – connecting with nature over sunset

It is dusk time; the students, teachers, and I walk up to a hilltop to see the sunset. Students hike up a hill quietly, with some of them lost in thought, some stopping to look at trees and butterflies, some touching the tree barks and leaves as they walk along. The students have developed an inherent connection and deep appreciation for nature. As I trek along, I am reminded of various comments that students have mentioned at other times like "look, how beautiful is this tree", "this is a wonderful rock", and "the hill looks very beautiful [as it is struck by sunlight]". Upon reaching the top of the hill, everyone sits quietly as they look out at the sunset. The vastness of nature is humbling and calming. It brings a notion of silence, and many of my immediate concerns melt away. Over dinner, I speak to a student that I have connected with and he comments that the evening walk is the most valuable part of the day for him. The 15-minute hike up, 15 minutes of sitting, and 15 minutes of hike back in complete silence allow him to connect with nature and any stress or concerns disappear. He mentions that even when he grows older he would look for similar opportunities every day. This reminds me of an alumni I met who shared "that old tree. It must have been here for far longer than I have been, and it will be there after me. Similarly, that mountain – it is quite huge. It allows you to see that you are quite tiny".

For a long time, I have cherished a deep connection with nature; and it feels like the students share a similar meaningful connection with it. They also have a strong understanding of nature around them; identifying, relating with, and appreciating nature (trees, birds, animals, flowers, sun, moon, stars, wind, rain …). Their campus, and other campuses of similar schools, are surrounded by nature, with one being located in a forest valley. Additionally, students frequently engage in bird watching, long hikes, cycling treks, and daily walks to watch the sun set.

As I head back to my room, walking along the moonlit path through the forest, I feel the forest has been charged through the day, and so have I. I don't feel tired but feel strangely recharged. I eagerly await tomorrow! I find myself drifting into thinking about why; and decide that the day was a day of *Sadhana*. It was a day of learning and living in harmony with nature, each other, and myself.

Reflecting back

Today, as I sit and reflect back on my experiences of my fieldwork schools from a couple of years ago, I feel my facial muscles relax, breathing slow down, and any stress and tension ease up. In hindsight, the schools were a space for everyone to learn to be their whole selves by integrating various aspects of themselves, forgoing any false compartmentalisation and fragmentation, and just being (learning to be)! I believe these schools were ashrams where everyone engaged in living, being, and learning — learning a different way of life. The process of putting this notional day together has brought back many memories and has been a stark reminder for me about the purpose of life. As I was writing this section, I noted down for myself "we often focus on becoming, and perhaps I should pay more attention to being in the here and now"!

Conclusion

Rewilding education, then, draws on scientific ways of understanding the world, but also on wisdom traditions and indigenous knowledge about living in harmony with nature that operate through myth and story and that help individual humans to know their place in complex ecosystems, and in the cosmos. This chapter has argued that a rewilded education needs to integrate the body, mind, heart, and soul. It has proposed that a focus on the body can challenge traditional understandings of cognition and offer new ways of knowing and learning. A focus on the mind can encourage mindfulness, critical thinking, and an understanding of how the brain works. A focus on the heart can enable young people to develop empathy, compassion, and healthy relationships with themselves and others. And a focus on the soul can support young people to connect with something deeper and more meaningful than the everyday world. The rewilded classroom as exemplified through the notional day across Indian alternative schools, offers both students and teachers the space, freedom, and opportunity to embody and embrace their humanity. It brings about the integrated development of the body, mind, heart, and soul as a whole. Such a rewilded education has the potential to foster a sense of wonder, belonging, responsibility, and interconnectedness; ultimately, creating a future where all of us live in harmony with ourselves, others, and the larger world. As William Blake suggests, by opening the doors of perception, we can see the world as it truly is, in all its infinite beauty and complexity. Rewilded education is a powerful tool for doing just that, enabling us to rediscover our innate wisdom and to live more fulfilling and meaningful lives.

Contributor Bio

Dr Jwalin Patel is a research scholar who has been working in the education developmental sector for the last 15 years. His research (MPhil, PhD, Postdoc at University of Cambridge, UK and ongoing research) focusses on educational philosophy, classroom and schoolwide ethos and practices, teacher professional development, and interventions for holistic education, education for harmony, and social emotional learning. He has published several academic papers, book chapters, educational reports and books; notably his book *Learning to Live Together Harmoniously: Spiritual Perspectives from Indian Classrooms*. He previously taught undergraduate and postgraduate students at University of Cambridge, UK, University College London, UK and St Xaviers College, Ahmedabad.

Dr Patel has also been actively involved in grassroots-level change in India since 2009 as the cofounder of two charities; Independent Thought & Social Action and Together In Development & Education Foundation. As the president of TIDE Foundation, he oversees several programs including education for social justice, activity- and application-based learning, school improvement, and teacher education and empowerment. Furthermore, he has also served as an education and international development consultant supporting various Indian and global education-focussed organisations including Global Innovation Foundation, Inter Network Agency for Education in Emergencies, and Cambridge Partnerships for Education.

Notes

1. Language adapted to be gender neutral.
2. Singleton, J. (2015). Head, heart and hands model for transformative learning: Place as context for changing sustainability values. *Journal of Sustainability Education*, 9(3), 171–187.
3. Patel, J. (2021). Learning to live together harmoniously: a conceptual framework. *Cambridge Journal of Education* 52(3), 327–347; Patel, J. (2023). *Learning to live together harmoniously: spiritual perspectives from Indian classrooms*. Palgrave Macmillan Springer.
4. Stanford Encyclopedia of Philosophy (2021) *Embodied Cognition*. Accessed January 2025. https://plato.stanford.edu/entries/embodied-cognition/.
5. Hooks, b. (1994). *Teaching to transgress: education as a practice of freedom*. Routledge.
6. Hooks, b. (1994). *Teaching to transgress: education as a practice of freedom*. Routledge, p.135–38.
7. Wahlstrom, K., Dretzke, B., et al. (2014). *Examining the impact of later high school start times on the health and academic performance of high school students: a multi-site study*. Center for Applied Research and Educational Improvement. St Paul, MN: University of Minnesota. Accessed January 2025. https://files.eric.ed.gov/fulltext/ED596205.pdf.
8. Eringfeld, S. & Cremin, H. (2022). Don't just do something … stand there! Two women dance their academic trajectories. In P. Burnard, E. Macklinay, D. Rousell & T. Dragovic (Eds), *Doing rebellious research in and beyond the Academy*, Brill, 224–37.
9. Smith, D. G. (2014). *Teaching as the practice of wisdom*. Bloomsbury.
10. Tolle, E. (2005). *A new Earth: create a better life*. Penguin.
11. Sellman, E., & Buttarazzi, G. (2020). Adding lemon juice to poison – raising critical questions about the oxymoronic nature of mindfulness in education and its future direction. *British Journal of Educational Studies*, 68(1), 61–78.
12. Tolle, E. (2005). *A new Earth: create a better life*. Penguin. p.214.
13. Kahneman, D. (2012). *Thinking, fast and slow*. Penguin.
14. McGilchrist, I. (2010). *The Master and his Emissary*. Yale University Press.

15 Taleb, N. N. (2010). *The Black Swan: the impact of the highly improbable* (2nd ed.). Penguin.
16 Peters, S. (2021). *A path through the jungle: Psychological Health and Wellbeing Programme to Develop Robustness and Resilience*. Mindfield Media Limited.
17 Buber, M. (1970). *I and Thou* (W. Kaufmann, Trans.). Charles Scribner's Sons.
18 Klaus, P. (2016). 'An ordinary day'. In H. Lees & N. Noddings (Eds.), *The Palgrave International Handbook of Alternative Education*. Palgrave Macmillan.
19 Miller, J. (2018). *Love and compassion: Exploring their role in education*. University of Toronto Press.
20 Miller, J. (2018). *Love and compassion: Exploring their role in education*. University of Toronto Press, p.5.
21 Miller, J. (2018). *Love and compassion: Exploring their role in education*. University of Toronto Press, p.35.
22 Office for National Statistics (2020). Child sexual abuse in England and Wales: year ending March 2019. Accessed January 2025. https://www.ons.gov.uk/peoplepopulationandcommunity/crimeandjustice/articles/childsexualabuseinenglandandwales/yearendingmarch2019#child-sexual-abuse-recorded-by-the-police.
23 NB Percentages go beyond 100% because some victims sadly identified more than one abuser.
24 Ofsted (2021). Review of sexual abuse in schools and colleges. Accessed January 2025. https://www.gov.uk/government/publications/review-of-sexual-abuse-in-schools-and-colleges/review-of-sexual-abuse-in-schools-and-colleges#what-did-we-find-out-about-the-scale-and-Nature-of-sexual-abuse-in-schools.
25 Moosa, S., & Bhana, D. (2022). 'Troubling men who teach young children': masculinity and the paedophilic threat. *Pedagogy, Culture & Society*, *30*(4), 511–528.
26 Hooks, b. (1994). *Teaching to Transgress: Education as a practice of freedom*. Routledge. p.199.
27 Hooks, b. (1994). *Teaching to Transgress: Education as a practice of freedom*. Routledge, p.195.
28 Duncan, R. (2018). *Nature in mind: systemic thinking and imagination in ecopsychology and mental health*. Routledge.
29 Kumar, S. (2017). *Soil, soul, society: a new trinity for our time*. Leaping Hare Press.
30 Abrams, D., Lama, D., & Tutu, D. (2016). *The book of joy: lasting happiness in a changing world*. Hutchinson.
31 Bai, H., Cohen, A., & Falkenberg, T. (2023). Inner work: foundational to contemplative and holistic education. *Journal of Contemplative and Holistic Education*, *1*(2), 6. p.7.
32 Dass, R. (2019). *Becoming nobody: the essential Ram Dass collection*. Sounds True.
33 Chodron, P. (2019). *Living beautifully with uncertainty and change*. Shambhala Publications Inc.
34 Loy, D. (2008). *Money, sex, war, karma: notes for a Buddhist Revolution*. Wisdom Publications.
35 Rohr, R. (2010). *The art of letting go: living the wisdom of Saint Francis*. Sounds True.
36 Bonnett, M. (2009). Education and selfhood: a phenomenological investigation. *Journal of Philosophy of Education, 43*(3), 357–70.
37 Lees, H. (2017). Hanging around, pottering about, chilling out: lessons on silence and well-being from Summerhill school. *Revista Hipotese*, *3*(2), 192–210.
38 Lees, H. (2012). *Silence in schools*. Trentham Books.
39 Shirley, D., & Macdonald, E. (2016). *The mindful teacher* (2nd ed.). Teachers College Press.
40 Shirley, D., & Macdonald, E. (2016). *The mindful teacher* (2nd ed.). Teachers College Press, p.5.

41 Osgood, J. (2010). Reconstructing professionalism in ECEC: the case for the 'critically reflective emotional professional.' *Early Years, 30*(2), 119–133. p.130.
42 Freire, P. (1973). *Education for critical consciousness*. Continuum.
43 Sheldrake, R. (2018). *Science and spiritual practices: reconnecting through direct experience*. Coronet.
44 Culham, T., Oxford, R., & Lin, J. (2018). *Cultivating the abilities of the heart*. International Handbook of Holistic Education, 170–177; Lin, J., Culham, T., & Edwards, S. (2019). *Contemplative pedagogies for transformative teaching, learning, and being*. Information Age Publishing; Miller, J. P. (2010). *Whole child education*. University of Toronto Press; Miller, R. (1991). Educating the true self: spiritual roots of the holistic worldview. *Journal of Humanistic Psychology 31*(4), 53–67; Patel, J. (2023). *Learning to live together harmoniously: spiritual perspectives from Indian classrooms*. Palgrave Macmillan Springer.
45 Radhakrishnan, S. (1959). *Sarvepalli Radhakrishnan (combined edition Oct. 1952 to Feb. 1959). Occasional Speeches and Writings*. Government of India Press.
46 Cajete, G. (1994). *Look to the mountain: an ecology of indigenous education*. Kivaki Press; Four Arrows, aka D. T. J. (2018b). From a deeper place: indigenous worlding as the next step in holistic education. *International Handbook of Holistic Education*, 33–41; Mani, L. (2013). *Integral nature of things: critical reflections on the present*. Routledge.
47 Dalai Lama, & Chan, V. (2013). *The wisdom of compassion*. Riverhead Press. Rinpoche, Lama. Z. (2008). *How to be happy*. Wisdom Publications.
48 Illich, I. (1971). *Deschooling society*. Harrow Books.
49 Jain, M. (2023). From factory schooling to Nai Taleem: a paradigm shift in education. *Journal of Contemplative and Holistic Education 1*(2).
50 The Mother (Mirra Alfassa) worked closely with Sri Aurobindo, an Indian spiritual leader. The mother called for integral education (physical, vital, mental, psychic and spiritual) and has inspired several alternative schools across India.
51 Patel, J. (2021). The role of dissent, conflict, and open dialogue in learning to live together harmoniously. *Educational Philosophy and Theory 55(6)*, 707–718; Patel, J. (2023). *Learning to live together harmoniously: spiritual perspectives from Indian classrooms*. Palgrave Macmillan Springer.
52 Patel, J. (2023). Learning to live together harmoniously: spiritual perspectives from Indian classrooms. Palgrave Macmillan Springer; Patel, J. (2020). *Education for togetherness and harmony; learning and teaching through lived experiences*. University of Cambridge. https://doi.org/10.17863/CAM.64123.
53 The Mother. (1977). *Collected works of the Mother; on education*. Sri Aurobindo Ashram Press.
54 Several alternative schools are exploring ways to support mainstream schools to bring about holistic education at scale.
55 Krishnamurti, J. (2013). *Educating the educator*. Krishnamurti Foundation India.
56 Patel, J. & Shakti, M. (2023). Life as/of Holistic Educators. *Holistic Education Review 3*(2).

Chapter 7

Nature as teacher

Introduction

As discussed in Chapter Two, the need to honour nature's integrity demands a different way of thinking about education. It points to us moving beyond merely human considerations and placing nature at the heart of processes of teaching and learning. This is not to abandon the humanities, but rather to include non-anthropocentric perspectives and study of the more-than-human in the curriculum. It involves taking the cycles and rhythms of nature as starting points for teaching and learning. Although not necessary for rewilding education, this will often involve learning out of doors and having direct experience of nature. This chapter discusses how students can have new opportunities to grow through testing their limits in wild settings and suggests that wild spaces can provide opportunities for young people to transition into adulthood with greater maturity and self-awareness. It explores the different possibilities that open up when we consider nature-as-teacher, and how overly narrow conceptions of child development can be 'rewilded' through more organic and indigenous views of the unique potential in each individual. Finally, the chapter presents two case studies: one discusses the role of nature in nature–based education in India, and the other presents a poetic narrative from a forest school in Germany.

Beyond a metaphysics of mastery

Much of this book has been about the need to think of ourselves as embedded within complex living systems, rather than as positioned at the top of hierarchies of domination. Michael Bonnett[1] refers to this latter tendency as 'rampant human supremacism,' and urges educators to reverse the metaphysics of mastery. Not only does this arrogance alienate us from the natural world, but it also alienates us from our own nature as we become 'spiritually constipated in a world that appears evermore human-authored.' Young people need to have a better understanding of their place within natural systems if they are to be enabled to thrive.

DOI: 10.4324/9781003627807-10

We need to educate young people to understand that nature is not just 'out there' – we are nature too. The word 'nature' means birth. 'Natal,' 'nativity,' 'native' and 'nature' all come from the same root. 'Nature' is whatever is born and will die. We too are subject to the rhythms and cycles of nature, and young people need support to come to terms with their natural existence of endings and beginnings in order to escape from the metaphysics of mastery and permanence that has been imposed by modernity's excesses. There is peace and joy in the acceptance of natural life stages and in the awareness that all things have their limits and must come to an end. There is a good deal of suffering (dukkha) that comes from their denial and from the desire to stand outside of the natural order of things – outside of time and space.

There is also a good deal of suffering that comes from the domination of nature and the sequestration of the earth's resources for the benefit of an elite minority. This is deeply problematic for individuals (whether as 'winners' or 'losers'), as well as for wider issues of equity and justice. Suffering comes too from an overly exploitative and acquisitional attitude towards nature. We could, for example, shift from an economy that's organised around domination and extraction to one that's rooted in reciprocity with the living world. A sustainable global future could be built around interconnectedness, de-growth and equality if young people could be educated for this ecocentric future. Such an alternative approach recognises the intrinsic value of all life, small or large, human or non-human. All living beings (including insects, trees, animals and birds) are treated as having a right to life, irrespective of their potential value (or danger) to humans. Non-living things like lakes, rivers, oceans, air and mountains are treated with the same care and respect[2]. Jwalin Patel and Carlotta Ehrenzeller,[3] and Michael Slote[4] argue that an ethics of reciprocity could support young people to become wise and ready for these challenges.

In order to reverse the metaphysics of human mastery that dominates education, it is important to recognise the essential autonomy that nature possesses. Michael Bonnett[5] has developed a phenomenology of nature as 'self-arising' to do this. Seeing it in this way acknowledges its alterity and mystery and restores its rightful place as co-author of all that we experience. He gives an example of looking up at the heavy clouds and seeing the sun break through. Although this experience is understood through human language, using terms such as, 'clouds,' 'sky,' 'sun,' and so on, it occurs independently of human intentionality. Our consciousness and ability to witness and articulate moments like this are a function of an extraordinary moment in time on this particular planet – but the planet and the wider universe have their own logic and flow that is independent of our existence. Putting ourselves in a position to notice and respond to the cosmos and nature's unfolding enables us to enter into relationship with it and to become aware of our position within the Earth's phenomenal biosphere. It reminds us that we are not at the centre of it all.

Nature as teacher

Several years ago, I was at the funeral of my friend's mum. Amongst the many things that made my friend thankful, she was grateful to her mum for teaching her to see green. This is the poem that wrote itself soon after and that expresses the delight of learning from nature as a child:

> **Forever changed**
>
> When her mum asked
> How many greens?
> She started
> With two
> Perhaps three.
>
> She counted
> The emeralds
> The mosses
> The ivy
> The stone.
>
> At thirty
> They stopped,
> Turned homewards.
> Laughing eyes
> Swimming with green.
>
> And now,
> At her graveside
> She mouths
> Her thanks.
>
> Because
> When someone
> Asks you
> 'How many greens?'
> You are
> Forever changed.

I've since learnt that we can see so many shades of green (less so with other colours) because of our evolutionary past, but this just adds to my sense of wonder.

Education needs to take place out of doors, at least some of the time, in order for learners to develop a sense of their place in nature as described earlier. Patel and Ehrenzeller[6] advocate for learning from, with, and within nature in order to go beyond merely learning facts about it. Spending extended time in nature enables it to act as a 'primary pedagogue,' teaching complex concepts like interconnectedness, diversity-based oneness, circularity, non-linearity, and impermanence. To achieve this, Kumar[7] has set up schools in the UK that are based on those that Tagore established in the last century in India. Tagore wanted children (and students in his university) to love nature. He insisted on holding his classes under trees and is reported to have told his students that they had two teachers – a human teacher and also the trees. Kumar's schools run along the same lines:

> The present system of teaching is mostly within closed walls in modern buildings where classes are held under artificial light and with artificial air-conditioning. I would like to suggest that universities and schools should be built in open fields and forests rather than in the congested streets of an urban metropolis. Universities and schools should be surrounded by trees, ponds and animals. Students should have the opportunity to roam, think, enjoy and celebrate Nature.[8]

Kumar believes that learning out of doors enables a sense of 'deep ecology' which can counteract the 'shallow ecology' of treating nature as subordinate. Deep ecology comes about through touching the soil, walking in the woods, swimming in the sea, watching the clouds and the sunset, and more. Only from such deep experience can commitment to care for nature arise. Deep ecology implies the same rights for nature as for humans. If our relationship with nature is forged through education that respects the principles of reverence for life, then we may more easily move from mastery to sustainability. If we had gardening teachers as well as PE teachers, and large gardens to grow food and flowers as well as playing fields, fewer young people might see dirt as dirty. They might find dignity in working with their hands and cultivating the soil. It is bizarre that people are considered illiterate if they can't read a label on a food packet, but not if they can't grow their own food. Indigenous communities, peasants and farmers, bushman and nomads who have profound knowledge of forest medicine, animal behaviour and changing seasons are thought of as uneducated if they can't read or write, whilst people who don't know how to sustain themselves in their natural environment are somehow seen as intelligent. This needs to change.

It must of course be borne in mind that, for now at least, many urban spaces are made almost entirely of concrete, and that this can continue for miles. In some settings it may also be challenging to find green spaces that are not just laid to grass (or worse, laid to artificial turf). There may be children's play areas, benches, and somewhere to buy coffee, but no wildflowers or trees.

Travelling out to find wild spaces (and thereby contributing to urban congestion and carbon emissions) is hardly a solution. It must also be borne in mind that some young people may not appreciate being removed from their comfortable, convenient, indoor areas, or from their toys and computers. If they have only known life in concrete high-rise apartments, they may not like the feel of bare earth beneath their feet. If animals have mainly featured on food packets, in plastic toys, or on the TV, they may fear coming into direct contact with them. If their toys are non-living, objectified and passive, children may be burdened with a material worldview that does not take account of basic human developmental needs.[9]

Although I have argued in this book that rewilding does not have to involve learning out of doors, I maintain that it should at least involve some exposure to wild spaces, and that solutions need to be found for young people who are reluctant at first. This is for many reasons. Firstly, and most importantly, our unnatural and unsustainable ways of living may well be coming to an end. If young people are not exposed to nature in times when they can learn how to live well as part of sustainable ecosystems, they almost certainly will be confronted with it through fire, flood, famine, and so on. If this does not apply to children in the global North who are currently alive, it certainly will to their children. If it doesn't concern all children, it certainly concerns those children (the vast majority) who do not make up global elites. We can no longer afford for the people of the planet to be so cut off from their life-support systems or the wider global community. Secondly, the benefits of changing perspectives following exposure to nature cannot be underestimated. New ways of seeing remain with young people as they grow older, and prompt healthier styles of learning and ways of being in the world.

If young people are anxious about exposure to nature, preparation work might include using sport or the arts to encourage participation. Jogging or fitness training might be attractive, or else stories, painting or work with clay could reawaken the senses. Listening to music might build sensitivity to the acoustic environment and enable young people to really hear and respond to sounds in nature. Spending time in nature can also be therapeutic in its own right and can reduce feelings of anxiety and depression more generally.[10]

Roger Duncan,[11] who has been a Steiner and Waldorf teacher and a nature-based educator, argues that nature-based education and eco-psychotherapy can work together to restore health and well-being to young people who have become lost and alienated. Eco-psychotherapy for young people involves promoting biophilia (love of nature), restoring deficits in attention, and working through the body to address psychophysiological stress. For this, he uses the senses of touch, balance, kinaesthetic awareness (movement in space) and somatic awareness (inside the body). He supports young people to think from a systemic perspective, and to see the whole of nature as a matrix of complex fractal patterns revealed through raw sensory experience. Drawing on Gregory Bateson,[12] he suggests that the search for patterns is not only an intellectual pursuit, but also a search for meaning that we can connect with aesthetically and emotionally. He finds useful scaffolding for the imagination in the biological processes of mitosis, seed formation, dormancy, germination, fertilisation, seed dispersal, fruiting and so on. These can be used to describe both psychological and natural phenomena. They can replace the familiar language of the machine with more organic language and metaphors. An ecological understanding of nature thus crosses over into language and a psychotherapeutic understanding of the self.

Roger Duncan calls for the rewilding of both psychotherapy and education. He compares modern humans to polar bears in an American zoo living unhappily outside of their natural habitat. We too are separated from our natural environment and are 'recovering refugees from a hunter-gatherer lifestyle.'[13] He notes that while our ancestors would have engaged for millennia in experiential learning and body-based daily activity, modern humans have transitioned to the intellectualisation and abstraction of the left brain, with its tendency to name, objectify and categorise. Like Iain McGilchrist,[14] he sees the origins of significant and growing levels of mental illness in this kind of thinking.

To be clear, I am not drawing on Roger Duncan here to argue that a return to premodern forms of education is warranted or necessary. As shown in the last chapter, I am arguing rather that education needs to draw on both the best of contemporary science and on the wisdom of nature-based societies. I am also arguing that all young people would benefit from some time learning in nature, even if this is not their overall experience. Primary education, for example, could be carried out mainly in Forest Schools, as is currently the case in many parts of Europe. If young children are exposed to nature early, it becomes a valued playground and source of ideas and adventure for them. They will not be as fearful as they might be if they did not encounter it before their teenage years. The first few years of life are particularly important for this as young children experience exceptionally rapid rates of brain growth, forming over one million neural connections per second as they create ideas about the world around them.[15] In this precious window of development, exposing them to safe green environments is both stimulating and nurturing. Although children in Early Years and primary education often have their capabilities underestimated, research suggests that they are highly responsive to innovative pedagogy that teaches them new ways of thinking and being.[16]

Rewilding child development

Drawing on the analogy of an acorn, Roger Duncan suggests that each person's uniqueness is already present before it can be fully realised. If we see human development from an eco-psychological perspective, we are more likely to 'hold a respectful position of curiosity and not-knowing ... and embrace the idea of each child as a potential and unique change agent, with the possibility of making a valuable and significant difference within our society.'[17] This is very different from a view of child development taken from education psychology, or theorists such as Piaget,[18] who see young people as progressing through a set of predetermined and age-related socio-cognitive stages.

Bill Plotkin[19] has adapted the Native American Medicine Wheel to show how we might replace modern ideas of child development with an ecopsychology of human development that lasts throughout the lifespan. He shows how fully and creatively people can mature when soul and wild nature are taken as a guide. He defines eight stages of human life: Innocent; Explorer; Thespian; Wanderer; Soul Apprentice; Artisan; Master; and Sage – and describes the challenges and benefits of each. He outlines a method for progressing from our current egocentric, aggressively competitive, consumer society to an ecocentric, soul-based society that is sustainable, cooperative and compassionate.

In the final section of this chapter, two extraordinary educators from the Cambridge Peace Education Research Group[20] share examples of rewilded education drawing on their own research. The first case study is once again provided by Jwalin Patel, who discusses the role of nature in a holistic alternative school in India, while the second case study from Carlotta Ehrenzeller uses the lens of educating for peace and Montessori education to present a poetic narrative from a German forest school.

Jwalin Patel: Rishi Valley School

I am interested in exploring alternatives to mass education because I have come to recognize that modern mass education systems and practices are based on materialistic, reductionist and anthropocentric epistemologies. Over the past six years, I have been researching education for togetherness and harmony[21] by exploring alternative and holistic education visions and practices stemming from India. Here, I share a small part of my work that explores the role of nature in holistic education.

Rishi Valley School, one of the schools that I have been researching, was inspired and set up by the Indian thinker Jiddu Krishnamurti. It is an alternative school that questions the purpose of mass education and aims to bring about holistic education and 'education for flowering in inner goodness'.[22] The school is surrounded by and embedded within nature. It is located in a valley very close to the Indian Eastern Ghats and is surrounded by hills and trees. Over recent decades the school has been actively involved in sustained reforestation and water conservation efforts; these have helped convert the barren hillside into a rich forest area. The region has been designated as a bird sanctuary and a special development zone with mandates to protect and conserve the rich and diverse environment.

Nature is deeply embedded within the school. Physically, the school is spread out across the valley with various built structures that are quite distanced from each other and interspersed by trees and the forest. Through the course of any given school day, the students spend considerable time walking through the forest as they walk between their houses, academic spaces, non-academic spaces and dining / recreation spaces. The houses and classrooms are surrounded by trees and have a noted open design which integrates the indoors with the outdoors. The school has many alternative learning spaces (including fields and grounds, spaces under trees, open huts) all of which are in close contact with nature.

Children's lived experience of the school also brings them into close interaction with nature in more structured ways. For example, the school actively engages students with nature through daily walks to see the sun set, weekly bird-watching hikes and treks through the Eastern Ghats once a semester. They also designate students to take care of a certain tree. Curriculum and pedagogy promote engagement with nature through deep observation, arts- and project-based learning, dialogic teaching and group work.

It is important to note the underlying non-anthropocentric worldview of the school. Human beings are considered to be a small part of the larger interconnected world (made up of the human, the non-human, and the non-living) and this is borne out through the teachers' ways of living, teaching and being. They are critical of modern perspectives on nature where mountains, trees and animals are seen as resources to be used for the development of human societies. Instead, they believe that nature has its own integrity as a sacred part of existence. Human beings should learn to respect, support and live in harmonious coexistence with it.

This non-anthropocentric epistemology leads to children developing a strong commitment to the well-being of the interconnected world. Students frequently note, comment on and appreciate the beauty of stones, rocks, hills, trees, flowers, birds and insects (during my immersive fieldwork at the school I heard such comments more than ten times every day). The students have an inherent appreciation of nature and a deep relationship with it. They intuitively know when a tree or animal is not well, and students and school alumni frequently speak about the hill or trees as friends, teachers and counsellors. As I now reflect back, I believe that my time at various *ashrams* and holistic education spaces have redefined my own relation with nature. I believe that my visit to Rishi Valley School was deeply transformative – it led me to recognize and appreciate nature as being sacred.

During my fieldwork in this school I made field notes. The following story is perhaps indicative of the transformative process that I myself went through:

> A teacher was telling a story about birds to the class.... As usual, during such storytelling sessions students had the freedom to listen, scribble, close their eyes, and look around and potentially daydream. I decided to focus on a boy who was not apparently listening; he seemed to be looking around and not necessarily following the story... After a couple of minutes, he commented to his teacher "Da [brother] even the birds are listening to the story".

It then struck me that I had lost touch with what the story was really about, despite listening intently. The child's comment helped me recall that the story was about birds and realize that there were many birds around, interacting with each other and potentially with all of us too.

Carlotta Ehrenzeller: Montessori Forest School

My research concerns Montessori education, and in particular ways of educating for peace in the 21st century. My contribution to this chapter draws on the voices of teachers and students (six to 11 years old) from a forest class in Germany. Although I have rearranged a multitude of voices and shaped a narrative, the words are direct quotes from the participants of my PhD research project. Moving away from a modern Western way of knowledge generation, this is my way of creatively exploring the meaning of being in the forest and fostering an innate relationship with nature as part of a forest-class community. I researched with both students and teachers through participative methods such as drawing, acting, conversational interviews and focus group discussions. As the researcher, I hope that the participants' voices let you hear their hopes, dreams and challenges through their words, rather than mine.

> **Into the forest school**
>
> The pressure to break away from these constraints, from these rigid school structures.
> The common element between all alternative schools and education: Focus on the child.
> Crucial point.
>
> How do we look at the children?
> How self-determined are they?
> Do we give them the opportunities to develop?
>
> The forest is absolute therapy:
> for everyone.
>
> Heartbeat of the earth.
>
> Go more into the forest. That's what simply does you good.
> Just go more
> into the forest.

Get rid of "ew, wet, dirty".

Just go for a walk.

I'm not a full-on ecologist.
Not everyone has to live *in* the forest.
Not everyone has to *go* to forest classes,
no.

What I am saying is
"just go outside".
Just do it.
Feel what the forest does to you. Not just the forest,
but Nature,
being outdoors.

Go outdoors.

Forests, meadow, water, parks, city.

I was unhappy for a while.
This being in the forest has helped me regain footing in life.
I changed incredibly.
Became totally calm.
Children feel the same way: they find
Peace
here.

When we go into the forest, it feels like you're freed from
bad
things.
Going outside somehow clears your heart.
This might sound strange.

In the forest I feel like
time stops
with the fears I have;
that these things
can not
happen.

I feel so much
Myself.
You see this light,

breaking
in the trees.
The air,
that you breathe.
The soundscape that is actually
there.

Just go outside.

A lot of my friends say
"I'm so well-balanced,
Relaxed, always in a good mood."
(even though I might earn less than them)
That's how being this kind of educator pays.

They,
earn twice as much.
Only stressed, only problems,
complaints all day.
Heart attack in their mid-50s.
Burn-out.

I'm a far away,
from that.

My Feeling: The forest
Is totally good
for all of us.

Why not learn *from* Nature, *with* Nature?

Just being outside.
Breaking
through these classic, confined
spaces.
No ties to spaces, and spatial thinking.

Flowing like a river.

Having that air outside, Nature around you, the sounds you have
there.
Experiencing seasons, the weather
permanently.

Opportunities to relax.

More freedom.

Run.

Run through the bushes. Walk slowly.
Play.
Play.
Walk slowly, run through the bushes.

Talk.

You can't name it. You can't paint it. You can't photograph it. That's just what's floating around.

Feel.

Trained eye: freedom to observe.

Explore:
All the time.
Freedom:
To Look. Feel. Smell. Taste.

To Look, differently.

Not environmental education, but
Nature education:
A contact
with Nature,
a relationship. Foundation stones for life.

For you to get a feeling, its fundamental,
that the environment is *worth* something
to you.

The environment is worth something to you.

So we don't stand up and say
"you, you, you".
You have to do this and you have to do that.

Relationship to Nature, awareness for and with Nature.

They value Nature. Arrive at the value system that they
want
to do *something*
for it.

> If you love something, you respect it,
> Protect it.
>
> Creating
> A
> Generation
> Of
> Dissenters.
>
> I couldn't teach without the forest anymore;
> the taste,
> the dirty hands,
> that's all part of it for me.
>
> Go outside.
>
> take that experience of being outside
> a lot more.
> This
> peace,
> this down-to-earth, back to the roots.
>
> Heartbeat of the earth.

As part of my PhD research exploring the contextualisation of Montessori education, I spent four months in two different Montessori schools: one, a public forest-Montessori school on the outskirts of a German city. The other, a private Montessori school in an affluent area in an Australian city. I was curious to explore whether Montessori in different contexts is adapted to local needs, or whether Montessori is another way of exporting dominant 'Western knowledge' to communities around the world.

The aims of the forest Montessori school in Germany, let's call it Malaya school, are: to reconnect children with nature; to allow freedom and time to truly follow the child's interests and needs; and to provide a learning environment where positive caring relationships in the multi-age class community are prioritised.

Twenty-eight children (coming from a diversity of backgrounds including: (dis)/abilities, migration background, genders, economic backgrounds, diverse family situations, mental health challenges) and six adults (teachers, educators, pedagogues, nature pedagogues, special needs educators) spend the majority of each seven-hour day in outdoor spaces. The school is ten minutes by foot from the nearest forest. About 30 minutes by foot are a lake, rivers, parks and meadows which the school frequently chooses as learning spaces. Moving away from the constrained structures of physical school settings allows both teachers and students to experience freedom and inner peace.

As the Italian scientist and pedagogue Maria Montessori[23] highlighted more than 100 years ago, 'It is not the child who should adapt to the environment, but we should adapt the environment to the child.' The whole-day concept of the school necessitates the sharing of duties such as setting the table for lunch, serving food during communal meals, collecting firewood, and cleaning or taking care of the outdoor environment. The forest-school concept enables teachers and students to honour nature's integrity and to value the more-than-human in its diverse forms. This provides children with freedom to test their limits in wild settings, to learn and explore real environments and to move freely. They are able to integrate learning from all five senses as well as the promptings of their inner lives.

A growing body of literature shows positive outcomes for learning with and about nature.[24] Malaya school values and promotes pedagogies that enable creative exploration with natural materials, meditation and silence, connection circles, storytelling, movement and music, animal and nature observation and more. Away from traditional foci of academic learning and a general belief in the dominance of humans over other species, the focus of this school is on integrating nature and mind in order to move away from the Anthropocene towards multiple ways of embodied knowing and being.

Conclusion

As these powerful examples show, education can take many forms, and nature can become the third pedagogue with children and teachers engaged in processes that draw on its inspiration. Business as usual (teaching and learning only taking place in artificial spaces) is strangling our planet through alienation and disengagement with our natural life support systems. We have to do better if we are to educate our children to build more sustainable futures.

Notes

1 Bonnett, M. (2019). Towards an ecologization of education. *The Journal of Environmental Education*, *50*(4–6), 251–258. p.255.
2 Mani, L. (2013). *Integral nature of things: critical reflections on the present*. Routledge.
3 Ehrenzeller, C., & Patel, J. (2024). Calling for eco-peace: reimagining interconnected peace education. *Journal of Peace Education*, 1–17.
4 Slote, M. (2013). *From enlightenment to receptivity: rethinking our values*. Oxford University Press.
5 Bonnett, M. (2019). Towards an ecologization of education. *The Journal of Environmental Education*, *50*(4–6), 251–258.
6 Ehrenzeller, C., & Patel, J. (2024). Calling for eco-peace: reimagining interconnected peace education. *Journal of Peace Education*, 1–17.
7 Kumar, S. (2017). *Soil Soul Society: A new trinity for our time* (3rd ed.). Leaping Hare Press.

8 Kumar, S. (2017). *Soil Soul Society: A new trinity for our time* (3rd ed.). Leaping Hare Press, p.112.
9 Duncan, R. (2018). *Nature in Mind: Systemic Thinking and Imagination in Ecopsychology and Mental Health*. Routledge.
10 Capaldi, C. A., Passmore, H.-A., et al. (2015). Flourishing in nature: a review of the benefits of connecting with nature and its application as a wellbeing intervention. *International Journal of Wellbeing*, 5(4), 1–16.
   Richardson, M., Passmore, H-A., et al. (2021). Moments, not minutes: The nature-wellbeing relationship. *International Journal of Wellbeing*, 11(1), 8–33.
11 Duncan, R. (2018). *Nature in Mind: Systemic Thinking and Imagination in Ecopsychology and Mental Health*. Routledge.
12 Bateson, G. (1979). *Mind and Nature: A Necessary Unity*. Bantam Books.
13 Duncan, R. (2018). *Nature in Mind: Systemic Thinking and Imagination in Ecopsychology and Mental Health*. Routledge. p.100.
14 McGilchrist, I. (2010). *The Master and his Emissary*. Yale University Press.
15 Britto, P. R. (2017). Early Moments Matter for Every Child. UNICEF. Accessed January 2025. https://www.unicef.org/reports/early-moments-matter-every-child.
16 Kurian, N. (2023). Building inclusive, multicultural Early Years classrooms: strategies for a culturally responsive ethic of care. *Early Childhood Education Journal*. 52. 863–878.
17 Duncan, R. (2018). *Nature in mind: systemic thinking and imagination in ecopsychology and mental health*. Routledge. p.104.
18 Jean Piaget was a Swiss psychologist who developed an influential model to explain how children learn and grow mentally. The stages include sensorimotor (exploring through senses), preoperational (using symbols and imagination), concrete operational (thinking logically about real things) and formal operational (abstract thinking and problem-solving).
19 Plotkin, B. (2008). *Nature and the human soul: cultivating wholeness in a fragmented world*. New World Library.
20 The Cambridge Peace and Education Research Group (CPERG) provides a hub for research students and faculty members at the University of Cambridge to exchange ideas and collaborate on projects that explore the relationships between conflict, peace, and education, both in the UK and internationally. Its website can be accessed at: https://www.cperg.org/.
21 Patel, J. (2023). Learning to live together harmoniously: spiritual perspectives from Indian classrooms. Palgrave Macmillan Springer.
22 For more details on the school visit https://www.rishivalley.org/.
23 Montessori, M. (1965). *Dr. Montessori's own handbook*. New York: Schocken Books. p.14.
24 E.g. Richardson, M., Passmore, H-A., et al. (2021). Moments, not minutes: the nature-wellbeing relationship. *International Journal of Wellbeing*, *11*(1), 8–33.

Chapter 8

Health, engagement, practical wisdom and an arts-based mindset

Introduction

As noted in Chapter Three, systems of schooling throughout the world are making people ill. They neglect the bodily needs of students and teachers and contribute to alarming and growing levels of poor mental health. As previously discussed, traditional schools enable the global dominance of Eurocentric thought over other alternative, common sense, indigenous, holistic and contextualised ways of knowing, and this epistemic monoculturalism leads to deep socio-cultural violence that can trigger feelings of alienation and disempowerment. When everything is required to fit a narrow, strait-jacketed way of living and being that is established by someone else, there are few options for marginalised groups (and even dominant groups) to feel a sense of purpose and control over their lives. The ways that some seek to control others' ways of living and being (whether in the workplace, the family or in the natural environment) need to be challenged through a rewilded education that foregrounds autonomy, diversity, respect, imagination, love, compassion and creativity. New kinds of relationships for teaching and learning are required if we are to thrive and reverse the global mental health crisis. This chapter identifies three areas of focus for achieving this: promoting self-efficacy and feelings of empowerment; practical wisdom, appropriate technology and situated learning; and imagination, narrative and an arts-based mindset. The three are linked and together they can take us from paralysis and despair to hope, creativity and change. The chapter contains several of the author's poems as a means of showing how alternative ways of knowing and writing are integral to the arguments being presented and also shares case studies from schools in the UK and India and from research into arts-integrated programs for social justice and change.

Self-efficacy and feelings of empowerment

It is essential for good mental health for people to feel in control of their lives. The climate emergency has taken away many people's sense of agency, and this has led to a kind of collective trauma that induces eco-anxiety and solastalgia. Young people's mental health can be bolstered if they are supported to move beyond depression and paralysis towards feelings of hope, engagement and empowerment.

Rewilded education improves mental health through educational approaches that foreground choice, agency and collective action. In a Buddhist tradition, David Loy,[1] for example, calls for eco-activism that is grounded in learning from both nature and Buddhist teachings. He outlines how 'ecodharma' can enable an urgent and effective response to ecological crises without inducing feelings of despair. Joanna Macy and Molly Brown[2] come from a different tradition but also lay out how it is possible to remain optimistic in the face of deepening global crises. Drawing on Native American teachings, they suggest that grief, anger and fear are healthy responses to these crises, and that education should reconnect people with the land, with ancestors and with beings-yet-to-be-born through drama-based dialogue and processes of imagination, healing and connection.

My own work in schools over the years has set out to empower young people to resolve their own conflicts and to establish strong interpersonal and community relationships. I have done this through the use of circles and through training peer mediators in hundreds of schools over many decades. I have outlined this work in depth in other publications,[3] and so for now I will limit myself to a brief discussion of the power of the circle.

Peer mediation empowers young people to resolve their own disputes and those of their peers in ways that lead to positive outcomes for all. In order for this to happen, circle pedagogy first sets the foundations of trust, open sharing, active listening, affirmation, emotional regulation, constructive dialogue, care, compassion and playfulness. These are essential for the transformation of conflict, but also for the maintenance of healthy relationships. Too often these things feature in school promotional materials without any meaningful engagement with how they might be enacted in the daily life of the school.

In circle pedagogy, children sit in a circle (on chairs or on the floor) and engage in activities that build speaking and listening skills, feelings of empowerment, and the social and emotional aspects of learning. There are two fundamental ground rules for the circle: one person speaking at a time and equal respect for all contributions. One of the main circle activities is the go-round. This involves each student around the circle taking a turn to speak whilst holding a talking object. Anyone who does not wish to speak can simply pass the object on without saying anything. The advantage of this is that the students learn to talk one at a time, and those students who find it hard to make the space to be heard have an automatic opportunity to contribute, or else to pass and still be included in the activity. It is important that adults also respect this convention as much as is practical and possible. In this way, inclusiveness, acceptance, empowerment and an atmosphere of trust are developed. Both timing and the language used by the teacher or facilitator in these situations is key. In the early stages of circle pedagogy, the teacher or facilitator needs to be more directive in order to establish a safe and conducive atmosphere for the circle work. As time goes on, however, the group can increasingly take responsibility for maintaining this ethos. The circle can be used for relationship building, but it can also be used to teach across the curriculum – from the humanities, to science, to mathematics and to languages and beyond. It can also be used for reflexive learning and to develop metacognition.

Kay Pranis[4] gives examples of the ways that circles can be used, such as: check-in/check-out circles, resolution circles, support circles, talking circles, community-building circles, celebration circles and reintegration circles. Above all, however, circle pedagogy should be about having fun together, sharing and valuing each other's insights, and moving forward as a group or community. This prepares young people to take action and work with others to bring about change, even if they have different starting points. This is harder when schools serve a monoculture of like-minded parents and children. Rewilded primary schools need to be sufficiently diverse to avoid reinforcing echo chambers and battle lines between disparate identity groups.

Circle pedagogy can be used for young people to learn the basics behind how to build community, a small business, or a social or political movement. Diffuse leadership opportunities abound in the 21st century, with the internet enabling groups of all kinds to connect both locally and globally, often for time-limited or task-specific purposes. Indeed, Godin[5] suggests that everyone now has an opportunity to lead a tribe or a movement. The ability to do this ethically begins with learning how to be in a circle. Circle pedagogy teaches empathy, cooperation, confidence and sharing in ways that build the kind of ethical understanding that are essential for human thriving, and perhaps even human survival.

For young people to feel empowered, however, teachers must feel the same. They cannot teach young people to lead and innovate if they themselves are being told what to do. Some have gone so far as to claim that a contemporary form of fascism operates at micro and macro levels in schools and in wider society.[6] This is seen to operate through a kind of 'biopower' that is entangled in everyday processes of discipline and control in schools. Pedagogical strategies such as circle learning are vitally important to enable teachers and their students to reclaim a sense of purpose, solidarity and power without losing track of the scale of the problems that they face. Teachers need to constantly navigate the ways in which they are both co-opted, and yet able to disrupt, the powerful relations that surround them.

Two examples of this come through the inspirational work of Tom Shaw and his colleagues in Carr Manor Community School in Leeds, UK, and Lee Farmer and Jenny Davis in Holte School in Birmingham, UK. These are both state schools in areas of high deprivation, and yet what they are able to achieve for their staff and students is extraordinary. The following case studies are narrative accounts of a typical day in their schools.

Tom Shaw: Rewilding education – pastoral systems in a Leeds Through School (2–19)

Monday Morning, 7:30 a.m.

My fingers are cold, stiff, numb with the chill of a November morning in a Northern English City. I've cycled into school, the biting wind still lingering in my bones. I approach the front door and fumble with my key card. There's a pause—there's always a pause—as the door lock processes my request. In that brief stillness, I turn to a colleague. "Good morning, did you have a good weekend?" The pause becomes a moment of connection, a subtle resistance to the cold securitisation of English schools over the last 25 years. At the next two doors, we continue to subvert this routine, our conversation inching forward with each swipe, each click. I feel a tingling at the tips of my fingers, a sign of warmth returning.

Monday Morning, 7:45 a.m.

I step into the room, greeted by a familiar sight: a circle of chairs—one for each member of the leadership team. Before my experience of the circle briefings were a quiet scramble for the right seat, a strategic dance of to hide or not to hide, to listen and speak when spoken to. In these meetings there was always some initiative or other to be informed about. In an area of high deprivation in the state-school sector the whirlwind of initiatives would normally be hard to escape from. Now, we begin the week with a check-in. There's no hiding here. No barriers of coats, bags, or notebooks to shield us. At first, this openness was uncomfortable—vulnerability always is. But over time, the predictable rhythm of the circle allowed me to breathe, to prepare. Now, I anticipate this chance to hear my colleagues' stories and share my own concerns.

This week's check-in question: "How would you describe your weekend if it was a weather forecast?" "Sunny with bolts of lightning," I say. We acknowledge the personal lives we carry into our professional space. Authenticity is not just welcomed here—it's essential. We are not just leaders; we are human beings. The circle's physical arrangement holds us in proximity, setting the stage for connection. We refine the week's messages, readying ourselves to share them with the wider school community. There is challenge from the principal – our commitment to each other is to sustain our commitment to the children; expectations are high. The circle is powerful because it fosters mutual trust, courage, and appropriate vulnerability. My fingers are still cold but no longer stiff.

8:15 a.m.

Together, we head to the school hall. Eighteen circles of ten chairs, each slowly filling up. Teachers, admin staff, IT support, site team, learning support workers—we all find our places. Warmth rises in me as I watch colleagues weaving through the space, finding their circle. The staff circle lead poses the same check-in question, and we each respond. In this space, titles dissolve and hierarchies are suspended. We listen, we share, we lean in with care and curiosity. I remember noticing this subtle shift for the first time: bodies leaning forward, postures signaling intent—to listen, to encourage, to hold the speaker in the safety of the circle.

We are not just here to share feelings. Important messages from the principal direct the session. We turn, we listen, we reflect on how these messages apply to our roles and our coaching groups. The energy flows smoothly, aligning us with shared inclusive values. I think of the visitors to the school — over sixty so far this year —who always remark on how adults speak to each other here. Passing in corridors, pausing in classrooms, presenting in workshops: respect, dignity and connection permeate it all. My fingers move freely now. The numbness is gone, and I am ready.

8:45 a.m.

It's time to meet our coaching groups—small, vertical communities of 8 to 12 children. The younger ones are aged 4 to 10; the older ones, aged 10 to 16. Every adult here is a coach, an advocate, a trusted guide. The children are already arranging chairs into a circle. It's hard to remember when they used to sit in lines, separated by desks, their connections limited to a few friends. How much effort it took to draw in the isolated ones. Now, it happens naturally. An older student leads the check-in. They pause to ask a follow-up question, to scaffold the response of a younger child.

I distribute the Coaching Chronicle, our school newspaper, or play CMTV, the video version. A child notices an opportunity that fits a peer and nudges them to take it. Peer mentoring unfolds organically. Voices are heard, agency is exercised, bonds are strengthened. I recall the old days of tutor groups: 30 children, same age, same routines. Compliance met the minimum requirement for 'personal development,' but the experience was shallow, especially for the most vulnerable ones.

Rewilding this system wasn't easy. Toby Greany[7] recognises that it demands leadership that move beyond pragmatic compliance to active agency—a willingness to disrupt the norm, do things differently and do different things. To invite people to draw on their lived experience, develop discernment and be willing to connect with themselves, each other and the wider world.

9:15 a.m.

By now, everyone—children and adults—has had a chance to speak, to be seen, to be listened to in a non-judgemental way, with an open heart. Guided by this sense of belonging, we face the week's challenges together. As I walk to my first lesson, I feel calm, confident, and curious. My hands are warm now, and I've forgotten they were ever cold. I see children moving through the school, each year group finding its way, the flow calm and connected. Lines form outside classrooms, a staff member heads to the safeguarding office—likely responding to information that was appropriately shared in their coaching group.

I feel a quiet pride: every person here has been invited to bring their authentic self. Our lives, fragmented though they may be, coalesce into a community ready to learn and grow toward human flourishing.

Wednesday, Friday, and Beyond

The week unfolds with a check-up on Wednesday and a check-out on Friday. We laugh, play, reflect, and share hopes and fears. I've heard it all: new siblings, house moves, weddings, funerals, football games, video marathons, parties, as well as anxiety, isolation and news of hospital visits and visits from the police. I've celebrated joys with cake, advocated for children with parents, and found help when harm was endured.

Once a term, Meet Your Coach Day deepens these connections. Coaches meet each child and their parents or carers, nurturing authentic partnerships and focusing on the whole person—social, emotional, intellectual, and academic. The meeting starts with 'pushing the paper to one side'—care, compassion and curiosity—these are the guide and create the conditions for high challenge and high support as the meetings address opportunities to learn and grow.

The Impact

For now I allow myself a moment to reflect that the benefits are undeniable. Children call their coaching groups "school families"—their words, not mine. Staff feel deeper connections. Support staff understand their roles in new ways. Parents and carers communicate early when they are concerned.

Rebecca Hibbin[8] describe this as a 'whole school ethos of care' and a 'distributed network of relational accountability.' Here, relationships and genuine accountability guide everything we do. Even Ofsted[9] (National Government Schools Inspectorate), with a good HMI (His Majesty's Inspector), reports 'Exceptional does not do this school justice. The School is a community by name and a community by nature . . . . The staff and pupils have a firm belief that when you connect with each other you can achieve wonderful things'. Last year the children achieved +0.56 progress 8—the national standardised measure for pupil progress. This means the cohort of children left school with qualifications that were well above national average. This is every child, there have been no permanent exclusions for 19 years; we do not select on entry or exit. Our goal, however, is where they are as adults and critical citizens at 25 or 35. How they navigate the pathways through opportunities to build families, careers, and communities. With strong staff retention, low levels of staff absence and over 10% of staff now alumni, the community is committed to pursuing positive peace for all.

Circles are more than seating arrangements; they shape a culture of care, connection, and community. We are warm and we are welcomed. By prioritizing authentic relationships, we create a space where everyone feels seen, supported, and empowered to flourish—in body, mind, heart, and soul. In this space, every adult and every child becomes an educator—connected to themselves, each other and the wider world—stepping fully into who we are meant to be.

Jenny Davis: Peace Circles in Holte

As I rush from my early morning meeting into our before-school staff peace circles, I know they have been designed to allow my colleagues and I space to build relationships and grow closer as a team. I enter the room and am joined by 14 other staff members, including an early career teacher, an assistant head, an art technician and the bursar. We all sit in one circle, just people, sharing our stories for 20 minutes. People of all ages, genders, faiths and beliefs, but all in our school make a difference to pupils who don't always find life easy. Our school is in a tough area, on a road that is becoming a byword for crime, with murders, drugs and gangs common problems. However, all the people in that circle are committed to helping our pupils become the best versions of themselves. I know that this time is precious and important. Precious because I have a million other things I could be doing, but important because the more I know the people around me, the more trust forms and the closer we can work together to help our community. We discuss two questions; often the answers make us laugh, smile, or occasionally cry. It is a space for growing vulnerability and building connection.

Straight afterwards I head to my Year 13 geography lesson. I plan to spend the first half of our lesson in another circle. This one is much smaller with only four pupils in the class, no one can hide! I ask them to put their chairs in a circle, they know the routine, we do this most lessons. The US election results have just come in and I want to talk about their reactions to it. I want to glean both their knowledge and feelings surrounding the results. A depth of understanding of this issue is clearly important for an A-level geographer, but I am just as interested in their emotions around the topic. We are emotional beings who need space and time to discover, understand and be able to articulate our feelings. A circle of people you trust is a wonderful way of doing this. I know that this can be a difficult thing for some pupils, so I let them have four minutes to write down their thoughts and feelings before sharing them. We have been in a circle many times before: we have done exam feedback; played games; shared articles we have read; or held good old-fashioned debates. It means that when it comes to a time to go deeper, the framework for doing so is already there – the confidence that you will be heard and taken seriously is established and powerfully felt. We go round the circle, one at a time, each young person having a chance to say their bit, knowing they will be listened to. The energy, opinions and emotions spill out easily and are discussed by every person in the circle. This time to share strongly held beliefs, insights and feelings is precious and leads to our students being articulate and high achievers, as well as compassionate individuals and community members.

Holte School and Carr Manor Community School are truly inspiring. New forms of educational leadership that take account of the potential contribution of every member of the community are part of this, echoing Seth Godin's ideas about everyone leading a tribe or movement for a limited time, and with a particular group of people.[10] Despite the dominance of structurally and culturally violent systems of schooling around the world, these schools show that there is hope. They point to other possibilities of schooling beyond business as usual that foreground autonomy, connection and empowerment.

Practical wisdom, appropriate technology and learning in context

Alongside empowerment of individuals and groups, practical wisdom is fundamental for positive mental health and human thriving. Practical wisdom and rewilding are connected. Ecologists Paul Jepson and Cain Blythe[11] argue for rewilding because it blends radical scientific insights with everyday innovations to revive ecological processes and benefit people as well as nature. Rewilding democratises knowledge, widening a narrow view of science to include hunches, interdisciplinary work, intuition, trying things out, thinking outside of the box, learning by doing and so on. Rewilding education enables more young people to be empowered to work in these ways.

Most of the world relies on basic technology to meet local needs in common sense and offline ways, despite the current obsession with AI and information technology. A better synergy is needed between information technology and other technological approaches for dealing effectively with the omni-crises we face. We need both high- and low-tech solutions.

There have been a number of technological initiatives over the past century that have sought to develop solutions to everyday problems in sustainable ways. These have gone under a variety of names, including intermediate technology, alternative technology, appropriate technology and sustainable technology. Gandhi was one of the first to promote small, local and predominantly village-based technology, and his work has continued to grow. One recent example of an education and training initiative that works along these lines is Barefoot College International.[12] It operates in over 90 countries, and is a women-centred, global network dedicated to sustainable development for marginalised rural communities. They work collaboratively with these communities, supporting them to sustainably address their most pressing challenges, including climate change, food insecurity, gender inequality and lack of access to education and economic opportunity. By putting knowledge into the hands of women, they ensure that it is passed on through the generations and stays within communities.

Not only does this approach improve the local environment, it also reduces migration to cities, and protects rural traditions, knowledge and ways of life. Core to this are experiential learning and practical skills training that actively drive change. For example, their solar programme brings clean, renewable energy to rural communities by training local women as solar engineers. Each woman is trained to build, install and maintain solar home lighting systems and goes on to electrify an average of 50 homes in her community. Installing clean, renewable energy in remote off-grid communities increases the hours for children to learn at home and for community members to earn a living. This reduces reliance on harmful fossil fuels, such as kerosene.

In their regenerative agriculture programme, the Barefoot College uses permaculture philosophy to collaboratively design solutions for the needs of farmers and their ecosystems. The resulting workshops build on an initial needs assessment to provide a curriculum that supports farmers' agency, IT literacy and essential knowledge about how to realise the value of their products through fair and sustainable supply chains.

This practical education is indistinguishable from the life-enhancing activities that enable it. It is an example of genuine learning-for-real within a deeply contextualised and sustainable system. This is at the heart of rewilded education, as are many apprenticeship schemes, communities of practice and situated learning approaches. As Jean Lave and Etienne Wenger-Trayner[13] point out, learning is not only an internal process. It is always mediated through social and cultural experience and practice, and it always occurs in a particular place. In this sense it happens all the time and is an interaction between the self and the environment. It does not primarily involve the acquisition of a bank of knowledge that can be stored in the brain for later use. Students in school studying physics, for example, participate in a community that may, at best, reproduce a community of school physics learners. There are 'vast differences between the ways high school physics students participate in and give meaning to their activity and the way professional physicists do.'[14] Thus, rather than acquiring knowledge transmitted in instruction, students could learn through participation in communities of practice. In this way it is possible to distinguish between talking 'about' and 'talking within' a practice.

None of this is to say that theory, literature and research are not necessary. It is merely to point out that deep learning comes about through trial and error, apprenticeship and experience. It is also to point out that learning through activity and experience is not secondary to some kind of reified disembodied experience. The learning that is involved in cooking, art, gardening, music, dance and drama is just as valid as learning that occurs in the lecture theatre. The body can be used to think through things in the same way that a sculptor thinks with materials, or a painter thinks with paint. Very often a gut feeling is an important first step in scientific discovery and innovation. It is rarely the case that brain-based activity alone results in significant new knowledge.

Imagination, narrative and an arts-based mindset

The arguments in this chapter about the importance of empowerment and embodied practical learning also apply to the arts. An arts-based mindset enables young people to explore the world, find their voice, express themselves and work towards the change they wish to see. This is not a narrow view of the arts, nor is it a view that values high art over craft or local forms of community engagement. It is a view that seeks to enable individuals and groups to give creative expression to different ways of seeing, feeling, thinking, doing and being.

The arts can support young people to work for the change they wish to see in at least two ways. Firstly, the arts can trouble or destabilise business as usual, providing critique and alternative perspectives. Music, poetry, visual media, dance and theatre, for example, can provide safe spaces for people to enter disequilibrium and experience personal and collective change. This point of instability that the arts can bring about creates emergent properties that are unimaginable beforehand. Secondly, the arts can support young people to work for the change they wish to see through their imagination. It is not possible to work for more just, peaceful and sustainable futures if we can't imagine them. Jean Paul Lederach,[15] reflecting on a career in peacebuilding, uses the concept of the 'moral imagination,' rather than technocratic conflict resolution, to suggest how change can happen at a personal and social level. He suggests that new ways of seeing, supported by the arts and storytelling, are necessary if violence is to be transcended. He foregrounds the importance of imagination to enable people to see beyond the confines of unsustainable futures. He draws on Freire[16] to suggest that this should involve making art *with* people, rather than *for* or *about* them.

The arts then can provide ways of encountering others and imagining possible futures that enable personal and collective transformation. This is already happening through storytelling and narrative[17], music[18], poetry[19] and dance[20] to name a few. More than this, however, the arts are able to provide new ways of thinking for social and educational change that avoid the limitations of standard reductionist social scientific thinking.

In 2010, Jean Paul Lederach and his daughter[21] used music as a metaphor for understanding dynamic social systems. Their definition of social healing is based primarily on an aural understanding of change and movement. This important metaphor shift – from a linear view of change to one that reflects the nature of sound and movement – enables voice, silence, resonance, echoes, vibration, harmony, dissonance, wave formations, amplification and more to capture the ways in which young people can be supported to develop a deep understanding of our changing world, and to take their place within it. For Lederach and his daughter, 'voice' is both internal (vibration within an individual) and external. In its external form it can become a social echo and resonate in collective spaces, building meaningful conversation, resiliency, and purposeful action in the face of violence.

These symbolic ways of thinking about imagination, creativity and change don't have to be abstract. Later in this chapter, Will McInnerney will share his research into using arts-based approaches, and poetry in particular, to support men to reimagine masculinities and reduce violence against women. Rewilded education can begin to take hold in schools that wish to foreground the arts and creativity. The Cambridge University Primary School,[22] for example, which is a UK state primary school, has drawn on Pam Burnard and Michelle Loughrey's book *Sculpting New Creativities in Primary Schools*[23] to realise its mission of, 'releasing the imagination: celebrating the art of the possible.' Their curriculum foregrounds 'creativities' as 'response-ability' to a series of existential crises. These crises emanate from threats to the survival of planet earth, to the cohesion of communities, and to individual's sense of purpose and meaning.

A poster presentation about the school created by James Biddulph, who was headteacher at the time, at an OECD Creativity in Education summit in 2023,[24] points out, along the lines of this book, that positive forces for change are held back by technocratic and unimaginative responses to these crises and by education systems that are no longer fit to reimagine, reinvent and reinvigorate our response-ability to the challenges we face. They call for a revolution of the social imagination through education, leading to a tomorrow of active and compassionate citizenship. They use a model of diverse creativities that range from creative being, to creative thinking to creative enacting:

Creative BEING

We consider ways of BEING creative. This is embodied, collaborative, and intercultural, bringing to the fore a holistic response to learning and teaching. We consider the physical, intellectual, social, cultural and spiritual dimensions of BEING.

Creative THINKING

We invite children to raise questions, to ponder, to philosophise, to reimagine ways of BEING, as intercultural and transcultural ways of THINKING. Our values of empathy, respect, trust, courage and gratitude are drawn together with the Habits of Mind literatures (self-regulation and metacognition) so that Creative THINKING includes criticality, stepping back, being in 'spaces of uncertainty' and thinking 'what if?'

Creative ENACTING

Creative BEING and Creative THINKING together manifest in Creative ENACTMENTS. These underpin the focus of our curriculum – to nurture compassionate citizenship. These ENACTMENTS are spontaneous (e.g. a child starting a chess club for quieter children) or whole community events (e.g. a school carnival taken to the streets of our local community). These are the moments of creative agency where children and teachers and teaching assistants find ways to express, respond to, develop and reimagine new ways of BEING and THINKING to improve the world for us all.

From paralysis and despair to hope, creativity and change

Hope then, is important. Despite the fact that the climate emergency can lead to feelings of paralysis as the enormity of what needs to change becomes apparent, it is important to hold onto hope. Paul Jepson and Cain Blythe[25] talk about how rewilding can support people to move from feelings of despair to feelings of joy. Rewilding tackles eco-anxiety through supporting people to make positive changes, however small, and to work together towards greater sustainability. It tackles solastalgia through moving beyond conservation towards the establishment of future-oriented sustainable ecosystems. It reconnects people with wild spaces and reminds them of their place in nature.

These benefits, amongst other things, prompted Robert Macfarlane[26] to undertake a journey to find wild places in the UK – in beechwoods, moors, saltmarshes and valleys, and to write about what he found. His beautifully written evocative prose is punctuated with comments on climate change and destruction of habitat, and with questions of human culture, time and belonging. He treads a delicate line between biophilia and anger at the human destruction of wild spaces. I too walk this delicate line in this book. On the one hand I wish to focus on positive action for change – but on the other, this can't happen without people having a deep understanding of why change is important. We need to allow ourselves to feel the pain of what we are doing to the environment without succumbing to hopelessness. This is tricky.

There are three examples of the negative impact of human activity on wild spaces in Robert Macfarlane's book that particularly resonate with me. I would like to share them here, and to show how his way of presenting them has affected me. I would like to share my own poetry in the hope that this will affect others. Robert Macfarlane's work has emboldened the particular stance towards rewilding that I am taking in this book. We both aim to create links between wild spaces, art, human culture, well-being and education. We aim to inspire positive action and not just intellectual debate.

More generally, if the arts can be reinvigorated as a vehicle for expressing deep sorrow at what is happening to our planet on the one hand, and love of nature on the other, perhaps we can have more meaningful connections and conversations with young people about the kind of world they wish to inherit. Perhaps also we can support them to take action to bring this about. This starts with artistic engagement with the world through poetry, music, visual media, drama and storytelling, literature and much more. What insights might young people have, and how might they surprise and delight us with creative and innovative ideas? How can the development of an artistic mindset support young people to remain optimistic and innovative in the face of challenge and despair?

Woodland

The first of the examples I would like to share here concerns forests and woodland. According to Robert Macfarlane, the Bronze Age marked the point at which the UK was no longer made up of 50% forest. Then in England between 1930 and 1990, over half of the remaining ancient woodland was cleared or replaced with conifer plantation. During this time, half of the hedgerows were also pulled up. Up until very recently then, people's lives in the UK had been deeply grounded in forests and woodlands. Much of this has been lost within the last century. As he[27] points out:

> Woods and forests have been essential to the imagination of these islands, and of countries throughout the world, for centuries. It is for this reason that when woods are felled, when they are suppressed by tarmac and concrete and asphalt, it is not only unique species and habitats that disappear, but also unique memories, unique forms of thought. Woods, like other wild places, can kindle new ways of being or cognition in people ... can urge their minds differently.

It seems to me that this is fundamental to rewilding – we need to reintroduce biodiversity following human impact – but we also need to enable human beings to reconnect with nature and sustainable ways of thinking and being. This includes our cultural, aesthetic and existential understanding of the world as well as experiences in nature. For example, we need to spend time with trees. The benefits for human health and well-being of being amongst trees are increasingly being recognised. Forestry England,[28] who grow, shape and care for the UK's forests, have a page on their website about 'forest bathing,' which is the popular Japanese practice (*shinrin yoku*) of being calm, quiet and observant amongst trees whilst breathing deeply. This is an important birth right of everyone living in the UK, and throughout the world.

The scientific evidence about trees as vital producers of oxygen is important, but only one side of the coin. The depletion of forests and the loss of trees certainly hastens the time when the planet becomes uninhabitable for many humans, but it also leads to feelings of alienation from our natural heritage. This is most significant amongst the urban poor, but it also affects cosmopolitan elites who live in air-conditioned apartments in gated complexes with small, manicured gardens. The need to communicate the scale of what is being lost and motivate young people to spend time in nature is becoming ever more urgent. Following is a poem that attempts to capture my own love affair with trees. I wrote it after I was particularly struck by an X-ray of a human lung that looks just like a tree in reverse. It connected me with the beauty of our symbiotic relationship with trees through our exchange of oxygen and carbon (Figure 8.1).

Health, engagement, practical wisdom and an arts-based mindset 135

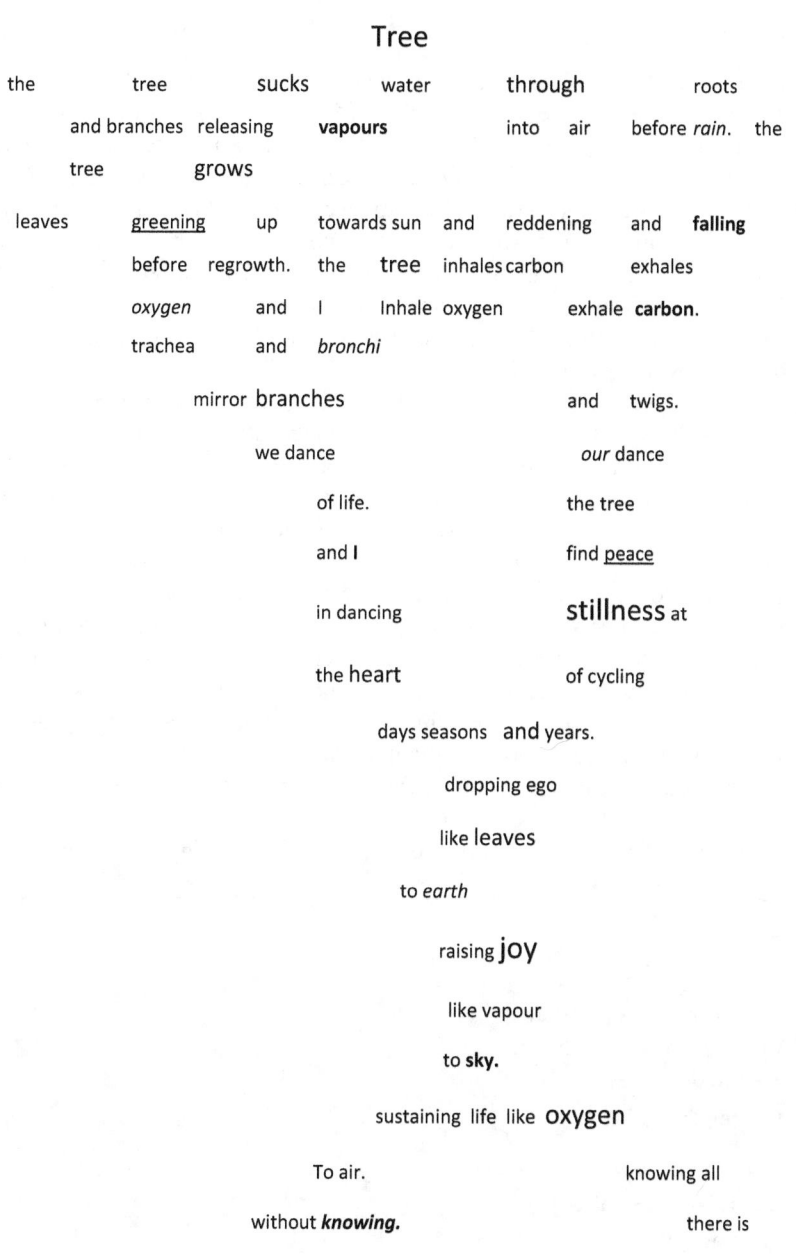

Figure 8.1 Tree poem

The sea

Another impact of human activity on wildness that particularly affects me is what we have done to the oceans. Robert Macfarlane speaks movingly about this. On the same page that he describes his visit to a remote island beach in Wales where there were oystercatchers ('neckless, in tuxedoed groups'[29]), he describes the debris that had washed up, even there. This included blue milk bottle crates, chunks of furniture foam, cigarette butts, bottle caps, aerosol canisters, and tetra pak cartons with faded writing from different parts of the world. I find it dizzying to think about how much single-use rubbish is produced in the households of the world every day, and how long it will take for it to degrade. Robert Macfarlane points out that thousands of tons of debris wash up each year on the coast of Britain and Ireland. This is increasing, and whales, dolphins and porpoises are dying from digestive tracts blocked by plastic. Seals and sea birds are becoming entangled in 'ghost' fishing nets which drift through the sea after being abandoned or lost by trawlers. Oil from marine traffic or offshore drilling kills forests of kelp and birds and seals. This transforms the beaches of our restoration and imagination into places of hazard, ugliness and death, as well as sending many sea-dwelling species into decline.

Beaches, like forests, have a special place in our shared culture and imagination, and have traditionally been spaces where people rest and play. Beaches are places of wonder for children making sandcastles, lovers at sunset, or people meditating to the (real or imagined) sound of the waves. The degradation of these restorative spaces is unthinkable. Again, I will share here one of my poems that's about my delight in beaches. As ever, it perhaps expresses the awe and wonder of the beach better than prose, and points to the centrality of the beach to existential questions around birth, death, meaning and love:

Beach

Where land meets sea,
Old dreams are re-born,
And new dreams
Glitter in sunlight.

Wave after wave
Brings sorrow, now joy.
Pushing, sucking,
An eternal dance.

Throwing up creatures,
And shells,
And sailors' souls,
Chuckling and stretching.

> And wood from shipwrecks,
> And distant shores,
> Licked dry and smooth,
> As old as old is old.
>
> And we, my love,
> Like land and sea
> Fall and tumble together
> Surrendering to each wave
>
> Creeping along the shore
> Pulled by unseen forces
> Our lunar love
> Is faithful, and still
>
> And old as old is old.

The Night

The third area that particularly affects me is the way that human activity is robbing all of us of the night sky. Robert Macfarlane[30] notes poetically that, 'towns stain their skies orange' and also points out that the release of this light disrupts the habits of nature. Migrating birds collide with illuminated buildings, thinking that they are daytime sky. The leaf-fall and flowering patterns of trees are disrupted because days seem endless throughout the year, and glow-worm numbers are declining because their pilot lights (by which they attract mates) are no longer bright enough to be visible at night. There are few sights more beautiful than a clear night sky. It powerfully reminds us of our place in the universe. If we are unable to make out the stars because of light pollution in towns and cities, the folly of assuming we are at the centre of the universe is rendered ever more possible.

One of my doctoral student colleagues, Portia Ungley, wrote this poem for this book to express her own feelings about the loss of the night sky. It is so much more eloquent than anything more that I could say here.

> **Portia Ungley: Twice 4 a.m.**
>
> i. On passage
>   Dark water and hissing waves
>   Gentle creaks of rope and sail and favourable tide
>   The night starless, tucked in with clouds
>   A container ship looms, a tower block on the move

> Bright wake disrupts night vision after it fades from view
> Return to breeze on cheek in inky blackness
> Companionable nothingness, alone with four senses
> Iodine and ozone, rope sore hands, wind burnt nose
> A glow appears, a smudge; sunrise? Too early
> Polluted light staining the horizon
> Depression's artist streaking sky greygreen, gangrene
> Murdering night with careless ease
> Sulfurous glow of public safety lights – safe from what?
> A thousand forgotten bulbs reflecting on clouds and streets
> Lightslick spreading across land and sea and sky
> Dawn's rosy fingers hidden by haphazard excess
>
> ii. Darkness
> A clatter of paws, howling at an unseen foe
> My limbs unwilling to soothe canine woes by trudging down
> Sleep shallow harumph and leaden steps, dressing gown askew
> An open door, lungs full of 4am and then the world spins, vertigo of breath
> A thousand thousand stars in yellow spider silk
> A sky so dark that I am lost to myself
> The milky way brightscattered stamp on eternity
> Fingerpainted by a child with light in their hands
> Lantern stars bobbing in the field of night
> Untouched finger-familiar constellations
> Traced by needles dipped in gold
> Tapestried tangle of forgotten fire
> Sphere of heaven rendering my words moot
> Humility of my dark against its brightness
> No manmade prints on this forever horizon
> Its wheel turning beyond time[31]

I am deeply grateful to Portia, and to all of my doctoral student colleagues for their contributions to this book.

I have shared my poems here to inspire others to find their own ways of creative expression. It would be incongruous in a book like this to argue against the dominance of traditional academic cultures of schooling using a traditional academic style. The point is that creative ways of expression open up dialogue with the reader / audience and invites them to engage with their own creative practice. This dialogue often takes place over several days, weeks or years in the minds of those who have been moved or challenged by a piece of art. Artists want their art to have transformative power. The brilliant musician Keith Jarrett, for example, is known to have said that he wants people to be fundamentally different after they have heard his music. The same can be said of another member of CPERG[32], Will McInerney, whose case study is shared here.

William W. McInerney: Reimagining masculinities

My research looks at the intersections of peace and arts education, with a specific focus on feminist theories of peace and men's violence prevention work. Men's violence against women is a severe and pervasive problem around the world. An increasingly popular way to address this violence has been to directly engage boys and men in feminist-informed education programs, otherwise known as the field of 'engaging men'. The focus of my research is on primary prevention group education programs which work with men from the general public in school and community settings. This is in contrast to programs that solely focus on men already identified as perpetrators. A primary prevention approach is rooted in the idea that not all men commit violence against women, but all men can and should play an important role in preventing it at home, school, work, and throughout their communities. Men can be particularly impactful allies and agents of change in challenging sexism within their male peer groups and in being gender equality role models as fathers, partners, coaches, and colleagues. Research shows that well-designed engaging men's programs can foster positive changes in men's violence-supportive attitudes and behaviours and promote their involvement in gender equality work.

This work remains challenging, however, and many programs are not well designed, resulting in limited engagement and impact. The field has faced a range of calls for reform and innovation, including concerns about a reliance on overly didactic approaches and cognitive-centric pedagogies. I've designed, taught, led, and researched these programs across the US, UK, Germany, and Australia for the past decade – and one strategy that I've found particularly helpful in addressing this concern is the use of the arts.

Aligned strongly with the insights shared throughout this chapter, my teaching and research shows arts-integrated approaches to engaging men have several potential benefits.[33] First, they can facilitate more holistic mind, heart, and body pedagogies that support learning in these programs. Second, the arts can make the work more personal and collective, thus supporting men in applying the knowledge to their own lived experiences and communities. My research shows that arts-integrated programs can help engage *more men* and engage *men more* – increasing the potential for larger mobilisations of men as allies for gender equality and deepening the learning in their efforts. Third, a holistic and humanising arts-integrated praxis drives what I find to be a *productively discomforting* imaginative process in the classroom which can help men stretch their understanding from a singular rigid idea of masculinity into a more expansive engagement with masculinities beyond gendered boundaries. This reimagining of masculinities is at the heart of engaging-men work and resonates deeply with Hilary's insights on the nexus of imagination, narrative, and an arts-based mindset.

However, an arts approach is not without its challenges, including the need for extra resources, time, and training; resistance to the arts by participants, institutions, and donors; and the risk of unintentionally doing harm to participants by creating uncritical art that re-affirms gender violence and inequality rather than challenging it. In short, art is not intrinsically 'good' or peaceful or feminist; rather it is powerful. Engaging with the power of arts requires careful planning and consideration, including the use of trauma-informed approaches to ensure that unintentional harm is not done through the often deeply personal and emotional work that can surface in these creative learning spaces. But when it is done with care and criticality, I've found, again and again, that the transformative power of the arts helps us see the world and its many problems more clearly, to better understand ourselves and our role as agents of change, and inspires us to work together to do something about it.

Building on my work with Hilary,[34] I've specifically found poetry to be a great example of this work in action. Poetry provides a way to tap into the complexity of people's narratives and emotions. It combines their analytical thinking – the crafting of metaphor and imagery with their affective entanglements in our world – tapping into the intangibles of our lived experiences. This is what I call both an analytic and affective meaning-making praxis. For example, my research shows poetry can be used as creative and culturally responsive learning texts for men to reflect upon, by hearing and reading the poetry of survivors of violence and allies speaking out for gender equality and by tapping into the long legacy of feminist and peace poetic traditions. Poetry can also be incorporated through writing and sharing exercises with the men, facilitating an opportunity to use creative writing to dig deep, explore their own conceptions of masculinity, reflect on their lived experiences – including the ways they have stood up to gender inequality and the ways they have remained silent or complicit with it.

Importantly, poetry invites us to imagine an alternative world, a new path forward. As bell hooks[35] has written, men (and all of us) must develop 'blueprints for change' to bring about feminist ideas of masculinity rooted in equality, justice, and peace. Hooks[36] called us all to action when she wrote, 'Clearly, we need new strategies, new theories, guides that will show us how to create a world where feminist masculinity thrives.' My teaching and research show us that the arts may be one way to help bring that about. As Hilary notes in this chapter, the arts and peace can be a part of a rewilding of education that helps us move from paralysis and despair to hope, poesis, and change.

It seems fitting to end here with a poem. In my research I often use a technique I call poetic mosaics. Drawing on various found poem techniques and my own career as a poet and poetry educator, I take quotes from research participants and I rearrange them in a single multi-vocal poem, creating a choir of voices across the line breaks and stanzas to reflect on key ideas and concepts. To be clear, the words in the poem are not my own. Rather, I've mixed and matched them together in a new light, combining the fragments of dozens of research participants' insights and experiences together to create something new, something greater than the summation of its individual components. The following poems brings the voices of 20 men's violence prevention educators and participants from the USA together in reflecting on the 'man box', a metaphor for the rigid and harmful gender norms dictate what it means to 'be a man', why it's important to break down those walls, and how the arts might help.

Will McInerney: A poem in 6 parts

I
it all starts
with the manhood definition
never be vulnerable
always be serious
harden yourself
build a shell
get defensive
tighten your grip
hold on to the
socialised system
and predetermined assumptions
about what being a man is
and is
not
see it's simple
if you're going to be emotional
then you're going to be weak
not necessarily true
but
that's how it appears in our patriarchal world
if you're not in control
you're
weak

II

you can't be weak
so stay
emotionally cut off
at a distance
silent
not my problem
just give me the facts
defending ourselves from our heart
defending you from my heart
we're so good at intellectualising
this work
the classroom
the field
the movement
you
me
us
we're stuck inside
the man box walls
of our minds
in dominant mental models
where I'm the expert teaching you
in TED talks
and statistics
preaching didactic prescriptions
and academic pedagogies
till the cows come home

III

but damn
does it even work?

IV

it doesn't work
if saying the facts was enough
things would have already changed
men need to change
and how matters

this work needs to change
to get deeper
to find the emotional core
a crack in the wall
we need a microscope
a new lens for masculinity
i don't think you get to people's heart through their head
i think you get people's heart through their heart
and you know
that's what the art does
painting and dancing and singing
weaving and sewing and whatever
art brings
other kinds of intelligences
minds, hearts, action
sparking conversations
unpacking emotions
arts open cracks in that defensiveness
cutting through the bullshit
get those walls down
get them in the door
a good piece of art
no matter what the medium
cuts through
finding ways to make resonant emotional connections with the material
with the problem
with our role in it
not just this theoretical piece
it's hands-on compassion and passion
applying and learning
bring it into your body
into your nervous system
it's visceral

V
no it's not easy
it's uncomfortable
vulnerable

this work is hard
going against the ways men have been socialised
and that's why it's so important
that's why we have to do it
this arts thing
this is the work
it leaves a mark in you
close your eyes
you can see it
so, impact?
absolutely
tears?
moment of truth?
yeah
trust me
i was sceptical
i didn't expect that
but here it is
we went there
so yeah
it worked

VI
we need balance
take the abstract and mix it with the concrete
the hard facts and the art
there's got to be
cultural
spiritual
embodied
emotional
and analytical
to reach
to inspire
to connect
to change what it means to do this work
to change what it means to be a man
engaging all parts of who we are
from the intellectual to the visceral

> a space where men can heal and be accountable
> an opportunity to look at their behaviours
> look at their attitudes
> and make some real changes
> it's holistic
> the heart
> the body
> and the mind
> art finds a crack
> and connects it all
> loosening the grip
> on the man box wall

Conclusion

Poetry is powerful. Rewilded education supports change through creative action. It values process over outcomes. It recognises that desired outcomes for education are now more unknowable than ever, and the work of building sustainable futures is unending. Young people need to learn how to dwell in the shifting sands of geopolitics, climate change and migration (to name a few) and how to be well in this space.

An emphasis on process allows space for deep and contextualised learning and the development of the whole person. It enables outcomes to be as varied as the people involved. Whilst schooling commonly values educational outcomes that are abstract or symbolic, or that are convenient for teachers and institutions to measure, rewilded education values processes that enable an embodied experience and a joy of learning. The various alternative schools mentioned in this book emphasise processes over outcomes, with students frequently engaging in activities and projects because they find them to be meaningful and enjoyable. This process-oriented approach also leads to educational excellence, and to a mindset that is comfortable with change, open-endedness and the arts.

Notes

1. Loy, D (2019). *Ecodharma: Buddhist teaching for the ecological crisis*. Wisdom Publications.
2. Macy, J., & Brown, M. (2014). *Coming back to life*. New Society Publishers.
3. Cremin, H., & Bevington, T. (2017). *Positive peace in schools: Tackling conflict and creating a culture of peace in the classroom*. Routledge; Cremin, H. (2007). *Peer mediation: citizenship and social inclusion revisited*. Routledge.
4. Pranis, K., Stuart, B., et. al. (2013). *Peacemaking circles: from crime to community*. Living Justice Press.

5. Godin, S. (2015). *We are all weird: the rise of tribes and the end of normal*. Penguin.
6. Zembylas, Michalinos. '(Un)Happiness and social justice education: ethical, political and pedagogic lessons'. *Ethics and Education 15*(1) 18–32.
7. Greany, T. (2024) Moral purpose in performative times: do school leaders' values matter?, *British Journal of Educational Studies, 72*(5) 587–606.
8. Hibbin, R. (2023): Relational responsibility, social discipline and behaviour in school: re-orienting discipline and authority through a distributed network of relational accountability, *Pastoral Care in Education, 42*(4) 492–512.
9. Ofsted (2023). Inspection of a good school: Carr Manor Community School. Accessed January 2025. https://files.ofsted.gov.uk/v1/file/50238157.
10. Godin, S. (2015). *We are all weird: the rise of tribes and the end of normal*. Penguin.
11. Jepson, P., & Blythe, C. (2020). *Rewilding: the radical new science of ecological recovery*. Icon Books.
12. Barefoot College International. Accessed January 2025. https://www.barefootcollege.org.
13. Lave, J., & Wenger-Trayner, E. (1991). *Situated learning: legitimate peripheral participation*. Cambridge University Press.
14. Lave, J., & Wenger-Trayner, E. (1991). *Situated learning: legitimate peripheral participation*. Cambridge University Press, p. 100.
15. Lederach, J.-P. (2005). *The moral imagination: the art and soul of peacebuilding*. Oxford University Press.
16. Freire, P. (1973). *Education for critical consciousness*. Continuum.
17. Monbiot, G. (2014). *Feral: rewilding the land, sea and human life*. Penguin.
    Nixon, R. (2011). *Slow violence and the environmentalism of the poor*. Harvard University Press.
18. Vass, E. (2018). Musical co-creativity and learning—the fluid body language of receptive-responsive dialogue. *Human Arenas, 1*, 56–78; Elwick, A., Burnard, P., et al. (2020). Young children's experiences of music and soundings in museum spaces: lessons, trends and turns from the literature. *Journal of Early Childhood Research, 18*(2), 174–188.
19. McInnerney, W. & Cremin, H. (2023) Poetic peace education: a curriculum connecting the mind, body, and heart in workshop spaces. In P. Trofonas & S. Jagger (Eds) *Springer International Handbooks of Education. Handbook of Curriculum Theory and Research*, Springer Cham.
20. Koppensteiner, N. (2020). *Transrational peace and elicitive facilitation: the self as resource*. Palgrave Macmillan.
21. Lederach, J.-P., & Lederach, A. J. (2010). *When blood and bones cry out: journeys through the soundscape of healing and reconciliation*. Oxford University Press.
22. The University of Cambridge Primary School. Accessed January 2025. https://www.universityprimaryschool.org.uk/.
23. Burnard, P. & Loughrey, M. (2022) *Sculpting new creativities in primary education*. Routledge.
24. Biddulph. J. (2023). Poster created for OECD Creativity in Education summit, Paris, September 2023. Accessed January 2025 https://www.oecd.org/content/dam/oecd/en/about/projects/edu/teaching,-learning-and-assessing-creative-and-critical-thinking-skills/ces-2023/CES%20Report%202023_brochure.pdf.
25. Jepson, P., & Blythe, C. (2020). *Rewilding: the radical new science of ecological recovery*. Icon Books.
26. Macfarlane, R. (2007). *The Wild Places*. Granta.
27. Macfarlane, R. (2007). *The Wild Places*. Granta, p. 98.
28. Forestry England. Your Guide to Forest Bathing. Accessed January 2025. https://www.forestryengland.uk/blog/forest-bathing.

29 Macfarlane, R. (2007). *The Wild Places*. Granta, p.52.
30 Macfarlane, R. (2007). *The Wild Places*. Granta, p. 194.
31 Portia Ungley, who wrote this poem, can be contacted via her website: https://rawlightco.wordpress.com/blog/.
32 The Cambridge Peace and Education Research Group (CPERG) provides a hub for research students and faculty members at the University of Cambridge to exchange ideas and collaborate on projects that explore the relationships between conflict, peace and education, both in the UK and internationally. Its website can be accessed at: https://www.cperg.org/.
33 McInerney, W.W. (2019). *Poetry, gender, and peace*. Bern, Switzerland: SwissPeace; McInerney, W. W. (2022). *Reimagining masculinities: arts-integrated approaches to engaging men in violence prevention in the United States*. University of Cambridge Repository. Accessed January 2025. https://www.repository.cam.ac.uk/items/59c418fa-58b0-4fc1-abaa-b335f9f1de9b; McInerney, W. W. (forthcoming). Arts-integrated approaches to engaging men in violence prevention: mapping a kaleidoscope of arts, masculinities, and feminist possibilities. *Journal of Gender Studies*.
34 McInnerney, W. & Cremin, H. (2023) Poetic peace education: a curriculum connecting the mind, body, and heart in workshop spaces. In P. Trofonas & S. Jagger (Eds), *Springer International Handbooks of Education. Handbook of Curriculum Theory and Research*, Springer Cham.
35 Hooks, B. (1994). *Teaching to transgress: education as a practice of freedom*. Routledge.
36 Hooks, B, (2000). *Feminism is for everybody: passionate politics*. Pluto Press. p.71.

Chapter 9

Education for peace, justice and inclusion

Co-authored with Nomisha Kurian

Introduction

This chapter takes ideas from permaculture about balance and flow and applies them to education. Speaking back to Chapter Four, it suggests that education can be rewilded by improving the flow and distribution of social, cultural, and educational resources amongst populations of the world. For this it will need to prevent resources from being sequestered by global elites. Inclusion in this chapter is envisaged as involving all young people globally in an education that is fit for purpose, rather than providing credentials for a minority who go on to exclude and accumulate. Peace is seen as the state that follows when inclusion and justice are strong.

The chapter begins by considering whether balanced, peaceful and inclusive systems of schooling are possible. It then turns to more radical, critical and anarchic ways of educating before finally exploring a real-life example of rewilding. What miracles and challenges emerge when a place commits to alternative ways of living and being for over a hundred years? Our case study of sustainable development is Kerala, a small coastal state in India. We reflect on the personal impressions of one of the authors of this chapter and then link Kerala's experience of sustainable development to the broader themes of rewilding discussed throughout this book.

Inclusive education for peace and justice

Inclusive education for peace and justice is the aim of systems of schooling throughout the world. Unfortunately, however, schools are often co-opted into the exclusionary practices of wider society. This is a sad reality. A question that I have wrestled with throughout this book is whether they exist to exclude (despite claiming the opposite), or whether they merely reflect the wider societies they serve. If the latter, can they be reformed to become inclusive, peaceful and just? There are plenty of local and global programmes that aim to do just this. In 2018, UNESCO,[1] for example, talks about global citizenship education as a means of working towards the 2030 Agenda for

Sustainable Development (most notably Sustainable Development Goal 4, Target 4.7) through promoting peace, sustainability and equity. In the UK there have been many initiatives to reduce inequality amongst young people. Brighton and Hove City Council,[2] for example, have developed a city-wide Attachment Aware Behaviour Regulation Policy that aims to support children's services, including schools, to move away from traditional punitive responses to challenging behaviour towards a more humanist, relational and universal approach that benefits local communities.

These local and global initiatives are clearly important, but care needs to be taken to avoid the impression that transformation is possible within social and educational systems that remain fundamentally unequal. In my work on positive peace with Terence Bevington[3], we have found the concept of indirect violence useful. This is the structural and cultural violence that is built into business as usual in systems of schooling. Our efforts to support schools to build social justice through conflict literacy and a culture of positive peace are grounded in a deep awareness of structural inequalities that do not disappear through peace education alone.

Positive peace in schools is a concept that has been taken from the fields of Peace Studies and International relations. It builds on the work of Johan Galtung[4] and addresses structural and cultural violence. Positive peace is preferable to negative peace because negative peace is unstable and unjust and merely addresses direct violence. Negative peace comes about when people merely tackle direct violence. Direct violence is more easily understood than structural and cultural violence – it includes physical attacks and verbal violence. It usually involves an episode – something that happens at a particular time, in a particular place, and with particular people. Direct violence is often tackled using peacekeeping strategies. This usually means that individuals or groups act to ensure that perpetrators are inhibited. This may be through avoidance (CCTV, clear rules and consequences, physical barriers) or through assertive responses (restraint, punishment, physical removal of offenders).

Structural and cultural violence are harder to identify because they are more indirect. They operate at the level of groups, institutions and societies, and they occur in multiple places and across long periods of time. Johan Galtung defined structural violence as indirect violence that causes death or harm. It is often linked to injustice or exploitation and results in certain groups and individuals doing less well than others. Cultural violence sustains structural violence. It makes structural violence appear natural or invisible. In 1990, Johan Galtung[5] defined cultural violence as:

> Those aspects of culture, the symbolic sphere of our existence – exemplified by religion and ideology, language and art, empirical science and formal science logic, mathematics) – that can be used to justify or legitimise direct or structural violence.

Galtung gives an example of people dying prematurely from starvation in one half of the world, and from cardiovascular disease in the other. This structural violence is maintained through cultural violence. He suggests that people who throw a stone in anger, or try to escape poverty or unequal power relations through criminal activity, are usually the focus of punishment or violence reduction programmes. Those who uphold unequal power relations through structural violence, and those who obscure and naturalise it through cultural violence, remain untouched, and feel justified in blaming victims. It is often the case that attempts to tackle violence in schools and elsewhere focus on direct violence and neglect its structural and cultural roots. This leads at best to negative peace through peacekeeping. In order to achieve positive peace, the focus needs to widen to include structural and cultural violence. This challenges our usual ways of thinking about violence in schools.

With Alex Guilherme[6] I have applied Johan Galtung and Franz Fanon's theories to education and given some examples of what these different forms of direct and indirect violence might look like in global education settings. Structural violence in education (e.g. students from certain cultural, social or colonised groups not doing as well in school as others) is often upheld through cultural violence (e.g. the myth of meritocracy). If direct violence (e.g vandalism, bullying) are to be avoided, a focus on reducing structural and cultural violence is needed. This is achieved through moving beyond peacekeeping into peacemaking and peacebuilding.

Peacekeeping then, is about preserving the status quo. It is about protection and strength. Although this may have a place in a school community that wishes to uphold values and safety, it is limited to maintaining order and does little to respond creatively to the gifts that conflict can bring, or to challenge the status quo. Peacemaking is about restoring relationships when conflict has occurred and involves power sharing. In my peace work in schools over the years, including latterly with colleagues in Cambridge,[7] peacemaking initiatives have often included peer mediation and restorative approaches that move away from punitive and authoritarian regimes towards more empowering and facilitative ways of responding to conflict and harm. At the level of outer peace and relationships, this involves, for example, using problem-solving circles. At the level of ecological peace, it involves reconnecting with nature in order to restore balance and well-being.

Peacebuilding is fundamental for peacemaking. It is not possible to make peace if the capacity is not there, and many conflicts can be avoided if schools build peace in proactive ways. Peacebuilding ideally enables all members of a school community to learn and use the language, skills and processes of transforming conflict and working towards peace. It takes place over a long period of time because it goes beyond concern with a particular episode. At the level of inner peace, for example, it involves learning to be mindful through the use of the breath; and at the level of the community and the world it involves reaching out to people with diverse backgrounds. I am currently working to develop positive peace in the UK, Kazakhstan,[8] Qatar, Colombia, Brazil, Europe and elsewhere. The schools who are using this framework are delighted with the results, but is it really possible to tackle structural and cultural violence in schools through re-focussing on peacemaking and peacebuilding? How do we address the fact that most schools are satisfied with negative peace though peacekeeping, and that this drives inequality?

Critical pedagogy and radical approaches

Some argue that positive peace in structurally and culturally violent schools is not possible. Much peace education research bears this out. Kathy Bickmore,[9] for example, found that initiatives to support critical dialogic pedagogy in schools in Canada were not able to deal with conflict in a meaningful way, or to involve the voices of non-affluent and marginalised students. In post-war Sierra Leone, Sean Higgins and Mario Novelli[10] found that peace education promoted a form of pacification derived from a decontextualized curriculum that treats victims as guilty and in need of attitudinal and behavioural change, while avoiding engagement with the structural and geopolitical drivers that underpin many contemporary conflicts. Basma Hajir and Kevin Kester[11] argue that the concept of structural violence needs to go further to promote (and not obscure) individual responsibility. They urge educators to consider an education for the privileged that would involve a 'pedagogy of discomfort' that might better support a decolonial praxis for critical peace education. Given that many efforts for inclusion throughout the world focus on what 'we' (the relatively wealthy) think 'they' (the poor, the dispossessed) should do in order to share our benefits (not possible with finite resources), it is perhaps time for research and development to focus instead on what 'we' need to do in order to stop our exclusionary practices.

For these reasons and more, Monisha Bajaj[12] and Ilan Gur-Ze'ev[13] call for new forms of critical peace education that transcend the ways in which it has been appropriated and domesticated. The challenge of responsible peace education, according to Gur-Ze'ev, is demanding, traumatic and dangerous. He draws on his concepts of response-ability and respond-ability to call for peace education that enables flourishing, love of life, and improvisation. He urges peace educators to reject forms of peace education that are mired in positive utopianism, the violence of self-evidence, and the maintenance of weak, marginalised and controlled collectives.

The argument here is that peace as a concept to support rewilding education is limited when it is naively or simplistically applied. Most people have a sense of what peace might look like, but it is different for different people, making consensus hard. It can be used to maintain the structural and cultural violence of business as usual. When taken seriously, however, peace can be an important cornerstone of rewilding education. As an aspirational state, it needs to be completed through discussion, decisions, actions and hard choices. Peace can be useful to help people imagine more hopeful futures, and thus to work for change. Peter Thompson and Slavoj Zizek[14] have reviewed the work of Ernst Bloch who wrote about hope in the late 1950s. They suggest that hope has become mired in the excesses and disaffections of contemporary capitalist society, and that it is important to attempt to revive it so that people can feel comfortable in a space of both being and 'not yet being' that grounds them and urges them onwards towards a better future.

The question that this chapter grapples with is: how can education for peace, justice and inclusion (and education more generally) break free of the values and practices of modern systems of schooling that work against it? This is a little like asking how to set up permaculture in a field that has been cleared of all life except for one crop. Clearly it takes time to reintroduce diversity and flow of resources. Our case study of Kerala shows what can happen when these conditions are met. Without suggesting that Kerala has found perfect solutions to the issues raised here, and without over-romanticising, we humbly share this autoethnographic account of Nomisha's travels in India. We want to share our sense of hope. Perhaps the case of Kerala will show that alternatives are possible, and that education can be rewilded in a state that foregrounds inclusion over profit.

Nomisha Kurian: Out in green paddy fields: a story of sustainable development

Kerala – India's southernmost state – is a sensory symphony. The feathery gold-green haze of the paddy fields. Rain-damp earth. The murmur of the backwaters. On my rambles, I encounter fields silver-ribboned by streams and lagoons brimming with water of the clearest blue. My days are canopied by teak and rosewood. When rain pelts, I take refuge under golden shower trees; so named after delicate blossoms that trail, feather-like, from their branches. At night, the blossoms darken into a thick midnight-black mass, huddled so close that they look like they are whispering secrets.

While journeying to this green state, I took two books with me upon Hilary's recommendation: Jason Hickel's *How Degrowth Will Save the World*[15] and Kate Raworth's *Doughnut Economics*.[16] Their arguments did not seem out of place in the stillness and peace of the paddy fields. Hickels calls for stopping the pursuit of endless economic growth, on the grounds that a myopic focus on Gross Domestic Product only drives climate change, ecological breakdown, and social inequality. Instead, he advocates for 'degrowth' – that is, cultivating human well-being and conserving resources. Raworth, in a similar vein, calls for 'doughnut economics': an approach to the economy that respects balance rather than unfettered growth. She employs the image of a doughnut to symbolise a 'safe and just space for humanity' ringed by both planetary and social boundaries. Planetary boundaries include threats and risks such as ozone layer depletion and climate change, while social boundaries include human needs such as water, food, health, education and social equity. Similar to Hickel's advocacy for degrowth, Raworth presents a vision of sustainable development by laying out seven principles:

1 **Change the goal**: Stop the conventional pursuit of boundless GDP growth. Instead, aspire to a new aim to meet planetary and social needs. This means expanding the definition of prosperity beyond financial metrics and adopting a broader notion of well-being.
2 **See the big picture**: Shift away from perceiving the economy as an isolated system. Instead, recognise its intricate embedding within society and the environment. Emphasise the interconnections and feedback loops that interweave economic, social, and ecological systems.
3 **Nurture human nature**: Challenge the conventional assumption of humans as solely self-interested and rational beings. Acknowledge the significance of human cooperation, altruism, and intrinsic motivation. Design economic systems that align with and cultivate these aspects of human behaviour.
4 **Get savvy with systems**: Cultivate a systems thinking approach to comprehending the dynamic relationships and feedback loops within complex systems. Analyse interdependencies and unintended consequences to develop more effective and sustainable policies.
5 **Design to distribute**: Prioritise economic systems that foster equitable distribution of resources and opportunities. Address systemic inequality and ensure a fair sharing of benefits and burdens across society.
6 **Create to regenerate**: Highlight the importance of regenerative practices in economic activities. Advocate for the designing production and consumption processes that restore and replenish the environment, rather than deplete or pollute it.
7 **Be agnostic about growth**: Challenge the assumption that economic growth should always be pursued. Instead, prioritise social progress and ecological resilience. Move beyond fixating on growth as the ultimate measure of success.

These seven principles resonate with Hilary's advocacy for long-lasting cultures of positive peace that tackle entrenched inequalities. By embracing these seven principles, Kate Raworth believes that economists can forge a new economic paradigm that is more sustainable, inclusive and responsive to the complex challenges of the 21st century. This multidimensional approach to economic thinking is envisioned as the key to a prosperous and resilient future.

In the green lap of Kerala, I am captivated by these arguments. The state has become globally acclaimed as a 'model of development'[17] and is lovingly nicknamed 'God's own country.'[18] Does Kerala – with its decades of investing in human welfare and rejecting excess industrialisation – represent degrowth and doughnut economics? How has Kerala become the golden child of development? And what does development mean, anyway?

Kerala lies on the southernmost tip of India. Shaped like a fish gazing out at the Arabian Sea, it is a small state filled with coconut trees. Flanked by the Malabar Coast, which spans 580 km of golden sand, Kerala brims over with waterways. Forty-four rivers, 34 lakes, and seven lagoons thread everyday life in this coastal state. *Kettuvallams* – traditional houseboats with thatched roofs, wooden hulls and furnished rooms – are popular. As an informal form of public transport, houseboats can be caught from almost all villages. Tourists can often be spotted reclining at the back of one as they float down palm-ringed canals.

In this tapestry of natural beauty, complex questions about human flourishing emerge. Kerala is one of the few regions in the world to have actively practised alternatives to the modern capitalist economy for over a hundred years. It has deprioritised the free market in favour of sustained state investment in social sectors such as healthcare and education.[19] Regardless of one's political affiliation, Kerala forms an interesting case study for applying Hilary's vision of rewilding, braided by Hickel's ideas about degrowth and Raworth's principles of doughnut economics.

On the one hand, Kerala has never been considered a beacon of material wealth. At the turn of the millennium, it was judged as 'poor even by Indian standards' with the gross domestic product per capita only $1,000 a year, approximately $200 less than the Indian average and only one twenty-sixth of the American average.[20] Kerala has historically had low per capita income. While this has increased in recent years, the lifestyles of most of Kerala's 34 million citizens continue to be relatively simple. Everyday clothing tends to be plain and without ornamentation. The tea stalls that dot the streets are often dilapidated, makeshift structures. Many roads are narrow and barely fit multiple vehicles.

On the other hand, Kerala's citizens enjoy some of the highest human development outcomes in the world. If you are born in Kerala, you can expect to grow and thrive by your first birthday. Neonatal care has been a key focus of state investment for decades. Consequently, Kerala enjoys one of the lowest infant mortality rates amongst low- and middle-income countries: 6 for every 1000 live births, compared to India's national average of 30.[21] You can also expect to confidently wield a pen. Kerala has achieved 94% literacy, which outstrips the literacy rate of the United States (92%). You can expect clean, well-maintained classrooms every few miles. As an economist put it at the turn of the century, 'children in Kerala are likely to beg for pens, not money.'[22] If a crisis strikes, you might well be able to trust the state to preserve your rights. For example, during the pandemic, UNICEF reported that 'Kerala is an exception' since 70% of parents of both younger and adolescent students felt that their child's overall learning progress was the same or better than it would be in school, since they were receiving equal access to education regardless of their socio-economic background.[23] UNICEF also noted that 'Kerala has been among the most proactive states in supporting students' and 'the only state' where almost all students reported receiving remote learning resources from the government and over 90% report regular contact with their teachers.

In addition, you need not worry about whether you have been born in a village or a city. Kerala's state planning has prioritised equity, resulting in human development outcomes that are not significantly affected by socio-economic disparities. For example, the fertility rate is the same in urban and rural areas and is only 1.8 births per woman – close to Denmark (1.7) and Sweden (1.7).[24] As you grow older, you can look forward to a long life; life expectancy in Kerala is 75 years, close to the American average of 77 and markedly higher than the Indian average of 70.[25]

What to make of statistics that seem incongruous for a small state to achieve in a country wracked by poverty and inequality? These patterns are unusual outside of modernised, industrialised nations in the Global North. Kerala compels a broader view of what makes for a good life beyond per capita income.

Kerala's doughnut economy: our shared reflections

In the following, we unpack how Hilary's vision of rewilding, threaded by Kate Raworth's principles of a doughnut economy and Sean Hickel's idea of degrowth, might be applied to Kerala. It is beyond our scope to capture all the political, economic and cultural complexities of state policy. However, we share examples and anecdotes as the textual equivalent of Polaroids: little snapshots of rewilded living.

1 *Change the goal*: Chapter One of this book explains why much of the world is caught in the 'death throes of modernity'. Developing countries,[26] however, have typically been pressured to adopt all the trappings of modernity, with neoliberal institutions making capitalist prescriptions for progress. In these prescriptions, rapid economic growth is the only way to improve ordinary people's standard of life – first comes the free market and a rise in GDP, and then comes the 'nice-to-haves' like social inclusion and universal education. Yet, Kerala reversed this teleology and became an 'enigma' and 'paradox' to developmental economists because it 'proved the experts wrong'.[27] In 1957, amidst high poverty and the ravages of colonialism, the state made a much-debated choice. Instead of setting up tax breaks and incentives for companies to invest in infrastructure and industry, Kerala invested in two things. One was basic needs: dramatically improving government services. The other was distributing food, housing, health services, and education equitably and efficiently. Crucially, Kerala did not wait to become rich before investing in the health, dignity, and learning of its citizens. Consequently, despite originating as a poor state and making relatively modest economic gains, Kerala continues, year after year, to have the highest amount of per capita spending on healthcare and education among all Indian states.[28]

Kerala was also the first Indian state to implement universal health coverage reform in 2012. It thereby achieved a paradox noted by Amartya Sen:

universal health coverage is often deemed a luxury only attainable by the richest nations, yet a small state in a high-poverty nation quietly achieved it at low cost by making sustained investment over time.[29] What this means for people's everyday lives is an unusually accessible set of social services. If you are sick, for example, you are likely to easily access free or highly subsidised treatment. If you are poor or unemployed, you are likely to access social security nets. Aside from investing in public healthcare infrastructure, the state invests in substantial social welfare schemes, such as the Comprehensive Health Insurance Scheme and the State Poverty Eradication Mission. Kerala's healthcare is not free of flaws; morphine access is notably low, for example.[30] However, the indignities and tragedies besetting healthcare systems in many developed nations – long waiting times, brief appointments and extortionate bills – are largely absent. We see this as evidence that there are alternatives to the logic of modernity.

As Chapter One points out, deprioritising human welfare only results in systems that exile many people from basic resources. If 'developing countries' can break away from the pressure of Western neoliberal institutions to prioritise human economic growth over human welfare, they may be able to replicate some of the benefits that Kerala has enjoyed. They need to be free to change the goals.

2 *See the big picture*: As Chapter Two discusses, we bear an ethical responsibility to maintain a respectful, reciprocal and reverential relationship with nature. Planning for biodiversity to thrive in the long term is not easy. However, places like Kerala offer a way to know and love nature without compromising human survival. To try and manage its lush coasts, Kerala has walked a delicate tightrope between allowing economic activity, conserving fragile ecosystems like mangroves, and protecting coastal communities against natural disasters. The result may be familiar to policymakers and indeed any person making decisions for a group: trying to please all may result in satisfying none. Some critics believe that, even though there has been a 'noticeable positive impact' ecologically, this has been at the cost of coastal people's property rights and economic development. They feel that prosperity has been 'severely hampered' because of 'unrealistic and unachievable' restrictions. These critics worry that efforts to protect the environment have been unduly zealous.[31] Others believe that Kerala needs to go still further to protect its coasts from littering, erosion, and climate change.[32]

Notwithstanding the difficulty of balancing economic and environmental priorities, Kerala has succeeded in one of the highest biodiversity conservation rates in the world, winning regular awards for innovation in conservation.[33] It has also succeeded in making sustainable agriculture a norm. It promotes organic and traditional farming techniques which minimise chemical inputs, conserve soil health, and make agriculture viable in the long term. It sees the bigger picture.

3 *Nurture human nature*: As Chapter Six suggests, developing practical wisdom that departs from mere abstraction is key to rewilding education. Practising such wisdom necessitates space to exercise agency and voice. In Kerala, ordinary citizens can be glimpsed jumping up to speak about global and local issues at every street corner – be it speeches about global wars, heated critiques of different governments, or personal visions of development. These vibrant voices belong to women, too. Despite tensions in feminist activism, women are a strong presence in local government, with a female quota of 50%.[34]

I witnessed this on my travels. Every street tea stall I visited was filled with men and women passing the newspaper to one another. They eagerly debate current affairs, unafraid to criticise the government and equally keen to become involved firsthand in creating the changes they want to see. On one occasion, whilst sitting in a tea stall, I saw a bus conductor stroll away from his bus to take up a position with a microphone in a dusty corner of a small village. He charted out a six-point plan for land reform before returning to his bus. The tea stall owner told me, with an affectionate grin, 'He speaks as though he is in a big stadium, even though it's just Raju (the stray dog) and a couple of kids milling around him!' Kerala's normalisation of everyday activism – as something which belongs to every citizen, rather than the preserve of the political elite – seems to manifest in vibrant acts of voice and agency, what Hilary calls 'an ethical, respectful and dialogic quest to understand the world.'[35]

In addition to everyday activism, Kerala holds the largest and most varied set of cooperative societies in India,[36] with almost 12,000 cooperative societies (including community-owned banks, hospitals, colleges, grocery stores and restaurants). This includes Uralungal Labour Contract Cooperative Society, which is the world's second largest cooperative. Community-led initiatives are common across the fields of politics, education, and healthcare. For example, when the Lancet commissioned research to investigate and improve palliative care in Kerala, its co-chair reported that a major reason for the success of the project was community participation.[37] Accustomed to grassroots initiatives, local people volunteered to act as links between the patients and the medical system, to make weekly or more frequent visits, or to help arrange financial aid. The people of Kerala share deeply contextualised, practical wisdom for the benefit of the whole community, nurturing human nature through cooperation, civic action, engagement, and care.

4 *Get savvy with systems*: As discussed in Chapter Three, governments are increasingly deploying 'nudge' approaches to manipulate people into behaviours they consider desirable. In this regard, we find it striking that Kerala decentralises its governance in ways that leave room for ordinary people to give back to their communities of their own free will. Kerala's decentralised governance entails complex ecosystems: empowering local governments to

make decisions and implement policies closely tailored to the community's specific needs. Combined with a long-standing history of encouraging and supporting ordinary citizens to be politically and socially active, this approach promotes participatory decision-making. What this has meant in times of crisis is that different systems for public welfare are used to working together.

During the pandemic, Kerala was routinely spotlighted in global media as an 'exemplar' of innovatively controlling COVID-19's spread. Its decades of investing in robust public healthcare and its cultural norms of volunteerism and community-led, grassroots movements bore fruit. Arun Elias[38] explains how systems thinking helped Kerala in this time of crisis. For example, on the principle of letting no citizen go hungry during lockdowns, community kitchens provided free food. This kind of charity may be observed in many places, but what was exceptional was the level of public coordination: in a mere 2 weeks, both national and grassroots stakeholders cooperated to form 1,255 community kitchens and hand out 250,000 to 280,000 packets of food every day, particularly to marginalised individuals like homeless people and migrant labourers. Although these community kitchens were initiated by the government, it was local networks that made them successful. From identifying vulnerable citizens to cooking and distributing food, actors on the ground included local self-governing bodies, 'Kudumbashree' long-standing the state's women community network, volunteer groups like 'Agrogya sena' (Health army), rural child care-centre teachers, WhatsApp groups, and ordinary neighbours.

A town called Thalassery even saw an unusual form of cooperation when two rival political parties laboured side by side in a hot community kitchen, rolling out mustard seeds on the pan together despite past histories of violent conflict with 200 lives lost.[39] The government mandated that volunteers dole out leftover curry and rice to stray dogs in their neighbourhoods before going home. Similar examples of national and grassroots collaboration were present across healthcare, policing, and education. Although Kerala did not emerge unscathed from the pandemic, health experts identified the state's decades of investing in healthcare, mutual trust between civil society and the government, and high social cohesion as key reasons why it succeeded in tackling the crisis so effectively.[40] These kinds of ecosystemic and organic approaches provide a useful antidote to command-and-control–style governance structures in which populations are nudged, coerced, and misinformed.

5 *Design to distribute*: As shown in Chapter One, property ownership is increasingly out of the reach of many young people coming of age in highly unequal capitalist societies. It would take drastic reform to reduce these toxic effects of modernity. In just such a dramatic move to unsettle long-standing power structures in the 1960s, Kerala abolished landlordism and redistributed land to reduce wealth disparities. The Kerala Land

Reform Amendment Act (1969) put a ceiling on how much land each person could hold and compelled land in excess of this limit to be surrendered to the state.[41] Meanwhile, the Kerala Agricultural Worker's Act (1974) enforced regular working hours, minimum wages, and other measures for the well-being of workers on farms and fields. These reforms are not uncontroversial and would of course seem quite impossible in modern capitalist economies, but they did have the effect of dramatically reducing income inequalities. Today, Kerala has one of the lowest levels of poverty in the country. Redistribution for global equity is not as impossible as it seems.

6 *Create to regenerate*: As Chapter Seven shows, reversing our history of dominating nature necessitates witnessing and responding to her rhythms and flows. Perhaps this means weaving the patterns of the earth into everyday manmade structures. When I landed in Kerala, I was struck by the bright glow of reflective panels all along the runway. 'Did you know we have landed in the world's first fully solar powered airport?' the air hostess smiled. Over 46,000 solar panels line the green field of Kochi International Airport, converting sunlight into energy. The first thing you will see as you drive away is a cheerful sign about the airport receiving the Champions of Earth award in 2018, the United Nations' highest environmental honour. This is one of Kerala's many significant strides in promoting renewable energy sources.

The state government has striven to incentivise households and institutions to reduce carbon emissions and ease the transition towards clean energy. For example, Kerala has become the first state in India to include hydrogen-powered vehicles as part of its zero-emissions mobility policy. This means promoting hydrogen gas as fuel, which produces zero carbon emissions when converted into electricity to power vehicles. In turn, air pollution decreases, and the lack of carbon dioxide and greenhouse gases helps fight climate change. Recognising that state support is vital to genuine change, the government has built the Kerala Hydrogen Economy Mission to help transform the state into a green hydrogen hub. Moreover, the Kerala State Action Plan on Climate Change 2023–2030 aspires to make Kerala a 100% renewable energy-based state by 2040 and net carbon neutral by 2050.[42] This spans diverse rewilding efforts: helping vulnerable communities withstand climate-induced hazards, producing green hydrogen, and tackling climate change across key sectors including agriculture, coastal fisheries, water resources, health, forests, and biodiversity. As previously argued, this is not about returning to a premodern state, but about marrying the best of contemporary scientific innovation to a commitment to environmental sustainability.

A highlight of my travel proved to be sitting on a houseboat dining on prawn curry made with coconut milk, surrounded by water so clear that I could even see *pearlspots* – the state's official fish, little green things with luminous scales – shimmering like emeralds at the very bottom of the river. The state emphasises rainwater harvesting and watershed management to conserve water, recharge groundwater sources, and keep water plentiful for farms and households. As a result, freshwater and marine life thrives. This is a strong example of creating to regenerate.

7 *Be agnostic about growth*: This can be a double-edged sword. Industries have long shown reluctance to move to Kerala, lamenting hyper-vigilant state inspections, slow manufacturing, and highly vocal trade unions that earn Keralite workers a reputation for being 'difficult'.[43] Perhaps the burden of a state being agnostic about growth is that *others* become agnostic about its potential. Economists have noted that potentially lucrative industrial leaders have shied away from Kerala, doubting whether it is dynamic enough for their industrial aspirations. Yet, Kerala has achieved remarkable human development outcomes despite relatively low levels of economic growth. The state's focus on social indicators like education, healthcare, and gender equality has resulted in high literacy rates, low infant mortality rates, and increased life expectancy. Perhaps this spells a different kind of economic success, one favouring citizens' well-being, quality of life, and sustainable development over GDP.

Kerala's doughnut-shaped economy thus challenges the conventional notion that economic growth is the sole measure of progress. The leading economist Amartya Sen,[44] when writing *Development as Freedom*, his magnum opus on progress as a matter of broadening people's abilities to 'be' and to 'do', spotlighted Kerala as an example of going beyond Gross Domestic Product. 'What ultimately matters,' he wrote, 'is the nature of the lives people can or cannot lead.' The United Nations draws on Sen and other social scientists who have called for broader visions of human flourishing in their own annual reporting. This has resulted in the paradox so often debated by development economists: Kerala has achieved human development outcomes comparable to richer developed nations, although its per capita income is a mere fraction of theirs.[45]

Of course, it is not the case that Kerala has translated the principles of degrowth and doughnut economics perfectly. For one, the economy has been judged by regional economists as at risk of 'jobless growth'.[46] Part of the reason for this is that many people from Kerala have chosen to migrate overseas in search of work opportunities. This migration of labourers to other countries, known as international labour migration, has provided an alternative avenue for employment for the labour force in Kerala. As an economist of Kerala puts it, 'international migration emerged as a safety valve' for a highly educated population restless in the face of 'lacklustre' production of material goods.[47] Instead of finding sufficient job opportunities within the local economy, people have opted to work in foreign countries. As a result, the local economy has not experienced the expected job creation and employment growth despite growth in other ways. In addition, sociologists have flagged continued imbalances in gendered and casteist power structures that mar Kerala's aspirations towards perfect equality.[48]

Yet, Kerala's indicators of human flourishing continue to thrive. As of 2023, state and local policies still prioritise social welfare agendas such as infant survival, nutrition, education, and public services. Workers' rights are taken for granted, producing a culture renowned for unusually vocal and assertive workers. I witnessed this spirit in a beauty salon: a young girl tweezing a tourist's eyebrows became the target of his fury. 'Why are you so slow? I'll take my money and leave!' he shouted. Uncowed, she said coolly, 'Then leave.' It is difficult to overestimate the significance of such confidence in India, where, like many other countries around the globe, class hierarchies can drive workers into a state of despairing compliance with the worst mistreatment.

While wandering Kerala's lapis-blue waterways, it sinks in how the complexity of planning for human welfare defies easy conclusions. Some might look at Kerala's slow economic growth and judge that the state desperately needs capitalist reform to bring it into line with 'modernity'. However, an alternative imaginary of peace might view Kerala as an *invitation* – a door left open to alternative ways of living and being. Even as we heed Kerala's struggles, we remain in awe of its record of human development. Kerala has upended the assumption that social justice is a luxury best left to fully developed economies. Instead, it has anchored its vision of success in social justice, achieving a high quality of life for its citizens without waiting to first acquire material prosperity.

Conclusion

This chapter on inclusive education began by focussing on structural and cultural violence in wider society and the ways in which this inhibits peace, justice and inclusion. It briefly reviewed education for peace as a way of tackling structural and cultural violence in schools, but was ambivalent about whether or not peace education, even critical peace education, can bring about necessary change in a system that remains deeply inequitable. The case of Kerala offers here a tantalising glimpse of a poor but inclusive society that has good educational and social outcomes. Like a river flowing upstream, Kerala has accomplished an act of teleological subversion: contrary to the neoliberal assumption that a state must grow its economy before nurturing human welfare, Kerala began investing in the dignity and well-being of its citizens when it was still a poor state. Social justice has been the starting point for the state's understanding of itself, rather than an end goal. Will Kerala continue to resist being steamrolled by neoliberalism? Is it a doomed experiment, or a living laboratory of possibility? The vast expanse of thriving paddy fields convinces us of one thing. From the fragrance of the tea plantations to the swaying of the coconut trees, every thread in this green tapestry whispers: *life*.

Contributor Bio

Nomisha holds a PhD in Education from the University of Cambridge and is currently an assistant professor at the University of Warwick, focussing on child well-being and child safety. Her recent publication on child-safe AI achieved 95 pieces of media coverage, including global outlets such as SkyNews, ABC News, and the *Times of India*. Nomisha has substantial experience in impact-focused research, having won both the University of Cambridge Vice-Chancellor's Award for Social Impact and the University of Cambridge Applied Research Award.

Notes

1 UNESCO (2018). 'Global citizenship education: taking it local.' Paris: UNESCO. Accessed January 2025. https://unesdoc.unesco.org/ark:/48223/pf0000265456.
2 Brighton and Hove City Council (2018). Developing an Attachment Aware Behaviour Regulation Policy: Guidance for Brighton & Hove Schools. Accessed January 2018 https://www.brighton-hove.gov.uk/developing-attachment-aware-behaviour-regulation-policy-0.
3 Cremin, H, & Bevington, T. (2017). *Positive peace in schools: tackling conflict and creating a culture of peace in the classroom.* Routledge.
4 E.g. Galtung, J. (1990) Cultural violence. *Journal of Peace Research 27*(3) 291–305.
5 Galtung, J. (1990). Cultural violence. *Journal of Peace Research 27*(3) 291–305. p.291.
6 Cremin, H., & Guilherme, A. (2015). Violence in schools: perspectives (and hope) from Galtung and Buber. *Educational Philosophy and Theory, 48*(11), 1123–37.
7 The Cambridge Peace and Education Research Group (CPERG) provides a hub for research students and faculty members at the University of Cambridge to exchange ideas and collaborate on projects that explore the relationships between conflict, peace and education, both in the UK and internationally. Its website can be accessed at: https://www.cperg.org/.
8 Positive Peace Education (2025). Nazarbeyev University Graduate School of Education. Accessed January 2025. https://positivepeacekazakhstan.com.
9 Bickmore, K. (2014). 'Peacebuilding Dialogue Pedagogies in Canadian Classrooms. *Curriculum Inquiry 44*(4) 450–68.
10 Higgins, S. & Novelli, M. (2020). Rethinking peace education: A cultural political economy approach. *Comparative Education Review. 64*(1) 1–20.
11 Hajir, B., & Kevin Kester. (2020). Toward a decolonial praxis in critical peace education: postcolonial insights and pedagogic possibilities. *Studies in Philosophy and Education, 39*, 515–32.
12 Bajaj, M. (2015). 'Pedagogies of resistance' and critical peace education praxis. *Journal of Peace Education, 12*(2), 154–66.
13 Gur-Ze'ev, I. (2005). *Critical theory and critical pedagogy today: towards a new critical language in education.* University of Haifa. p.26.
14 Thompson, P., & Zizek, S. (2013). *The privatiisation of hope: Ernst Bloch and the future of utopia.* Duke University Press.
15 Hickel, J. (2020). *Less is more: how degrowth will save the world.* Penguin.
16 Raworth, K. (2017). *Doughnut economics: seven ways to think like a 21st century economist.* Random House.
17 Kannan, K. P. (2023). Revisiting the Kerala 'model' of development: a sixty-year assessment of successes and failures. *The Indian Economic Journal, 71*(1), 120–51.

18 Suchitra, M. (2020). A toxic hotspot on the River Periyar in Kerala: corporate crimes in God's own country. In *Water Conflicts in India* (pp. 143-49). Routledge India.
19 Kaul, N., & Kannangara, N. (2021). The persistence of political power: a communist 'party village' in Kerala and the paradox of egalitarian hierarchies. *International Journal of Politics, Culture, and Society*, 1–31.
20 Kapur, A. (1998). Poor but prosperous. *The Atlantic Monthly*, *282*(3), 40–45. p.40.
21 Office of the Registrar General & Census Commissioner, India (2022). *Sample Registration System – Abridged Life Tables 2016–2020*. New Delhi: Government of India. Accessed January 2025. https://censusindia.gov.in/nada/index.php/catalog/44377.
22 Kapur, A. (1998). Poor but prosperous. *The Atlantic Monthly*, *282*(3), 40–45. p.41.
23 UNICEF (2021). India Case Study: Situation Analysis on the Effects of and Responses to COVID-19 on the Education Sector in Asia. UNICEF. Accessed January 2025. https://www.unicef.org/rosa/media/16511/file/india%20case%20study.pdf.
24 Government of India Ministry of Health and Family Welfare (2021) *National Family Health Survey (NFHS-5) 2019–2021*. Accessed January 2025 https://dhsprogram.com/pubs/pdf/FR375/FR375.pdf.
25 Office of the Registrar General & Census Commissioner, India (2022). *Sample Registration System – Abridged Life Tables 2016–2020*. New Delhi: Government of India. Accessed January 2025. https://censusindia.gov.in/nada/index.php/catalog/44377.
26 While this book uses the term 'lower- and middle-income countries', we use the term 'developing countries' in this instance to flag the power dynamic between neoliberal institutions based in the Global North (consisting of Western industrialised higher-income nations) and countries such as India which were under heavy pressure to follow their economic approaches in this time period.
27 Parayil, G. (2000). *Kerala: The development experience: reflections on sustainability and replicability*. Zed Books. p.1.
28 Kannan, K. P. (2023). Revisiting the Kerala 'model' of development: a sixty-year assessment of successes and failures. *The Indian Economic Journal*, *71*(1), 120–51.
29 Sen, A. (2015). Universal healthcare: the affordable dream. *The Guardian*. Accessed January 2025. https://www.theguardian.com/society/2015/jan/06/-sp-universal-healthcare-the-affordable-dream-amar.
30 Rajagopal, M. R. (2022). *Walk with the weary: lessons in humanity in health care*. Notion Press.
31 Ramachandran, A., Enserink, B., & Balchand, A. N. (2005). Coastal regulation zone rules in coastal panchayats (villages) of Kerala, India vis-à-vis socio-economic impacts from the recently introduced peoples' participatory program for local self-governance and sustainable development. *Ocean & coastal management*, *48*(7–8), 632–53. p.650.
32 Athikalam, P. T., & Karur Vaideeswaran, A. (2022). Vegetation bioshield for coastal protection in South Asia: status and way forward. *Journal of Coastal Conservation*, *26*(1), 3.
33 Nilayangode, P., Laladhas, K. P., et al. (2017). Grassroots initiatives for environmental sustainability. In K.P. Laladhas, Preetha Nilayangode (Eds) *Biodiversity for sustainable development*. p.185–92. Springer International Publishing.
34 Devika, J. (2016). The 'Kudumbashree Woman' and the Kerala model woman: women and politics in contemporary Kerala. *Indian Journal of Gender Studies*, *23*(3), 393–414.
35 Cremin, H. (2018). An autoethnography of a peace educator: deepening reflections on research, practice, and the field. *Emotion, Space and Society*, *28*, 1–8. p.1.

36 Kuruvilla, B. (2019). How Kerala's cooperative model is making strides despite odds. *Newsclick*. Accessed January 2025. https://www.newsclick.in/Kerala-Cooperative-Model-Making-Strides-Despite-Odds.
37 Rajagopal, M. R. (2022). *Walk with the weary: lessons in humanity in health care*. Notion Press.
38 Elias, A. A. (2021). Kerala's innovations and flexibility for Covid-19 recovery: storytelling using systems thinking. *Global Journal of Flexible Systems Management*, *22*(Suppl 1), 33–43.
39 Bechu, S. (2020). Army of volunteers: how a Kerala community kitchen feeds the needy amid COVID-19 lockdown. *The New Indian Express*. Accessed January 25. https://www.newindianexpress.com/states/kerala/2020/mar/31/army-of-volunteers-how-a-kerala-community-kitchen-feeds-the-needy-amid-covid-19-lockdown-2123912.html.
40 Chathukulam, J., & Tharamangalam, J. (2021). The Kerala model in the time of COVID19: Rethinking state, society and democracy. *World development*, *137*, 105207. Accessed January 2025 https://www.sciencedirect.com/science/article/pii/S0305750X2030334X.
41 Mannathukkaren, N. (2011) Redistribution and recognition: land reforms in Kerala and the limits of culturalism, *The Journal of Peasant Studies*, 38(2), 379–411.
42 Government of Kerala (2022). Kerala State Action Plan on Climate Change 2.0 (2023–2030), Directorate of Environment and Climate Change, Department of Environment, Government of Kerala. Accessed January 2025. https://climatechange.envt.kerala.gov.in/kerala-state-action-plan-on-climate-change-2023-2030/.
43 Kannan, K. P. (2023). Revisiting the Kerala 'model' of development: a sixty-year assessment of successes and failures. *The Indian Economic Journal*, *71*(1), 120–151.
44 Sen, A. (1999). *Development as freedom*. Knopf. p.1.
45 Parayil, G. (2000). *Kerala: the development experience: reflections on sustainability and replicability*. Zed Books.
46 Kannan, K. P. (2023). Revisiting the kerala 'model' of development: a sixty-year assessment of successes and failures. *The Indian Economic Journal*, *71*(1), 120–151. p.132.
47 Kannan, K. P. (2023). Revisiting the kerala 'model' of development: a sixty-year assessment of successes and failures. *The Indian Economic Journal*, *71*(1), 120–151. p.135.
48 Devika, J. (2016). The 'Kudumbashree Woman' and the Kerala model woman: women and politics in contemporary Kerala. *Indian Journal of Gender Studies*, *23*(3), 393–414; Kaul, N., & Kannangara, N. (2021). The persistence of political power: a communist 'party village' in Kerala and the paradox of egalitarian hierarchies. *International Journal of Politics, Culture, and Society*, 1–31.

Conclusion

As I turn to write the conclusion of this book it is January 2025. I am relieved, but also sad, to come to the end of this particular journey. It has been a labour of love that started five years ago, and it has involved even more re-draftings and updatings than usual. This work feels special for several reasons. It's the first time that I have had the courage to include my poems in my academic book-writing. It is also significant for me that so many of my colleagues and students have contributed and shared their arts-based approaches. This feels like a communal enterprise. Writing about rewilding is a departure from my specialism of peace education, although of course they are connected. It feels important to have finally written about my deep connection with Nature, and the need to educate future generations to protect it.

I think that the reason for the many re-draftings (apart from my perfectionism) is that this book feels both important and always a work in progress. Rewilding is a process, not an outcome. It will never be complete. I offer the book to you in the same spirit as a summary of my reflections and analysis at a particular moment in time. Several colleagues have recommended that I read Nora Bateson's book *Combining*,[1] for example, and it would have been perfect for inclusion if I were starting the book from now. This makes concluding difficult.

Because of this, I have decided to conclude with a series of letters to my readers which follow next. The letters aim to encourage a dialogic relationship with you, my reader, despite the restrictions of written prose. What will you do next with what you have seen in these pages? In what ways do you agree or disagree with what I have written? The letters are offered, not as a blueprint for change, but as a series of creative provocations.

However it is done, rewilding and educating for a rewilded future are two of the most important existential challenges that we face. The year 2024 was the warmest on record, according to the World Meteorological Organisation,[2] and we may have surpassed the lower limit of the Paris Agreement Long Term Temperature goal. Greenhouse gases reached record levels in 2023 and continued to rise in 2024. Antarctic and Arctic sea ice in 2024 were well below average. Ocean heat content and sea level continue to rise. In 2023, the ocean absorbed around 3.1 million TWh of heat, equal to approximately 18 times the world's total energy consumption. Glaciers around the world lost an estimated water equivalent of about five times the amount of water in the Dead Sea.

The catastrophic consequences of climate change are not a thing of the future – they are with us now. Food insecurity, migration and displacement are already being faced by populations around the world. The reduced cereal harvest across the globe in 2024 is the result of a widespread El Niño–linked drought that caused crop failures, steep declines in yields and reductions in harvested areas. Nigeria, Sudan, Myanmar, Ethiopia, Zimbabwe, Malawi, Chad and Yemen all had at least one million more people facing high levels of acute food insecurity in 2024 than in 2023. Global hunger levels have risen sharply from 2019 to 2021 and have been persistently high since. Extreme weather events in 2024, including flooding, droughts, cyclones, typhoons, and hurricanes have led to new, onward and protracted displacement of significant numbers of people in diverse places across the globe. Whether it was floods in Chad, Nigeria, Europe, Brazil, Afghanistan, Kenya and Tanzania; wildfires in Canada, Western USA, Australia and Chile; or hurricanes and typhoons in Vietnam, the Caribbean and China, the destruction of homes, critical infrastructure, forests, farmland and biodiversity loss continues to undermine global security.

Can we reverse this? Sometimes it feels too much to bear – too big to tackle. And yet we must. If we can begin with our precious duty to educate the next generation, perhaps this is as good a starting point as any. My twin grandchildren are currently 9 months old. Will you join me in ensuring a viable future for them, and for all of the children of the world?

Notes

1 Bateson, N. (2023). *Combining*. Triarchy Press.
2 World Meteorological Organisation (2004). *State of the Climate 2024: Update for COP29*. Accessed January 2025. https://library.wmo.int/viewer/69075/download?file=State-Climate-2024-Update-COP29_en.pdf&type=pdf&navigator=1.

Rewilding education: Letters to my readers

This part of the book puts the themes and ideas discussed throughout into conversation with you, its readers. Here, I speak directly to you, encouraging you to engage in reflection on your own educational experiences and on possibilities for the education of young people in the future. Whether you are a teacher, policymaker, NGO worker, parent or young person, you will be invited to reflect on the implications of the book for your own life and hopes for education.

These letters suggest how teachers can reclaim personal and professional integrity and become 'wild' in the sense that they are freed from the modernist structures that regulate and constrain their practice. The letters draw on the ideas in this book to reclaim the heart and soul of what it means to be a teacher. Without romanticising teachers, or the teaching profession, they go beyond technicist and performative considerations to talk about ideas for change – asking the kinds of questions that might begin the rewilding journey and bring about an education worthy of its name.

Letter to an education policymaker

Dear policymaker,

You hold the educational futures of so many young people in your hands. What will you do with this precious task? No doubt you arrived where you are because you care. You want an inclusive, equitable and sustainable education for all. The question is, what kind of system might enable wild education? Would it be possible to rewild standard state education systems? Clearly, for this to happen significant change would be necessary at all levels, including curriculum, pedagogy, learning relationships, teacher education, leadership, policy and overall infrastructure for education.

From the point of view of the curriculum, the reality of the climate emergency needs to be taught alongside a recognition of speciesism and its consequences. This can be done in ways that bring about hope and engagement, as well as critical awareness. Curricula throughout the world that focus on preparing young people as economic citizens need to take a wider view and prepare them for human flourishing, social justice and sustainability. That might involve drawing upon wisdom traditions and what they can teach us about living in harmony with nature and each other. It might also involve a greater emphasis on art, music, dance, sport and movement, as well as science that is deeply contextualised, applied and practical. Learners need to feel curious and confident in all subjects, and to feel able to have a go at tackling real-world problems at local and global levels. This includes the ability to speak other languages (or use translation AI expertly) and relate to other cultures.

Rewilded pedagogy is learner-oriented, embodied, relational, holistic, contextualised and open-ended. It takes account of a diversity of learning preferences and paces. It enables young people to find teachers and learning spaces that inspire and engage them. This might involve introspection and 'hanging out,' on the one hand, or activism and real-world projects on the other. Relationships with teachers are key. Rewilded teachers feel freed up to engage meaningfully with students. It feels normal for them to experience joy and love in all its infinite variety. How can you enable this?

Rewilded teachers need to feel that they are engaged as public intellectuals and lifelong learners, and not simply as technicians. They need to feel in control of their own teaching spaces. Planning for learning should feel creative and experimental, teaching should feel exciting and engaging, and evaluation should feel honest and meaningful. Teacher education, both initial and continuing, needs to be seen as important. Teachers need to feel that colleagues and mentors are interested in them throughout their career, and support should not fall away after the initial stages of teacher education. It goes without saying that the same applies to education leaders. They should feel free to work with teachers, students, and local and global communities in ways that are fit for purpose and enabling. They should also enjoy continuing education opportunities, and feel able to engage in research, reflection and development.

But is this enough? So far, I have been using language that refers to modern systems of schooling (albeit highly altered), but I now want to move on to discuss what is possible through revolution and not just through evolution.

It must be said that – overall – I feel that schools are pretty awful places, and that, as will be obvious from my critique in Part One, they may be beyond redemption, despite decades of reforms (I hope I am wrong). This means that some of your efforts as a policymaker must be directed towards more long-term radical change – reimagining education for a time when transformation becomes either possible or unavoidable.

As I have already shared with you in this book, I believe that the existential threats that we face as humans are immense, multifaceted and immanent. To continue business as usual is to perpetuate significant harm, and to take enormous risks with likely cataclysmic consequences. This is not how we tend to think about business as usual. Keeping things as they are is usually presented as the safer option. We say things like, 'let's wait and see,' and 'better the devil you know....' The status quo, however uncomfortable, often feels preferable to change, because change takes us into unchartered territory. It also feels preferable because change normally involves being held to account in ways that do not apply to maintaining business as usual. This is particularly true for education. Perhaps change in education is hard because schooling takes us back to our own childhood, and it involves children. This makes us feel both vulnerable and protective. This is hard territory for education policymakers to occupy.

Nevertheless, radical change is necessary if we are to avoid catastrophe. So what might it look like? It would involve no less than a paradigm shift. As I argued in 2018 with reference to transrationality,[1] the rewilded paradigm of education implies a discontinuation of schooling and higher education as they are currently conceived. They could be replaced by voluntary, flexible, lifelong learning for all from the end of the primary years. This would be centred around learning 'hubs' that would make a range of courses available to learners throughout the life course, with primary education functioning to prepare young people to be active, confident, informed and creative choosers. Learning would also take place in a wide range of home and community learning settings, including workplaces, art galleries, charities, libraries, science laboratories, outdoors and online. Under the rewilded paradigm, attainment would be recognised through smart assessment, portfolio accreditation, research findings, business start-ups, artwork, performances and civic participation, to name a few examples. Examined coursework or standardised assessment would only be used where it was felt necessary. World-class higher education would be available for those who wish to access it.

This new paradigm implies greater involvement from a wider range of adults in the education of young people, with teachers retaining a unique role. Each young person could have access to a weekly meeting with a teacher to support their choices and plan their progress. Whilst some same-age and peer learning would no doubt continue, new actors such as town-planners, curators, web designers, scientists and architects could be involved in creating learning opportunities, with a range of adults providing apprenticeships and individualised learning programs for young people in authentic settings. Teachers, lecturers and other adults would spend a significant amount of time engaged in their own learning and development. This might involve further study or research or continuing to develop the language / music / sport / historical / scientific / mathematical (etc.) knowledge and skills of their subject specialism. This kind of education involves everyone, and takes risk, humility, solidarity and transformation as its foundations. It remains open-ended and subject to adaptation to local circumstances, as well as holding on to inclusive and justice-oriented goals.

Since I first started to think about this, generative AI has grown, and we have had the experience of the pandemic with many schools throughout the world being closed for months at a time. Both have radically altered the education landscape and what it means to teach and learn outside of school buildings. Much of what happened educationally during the pandemic exacerbated inequality and was poorly conceived and executed – but some of it was game changing. People who could (such as musicians and scientists) stepped up from their living rooms to provide online material that was truly extraordinary. We are already learning what might be possible through massive open online courses (MOOCs), especially those provided freely by some of the best universities in the world. Although face-to-face contact and embodied and contextualised experiences are at the heart of rewilding education, there is certainly a place for the internet to open up hitherto unimaginable opportunities for the children of the world.

The question that presents itself, however, is whether we trust young people, and the adults who support them, to create unique education pathways through self-organising eco-systems. Can learners make responsible choices?

Large numbers of young people already do. Some young people enjoy the freedom to choose their own curriculum and ways of learning, but they tend to be at the top and the bottom of the socio-economic spectrum. They have either dropped out for some reason, or else their parents can afford for them to be educated at home, or privately in schools with an alternative ethos. These learner-centred methods result in strong rates of satisfaction and good education outcomes.

Could these benefits be mainstreamed? Could we work towards a system that provides student-centred education that foregrounds choice, freedom, support, and responsibility? There would of course be drawbacks. As we said in 2018:[2]

> Perhaps some young people would make mistakes, waste time and come out of the system ill-prepared for adult life – but probably far fewer than is currently the case.... The least that could be achieved is that education systems that favour global elites would have their fig-leaf of respectability lifted, and the majority who will never win the educational credentialing game would simply stop playing. Far more likely is that young people would engage with learning because they see the intrinsic benefits of doing so, because they are engaged, and because they see a future for themselves beyond the acquisition of grades.... Some young people might initially fall short of their goals: but what really matters is that doors would never be closed; and it would always be possible to return to learning and to start again. Education would be reclaimed as a life-long process.

Is this wishful thinking? Could rewilded education be the norm? Would it be so difficult to join up the Left and the Right of politics? Could we work towards a system that provides student-centred education within local and global marketplaces that foreground choice, freedom, support and responsibility?

I look forward to your response.

Yours
Hilary

Letter to a teacher

Dear Teacher,

First of all, congratulations on choosing the best profession in the world! Despite my critique of cultures of schooling, I have huge respect for what you do, and I care about you as a teacher in the system right now. I was a teacher once, and I have been involved in initial and continuous teacher education over several decades. Some of what I am suggesting here is quite radical, but I rely on you to know which parts of rewilding education can best be integrated into your practice now and in the future.

From the point of view of valuing nature, I would want you to be able to teach in beautiful, natural spaces. Not all teaching can or should take place out of doors, but teaching needs to enable a felt connection with wild nature (including in urban spaces). In this way, nature can be 'in conversation' with what takes place in learning spaces, and you can work with the rhythms and cycles of nature in ways that promote your well-being, as well as that of the young people in your care.

Your body as a teacher needs to be taken seriously, with time for nourishment, rest, movement and toilet breaks built into the day. There should be due concern for your work-life balance and need for a meaningful family life. In radically rewilded education systems you would also have time for further study (including researching your own practice) as well as opportunities to continue the pursuit of your subject specialisms. Your achievements and enthusiasm for your subject should inspire young people, and they can learn from you how to maintain balance and well-being. If you can be the teacher you entered the profession to become, a deep appreciation for beauty, brilliance, expertise, talent, genius, tenacity and flair could replace the fetishisation of exam results.

In rewilded education, you would be able to develop practical project-based teaching, learning alongside your students and tackling real-world problems. From there you could extrapolate further questions about theory, sustainability, history, art, culture and scientific research. You and your students would not be afraid to make and learn from mistakes, and you would draw on a range of expertise from people who might want to help with particular projects. No enthusiastic learner would be considered too young or too ill-informed to participate.

Sometimes learners might work directly on other people's business, community or arts / sport-based projects with the support of a teacher. Here your role would be to encourage high quality mentoring and to work with mentors to accredit skills and knowledge as they emerge, where needed. The basic impetus behind project-based teaching is that it is important to have a go – to make changes and tackle problems in ways that contribute to well-being and human and non-human thriving. This cannot be left to other people or to 'experts' alone. Feelings of inadequacy and powerlessness will become increasingly dangerous as the climate emergency, economic downturns and geopolitics throw up challenges that will affect people in the affluent global North, as well as in the global South.

In radically rewilded education systems you would have variety in your working life. This would require high levels of skill across a range of areas. You might be coaching a young person to make choices about future study at the start of the day, giving a lecture to 200 people before lunch, and leading project-based learning in a forest with a group of 25 learners aged between 12 and 75 in the afternoon. You would also visit (sometimes online) workplaces, science laboratories, libraries, museums, residential homes for the elderly, sports facilities, and so on to support mentoring and accreditation of individuals and groups, as well as taking time out for your own personal and professional development. Your role as a facilitator of young people's education would remain unique in a wider ecosystem where adults from various local and global communities would step up to support learning of all kinds.

If you are a primary teacher, you might spend more of your time in classrooms that look a bit like those that we are familiar with, but mixed-age groups, project-based learning and individualised learning would result in greater diversity of opportunities, even in primary schools, than is currently the case. Your aim would be to prepare young people as curious, confident, healthy, self-motivated learners who are literate and numerate, and understand the basics of what a wider education might offer them. Topics for lessons might include, for example: silence; food; global justice; waves; love; learning; time; evolution; money; health; trees; utopia; truth; bodies; measurement; community; stars; paint, and so on. Topics could be explored in cross-curricular ways, with stars and waves, for example, stimulating activities grounded in science, culture and the arts. Each lesson might begin with a stimulus (a text, a video, a visit, a website, a game ...) which would be followed by research and development activities and a synthesis of what has been learned through the creation of an artefact / text / presentation. Teaching like this would slow things down and enable time for reflection and connections to be made.

All of this would lead to different kinds of relationships between teachers and learners. This is an alternative 'aesthetic' of being a teacher. Is this what you would want for your life as a teacher? If so, how might you begin to make the changes that you want?

I wish you all the very best for your work.

Yours
Hilary

Letter to a parent

Dear Parent,

Your job is one of the most important, delightful and challenging in the world. Tell me about it! (I have two grown-up children and two baby grandchildren). It's a job that veers between boredom, ecstasy, fury, delight, shame, irritation, pride ... but, let's face it, a lot of the time – drudgery. It is hard work, and it is relentless. And yet most parents would sacrifice anything for their child to do well. Often that is understood as them doing better than other people's children ;-0. We want our child to be happy, but the real journey starts when we join them in discovering who they are. Happiness is about the power of now, and yet we often neglect the now in order to focus on the 'not yet'. The idea that pain now means gains later runs deep. The problem is that later never comes, and the habits of constantly deferring happiness become settled.

In order for our child to be happy we give up our time to drive them wherever we want them to go. We host their friends, we invest in understanding and correcting them when they go wrong, we create opportunities for them to learn and grow and achieve. If we are honest though, many of our decisions are framed by our desire to be held in high esteem by our peer group of other parents, friends, and our own parents and siblings. We have an idea of the kind of parent we should be, and we do our best to live up to that. We feel awful when we think that we have fallen short. Sometimes that means that we fail to hear what our children actually want. In my experience, parenting is a long journey of learning to inspire and motivate, but more importantly to listen, accept, accommodate and be transformed.

The problem with many schools is that most are not so interested in who our children actually are. They are set up to ensure that young people become who society / the state need them to be. This leads to the kinds of monocultures, thin communities and lost opportunities discussed in this book. Most of us have a nostalgic view of our time in school (the best days of our lives?) and we want to believe that we were well served and that our own children can benefit from the certainties that we grew up with. We tend to believe (despite evidence to the contrary) that the benefits that we have always enjoyed will continue to be available, and that the challenges that we have faced cannot be so bad because we are still here. This is not what is needed under current social, political and environmental conditions, however. The opposite is the case. The consequences of business as usual are more dangerous than the consequences of radical change. As parents we need to wake up and think about how we can prepare our child for a future that is utterly unknowable and that presents all kinds of existential threats. We can't rely on schools to do this.

How then will you make the most of this precious time with your child, despite the many challenges? How will you join your child on the journey of self-discovery, and how will you support them to achieve the kind of settled happiness and rewilding mindset that will be with them for life, regardless of what the future holds?

Yours in awe and respect for all that you do

Hilary

Letter to a young person

Dear friend,

What do you think about school? School is supposed to be a place where your mind can grow. Many schools don't do this very well. It is quite common for schools to try to make young people fit into school, rather than making schools fit for young people.

You may be lucky enough to go to a good school that helps your mind to grow and that helps your body, heart and soul to grow also, but you are quite unusual if so. Schools that are able to achieve this are the most amazing places. They are more holy than churches, more inspiring than museums! Treasure your school and your teachers if you go to a school like this.

Most schools are pretty awful places most of the time. Who ever thought that it was a good idea to put people of the same age in the same place at the same time to do the same things? Where else do we do that? Where else do we require people by law to go? The only other place is prison. Some schools can feel like an old-fashioned prison. You get yelled at. You are made to line up, to shut up and to wear a uniform. It is as if your body does not belong to you. You have your freedom taken away. Bells control your time. You can't just say, "I know that the bell has just gone, but I want to go for a short walk to figure out this science experiment" or, "I want to explore this period of history by making up a play about it" or, "I already know most of what you have just told me, and I want to find out about different things".

Many adults act as if children and young people were different from everyone else, and do not deserve the same kinds of respect and freedom. When you are in school you feel separate from everyone. You can even forget that a world outside exists. In fact a school is part of everything that surrounds it. It is like a pile of leaves that have been swept up together for the time being. Leaves can be blown away and the pile will disappear if someone stops sweeping.

A school is a place of learning, but learning takes place all of the time and everywhere. You learn when you look at a building, when you give to charity, when you visit a hospital. You can learn about the things that teachers want you to learn on the Internet, in a museum, in a library, in the sports centre, at the seaside, in a youth club. There are places where you would not normally go (because you are at school) that could teach you so much better. You could learn about science in a real laboratory, you could learn about art in an artist's studio, you could learn maths in a shop or university, you could learn about caring for people in a hospital. People who already work in science laboratories, or studios or shops or hospitals, say that school is really bad at teaching young people what they need for work. They are probably right.

Some people love knowledge for its own sake. They want to devote their lives to studying and researching and writing. That is a wonderful thing to do, but it is not for everyone. Schools should not be places where the only people who seem to matter are people who think like that. Schools have become places where people think about knowledge in the same way that they think about money. You are taught to save up and cash in your knowledge. Exams and testing have become more important than knowledge itself. Schools are teaching you to love certificates more than learning. Exams should be collected along the way, they should not be the reason you do things. Exam results are used to keep people out of many jobs. We tell young people that they need to do well in exams to keep doors open for them in the future. This often makes them act in ways that are not very balanced and healthy. It also makes them behave as if everyone else were a competitor, like in a game with only a few winners.

If you are reading this and thinking – this is exactly what I think, I am going to stop working and being polite to my teachers – then I have not done my job very well. You still need to get an education and be polite to your teachers. For better or worse, schools are the main places where young people receive their education. It happens like this across the planet. Everyone wants to get a good education for themselves and their children, especially those who can't afford to go to school. You can't just opt out. The difference is that you can perhaps start to think about the whole thing as a bit of a game. You may have to ignore some things and not mind too much about others. But if you can do this, you can learn a lot.

If you have a good attitude towards learning, you can achieve anything you like. You are in control of your own life, and you are guided by your own curiosity, strengths and desire to make progress. You can become the best person you can be. You can think about the ways in which only you can live your life. That might sound a bit odd, but there is a deeper meaning inside it. You are unique. You have a face and a body that might look like your mum or your dad or a grandparent, but it is yours. You have a personality that changes in different situations but is essentially yours too. You may be quite shy, or quite friendly. You may find maths really easy, or you may be better at languages. You may be a calm person, or someone who gets quite anxious. These are the things that make you who you are. Some of these things come from your genes (what you get from your mum and dad); some of them come from the way that you are brought up. Some things will stay with you for life; others will change over time. The point is that no one else on the planet is just like you, not even a twin.

You have talents and abilities that everyone else needs. You need them too, in order to make your way in the world. It may take some time for you to find them, but that is your life-long task. Once you find your thing (and there may be more than one) the thing that makes you light up, that you can do effortlessly, you should treasure it. That is your gift. Don't be put off if your gift is unusual, or impractical, or not what you wanted it to be. Work on it, shape it, celebrate it. Don't let other people change your mind. There may be things that you can't do if you are going to realise your gift, but that is what the word dedication means. You can dedicate your life to whatever it is that only you can do, but this also involves connecting with other people. It is important not to act out of ego. You are acting out of ego when you think that you are better than someone else because you are clever, or when you cheat, or let someone down, or waste people's time, or speak disrespectfully. No one should make you feel bad, and you should not make anyone else feel bad either. That is easy to say, but sometimes harder to do than you might think.

If you treat people with respect and generally try to do well at school, you can hold your head up high. Wherever you are, and however you learn, I wish you all the very best for your education. Remember, the aim is not to know all the answers, it is to keep getting better at asking questions.

Good luck with your studies!

Love
Hilary

Notes

1 Cremin, H. & Archer, D.T. (2018) Transrational Education: Exploring possibilities for learning about peace, harmony, justice and truth in the twenty first century. In J. Echavarría Alvarez, D. Ingruber & N. Koppensteiner (Eds.) *Transrational Resonances: Echoes to the Many Peaces*: Palgrave Macmillan.
2 Cremin, H. & Archer, D.T. (2018) Transrational Education: Exploring possibilities for learning about peace, harmony, justice and truth in the twenty-first century. In J. Echavarría Alvarez, D. Ingruber & N. Koppensteiner (Eds.) *Transrational Resonances: Echoes to the Many Peaces*, Houndsmill: Palgrave Macmillan. p.299–300.

Index

Pages followed by "n" refer to notes.

activism: eco 123; everyday 157
Albrecht, G. 31
Apple, M. 18
arts-based mindset 131
attainment gap 56, 61–63

Bajaj, M. 151
Barefoot College International 129–130
Bateson, G. 111–112
Bauman, Z. 19
behavioural psychology 26, 46–47, 49
Bevington, T. 149
biotechnology 21; see also Harari, Y. N.
Blake, W. 80
Blythe, C. 72–74, 129, 133
Bonnet, M. 37, 93, 107–108
Borrett, A. 18
British Medical Journal 40
Brown, M. 123
Buber, M. 87–88
Buddhism 92; interconnection 95–96; learning from nature 123
Burnard, P. 132
Burton, S. 41
Buttarazzi, G. 86

capitalism: definition 17; problems with modern capitalism 17–18; see also post-capitalism
Center for Disease Control and Protection 43
Child Poverty Action Group 56
Chimp Management Mind Model 87
Chodron, P. 92
circle pedagogy 123–124
climate emergency 12, 165–166; consequences on people 122–123; roots 33–37

Cohen, A. 92–93
cognitive bias 25–26
compassion 89, 91
conflict: global trade 33–35
COVID-19 pandemic 19, 47–52
creativity 132–133
Cremin, H. 130, 152, 155, 157
critical peace education 151–152
curriculum: failure of 39–40, 42, 61–62; physical education (PE) 40

Dalai Lama 89, 96
Dass, R. 92
Davis, J. 124, 128
de Sousa, S. 23
deep ecology 110; see also shallow ecology
degrowth 19, 152; see also Hickel, J.
dehumanisation 22
direct violence 149–150
discipline 62–63
doughnut economics 152; see also Raworth, K.
Duncan, R. 91, 111

early years education *see* primary education
eco-anxiety 123, 133
eco-psychotherapy 111–112; see also Duncan, R.
education: contributor to unsustainable mindset 36–37; deficit models 44; failed modernist project 16; grand narrative of modernity 13–14; perpetuator of capitalism 18–19; reproducing and magnifying violence 64–65; reproducing inequality 57, 65–66

educational psychology: assertive discipline 46–47; behavioural psychology 46; influencing behaviour 47
Ehrenzeller, C. 108, 110, 113, 115
Elias, A. 158
embodied cognition 81–82
empirical truth 22–23; *see also* post-truth
empowering young people 123–124; *see also* peer mediation
empowering teachers 124; pastoral systems 125–128; peace circles 128–129
environmental degradation 30–31, 35
Erignfeld, S. 84
Eurocentric thought: dominance 23, 25, 80, 122
European Enlightenment 11–12
exclusion in schools 63–64
exposure to wild 111

failure of: curriculum 39–40; education system 36–37, 41–42; inclusive schooling 45–46; peace education 65; reforms 61–66
Foucault, M. 14–15
fractious twins 13–14, 17, 20, 22, 26; *see also* capitalism; empirical truth; humanism; modernity; post-capitalism; postmodernity; post-truth; posthumanism
Freire, P. 95, 131

Galtung, J. 149–150
Gandhi 129
Gee, H. 75–76
global North 20, 22–23, 45
global trade 33–34
Godin, S. 124, 129
Gove, M. 61–63
grand narratives 13
Guilherme, A. 150
Gur-Ze'ev, I. 151

Hajir, B. 151
Harari, Y. N. 20
Harber, C. 65
healing: social 131
health in schools: physical 39–41; psychological 41–43
Hickel, J. 152–155
Higgins, S. 151

holism 95–96
holistic schools in India 96, 113–114; caring and connected community 100; collective responsibility 99–100; connecting with nature 102; sacred silence 97; space for flourishing 101; transdisciplinary teaching 97–99
hooks, B. 83–84, 90, 140
hope 133; *see also* posthumanism
human impact on: night 137–139; *see also* Macfarlane, R.; sea 136–137; woodland 134–135
humanism 20

imagination 131–132
inclusion 45, 148
indigenous: genocide of people 30–31; knowledge 103
indirect violence 149–151, 161–162
industrial mindset 12–13, 33–34
inequality: complex intersectional 18; gender 18, 56; income 56
inequality in schools 55–57; selective admission 15–16; structural inequality 58
inner peace 91, 150
international Monetary Fund (IMF) 56

Jepson, P. 72–74, 129, 133

Kahneman, D. 86
Kerala 152, 154, 161
Kerala's doughnut economy: being agnostic about growth 160; change the goal 155–156; see the big picture 156; design to distribute 158–159; navigating systems 157–158; nurture humans 157; regeneration 159–160
Kester, K. 42, 151
Klaus, P. 88
Knowledge is Power Program (KIPP) 62–63
Kumar, S. 33–35, 91, 110
Kurian, N. 152, 162

Lave, J. 130
learning: contextualised 36; new paradigm 169–170; out of doors 110–111, 120; planning for 168
Lederach, J.P. 131–132
Lees, H. 93
leg-up politics 58

letters: to a parent 173–174; to policymaker 167–171; to a teacher 171–173; to a young person 174–176
LMIC *see* low-and middle-income countries (LMICs)
Loughrey, M. 132
love 88–91
low-and middle-income countries (LMICs): international schools in 45; labour in 22; social mobility in 57; terminology of 28n27; Loy, D. 92, 123
Lyotard, J.-F. 13

Macdonald, E. 93–95
MacFarlane, R. 30, 71–72, 133–134, 136–137
Macy, J. 123
Marxism 13
Mbembe, A. 20
McGilchrist, I. 86–87, 112
McInnerney, W. 132, 139
McIntyre, L. 25
mental health: improving 123, 129; poor 39, 43–44
metaphysics of mastery 36, 107–108; *see also* Bonnet, M.
Midgeley, M. 13
Millennium Cohort Study 41
Miller, J. 88, 90
mindfulness 86
mindful teaching program 93–95
modern child 30
modernist movement 12
modernity: defining 11–12; problems with 13; toxic effects of 12–13, 19; *see also* postmodernity
Montessori, M. 120
Montessori forest school 115, 119–120
moral imagination 131; *see also* Lederach, J.P.
Morris, J. 30
myths: enlightenment 11–12; social mobility and meritocracy 18, 55–61

NASUWT 43
National Health Service (UK) 40
nature 108; relationship with 29–30, 34–35, 78; as teacher 30, 72, 107–112
nature-based education 111–112
negative peace 149; *see also* positive peace
neuroscience 86–87

new economic paradigm 153; *see also* Kerala's doughnut economy
Nixon, R. 33, 35
non-anthropocentric perspective 107, 114
Novelli, M. 151
Nudge theory 47

obesity 39–40
Ofsted 90, 127
Osgood, J. 95

parent *see* letters: to a parent
passive rewilding *see* rewilding: types
Patel, J. 96, 103–104, 108, 110, 113
PE *see* physical education
peacebuilding 150
peacekeeping 149–151
peacemaking 150
pedagogy of vulnerability 42
peer mediation 123; *see also* empowering young people
Peters, S. 87
physical education 40
Piaget, J. 113, 121n18
Pleistocene rewilding *see* rewilding: types
Plotkin, B. 113
poetry 23, 25, 32, 131–133, 140–141, 145, 147n33
policymaker 14, 19, 47; *see also* letters: to policymaker
population decline 75–76
positive peace 149–151; *see also* negative peace
post-capitalism 19–20; *see also* capitalism
posthumanism: consequences of technological advancement 20–22; *see also* humanism; in contrast to humanism 20
postmodernity: de-centring of the subject 14–15; *see also* modernity; discourses of power 14–16
post-truth 25–26; *see also* empirical truth
practical rewilding *see* rewilding: types
Pranis, K. 124
primary education 112, 169
Pring, R. 19
Programme for International Student Assessment (PISA) 16, 27n10

Radhakrishnan, S. 95
Raworth, K. 152–155
reimagining masculinities 139–141

Index

rewilding: agriculture 73; definition 72; future of 75; root 71; systems thinking rather than conservation 73–74; types 72–73
rewilding child development 112–113
rewilding education 3, 49, 103, 129, 151
rewilded education foundation 80–81, 95–96
rewilding the body: body 81; embodied cognition 81–82; integration of body and mind 84; socio-cultural understandings and body 83
rewilding the mind: the embodied brain 85; mindfulness 85–86; neuroscience 86–87
rewilding the heart: compassion 89; constraints 89–91; love 88–89; relationship with self and others 87–88
rewilding the soul: concept 91; constraints 95; transformative spaces 93–94; ways soul gets lost 92
Rishi Valley School 113–114
Robinson, K. 14
RSA 63–64

schools: intolerable institution 11; principles of the factory 14; principles of the military 14; contributors of poor physical health 39–40
Schumacher, E. F. 29, 33–34
self-harm 41, 43
Sellman, E. 86
Sen, A. 160
SEND *see* special educational needs and disabilities (SEND)
sexual abuse 89
sexual harassment 90
shallow ecology 34, 110; *see also* deep ecology
Shaw, T. 124–125
Sheldrake, R. 95
Shirley, D. 93–95
silence: as sacred 97; as silencing 20, 62; as strong 93
Slote, M. 108
Smith, D. 86
special educational needs and disabilities (SEND) 15, 44–45, 63

speciesism 34, 108
Spivak, G. C. 20
suicide 41, 43
Susskind, D. 21
Susskind, R. 21
sustainable communities 19
sustainable development: seven principles 153; *see also* Raworth, K.
Sutton Trust 56–58

teacher *see* letters: to a teacher
teacher's agency 16
teachers' well-being 43
technology: consequences of advancement 20–22; village-based 129–130
Thompson, P. 152
Tiny Houses movement 19
Tolle, E. 86
translocation rewilding *see* rewilding: types
trophic rewilding *see* rewilding: types

UK Office for National Statistics 89
UNESCO 148
UNICEF 40
UN Sustainable Development goal 64, 148–149

violence: forms 149–150; over nature 35; in schools 65
vulnerability: students' 41–43

Wenger-Trayner, E. 130
Western humanism *see* global North
Western view of the world *see* global North
wisdom: practical 129; traditions 80–81, 89
World Health Organisation 43
World Inequality report 18
World Meteorological Organisation 165

young person *see* letters: to a young person
Youth Sport Trust 40

zeitgeist 74
zero tolerance approach 62
Zizek, S. 152

For Product Safety Concerns and Information please contact our EU representative GPSR@taylorandfrancis.com
Taylor & Francis Verlag GmbH, Kaufingerstraße 24, 80331 München, Germany

www.ingramcontent.com/pod-product-compliance
Lightning Source LLC
Chambersburg PA
CBHW051542230426
43669CB00015B/2689